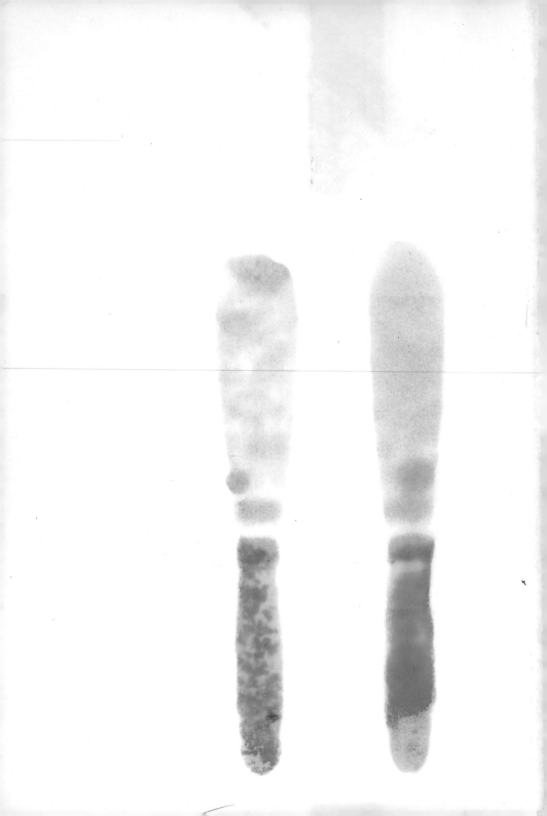

ELEPHANTS

ELEPHANTS

S. K. ELTRINGHAM
B.Sc., M.A., Ph.D., F.I.Biol.

WITHDRAWN

BLANDFORD PRESS
POOLE   DORSET

First published in the U.K. 1982 by Blandford Press,
Link House, West Street,
Poole, Dorset, BH15 1LL

Copyright © 1982 Blandford Books Ltd.

Distributed in the United States by
Sterling Publishing Co., Inc.,
2 Park Avenue, New York, N.Y. 10016

British Library Cataloguing in Publication Data

Eltringham, Keith
    Elephants. – (Blandford mammal series)
    1. Elephants
    I. Title
    599.6'1   QL737.P98

ISBN 0 7137 1041 1

Typeset by Permanent Typesetting and Printing Co. Ltd.
Printed by Butler and Tanner, Frome, Somerset

Contents

	Acknowledgements	vii
	Preface	viii
1	General characteristics	1
2	The study of elephants	23
3	The social life of elephants	52
4	Reproduction in elephants	74
5	Food and feeding habits	89
6	The daily round	107
7	Physiology and growth	118
8	Population dynamics	132
9	The elephant problem	145
10	Diseases of elephants	169
11	Elephants and man	186
12	The ivory trade	205
13	The ancestry of elephants	211
	Appendix: Numbers and distribution	244
	Bibliography	248
	Index	256

Illustrations

Some of the black and white photographs in the book were provided by the author, S.K. Eltringham. Other sources, which the author and publishers gratefully acknowledge, are listed below.

Black and white photographs

J. Allan Cash Ltd: Fig. 6.2
C.L. Cheeseman: Fig. 10.2
J. Dragesco: Figs 2.9 and 2.11
R.C. Malpas: Fig. 2.6
Ernest G. Neal: Figs 3.4, 4.3, 5.2, 5.3 and 9.1
David Travers/*Camera and Pen*/J. Allan Cash Ltd: Fig. 10.3

Colour plates

J. Allan Cash Ltd: 1 and 4
Colour Library International: 3
Hugh B. Cott: 5 and 7
Peter Johnson/Natural History Photographic Agency: 2 and 9
Ernest G. Neal: 8
Dieter & Mary Plage/Survival Anglia Ltd: 11 and 12
E.H. Rao/Natural History Photographic Agency: 10
Peter H. Ward/Natural Science Photos: 6

The line drawings were specially prepared by Michael Clark.

Acknowledgements

Many people have helped me in the preparation of this book. I am particularly grateful to Robert Malpas, who read most of the first draft although he is not responsible for any errors that remain. Robert Olivier gave me several unpublished reports on his studies of the Asian elephant and drew my attention to some published papers that I had overlooked. Peter White sent me a pre-publication copy of his review with I.R.F. Brown of the blood chemistry of elephants. Cynthia Moss was especially generous of her time in describing to me her unpublished work in Kenya, particularly her discovery of musth in the bulls of Amboseli National Park. My debt to the work of many other elephant biologists is obvious but my best thanks must go to my colleagues in Uganda, notably Robert Malpas, Michael Woodford and John Wyatt, who shared long hours with me either watching or counting elephants.

I am grateful to Ernest Neal, who persuaded me to take on this enjoyable task and whose gentle and patient exhortations ensured that I finished it. Beth Young and Maggie O'Hanlon of Blandford Press have been most helpful in preparing the book for publication. My warmest thanks go to Michael Clark for his friendly co-operation in preparing the figures and drawings. His skilled draughtsmanship and artistry greatly embellish the pages of this book.

Finally, I would like to thank the following publishers and learned societies for permission to reproduce material from their books or journals: American Philosophical Society; American Society of Mammalogists; Blackwell Scientific Publications; Carnegie Institute; William Collins & Sons; East African Wild Life Society; Fauna & Flora Preservation Society; International Union for the Conservation of Nature and Natural Resources; Oxford University Press; The Royal Society; Smithsonian Institution; Society for the Study of

Fertility; South African Wildlife Management Association.

The authors of the tables and figures reproduced in this book have also kindly given me permission to use their material and each is acknowledged by name in the captions. The stanza on page x is taken from 'The blind men and the elephant' by John Godfrey Saxe in *Elephants Ancient and Modern* by F.C. Sillar and R.M. Meyler, which was published by the Viking Press, New York, in 1968.

Preface

It is surprising that the elephant figures so prominently in the mythology of European countries, considering its absence from the continent. The appearance of an elephant is familiar to everyone today through books and films and most people have seen one alive at the zoo but, in mediaeval times, the elephant was a fabulous beast, no more and no less real than the griffin and cockatrice. We may laugh at the illustrations from those days, at the trumpets and hose pipes that served for trunks, at the impossibly angled tusks or bat-wing ears, but could we draw an elephant accurately from a description? I often wonder what we would make of an elephant if it were known only from fossils. What palaeontologist would dare to fit it with a trunk? What bold illustrator would draw the ears of an African elephant to their proper scale? Today we accept the elephant as just another animal but perhaps its very familiarity tends to blind us to its many peculiarities.

First there is its size. It is bulkier by far than any living land animal — over twice the weight of its nearest rivals, the rhinoceros and hippopotamus. Only the giraffe is taller but it is a much more delicate creature. Then there are the tusks, which gave the mediaeval artists such trouble and, the most peculiar organ of all, the trunk. The trunk has no parallel in other mammals and we have to go to the invertebrates, to the octopus with its tentacles, to find anything remotely similar. But no octopus tentacle can match in versatility the elephant's trunk, that 'lithe proboscis', with its multiplicity of uses. Then what can we make of the skin? It seems to have been roughly thrown over the body and not properly tucked in and stitched together. Its thickness is proverbial and was the feature selected by Victorian naturalists in naming the group Pachydermata, although today we no longer classify elephants with hippos, rhinos and tapirs.

There are many other peculiarities of the elephant but I have said enough to show that the elephant is indeed a wondrous beast that would be quite mystifying if seen for the first time. We can sympathize with the six blind men of Hindustan who wanted to find out what an elephant was like and quarrelled over their conclusions after meeting one for the first time. The first, stumbling against its side, thought that the elephant must be like a wall; the second, feeling the tusks, assumed it was like a spear; the third, holding the trunk, was sure it was like a snake; the fourth, stroking the leg, knew it was like a tree; the fifth, examining the ears, considered it was like a fan; and the last man, grabbing the tail, could tell that the elephant was like a rope. The moral is worth quoting:

> So oft in theologic wars,
> The disputants I ween,
> Rail on in utter ignorance
> Of what each other mean,
> And prate about an elephant
> Not one of them has seen!

There are plenty of theologic wars in elephant conservation and I shall no doubt do a lot of prating in the following pages but, I hope, not in utter ignorance, for at least I have seen an elephant.

S.K. Eltringham
Cambridge

1 General characteristics

Evolution

Elephants are members of the broad evolutionary line leading to the ungulates or hoofed mammals. The great diversity of mammals leads to problems over classification but most arrangements rely on the principles put forward in 1945 by Simpson, who divided the placental mammals into two main groups or 'cohorts': the Unguiculata, containing the insectivores, bats, primates and some smaller groups, and the Ferungulata, containing the carnivores and ungulates.

It is extremely difficult to distinguish between fossils of ancestral carnivores and ungulates but, later, recognizably ungulate-like creatures began to evolve. These early forms, the Protoungulates, enjoyed quite an extensive radiation in the Eocene and developed into large animals of many species, particularly in South America where they dominated the fauna. Although some continued into the Pleistocene, all are now extinct except the aardvark, whose precise taxonomic position is somewhat conjectural.

Later fossils show further development towards the ungulate condition but the limbs remain primitive and the nails have not evolved into proper hooves — the diagnostic feature of the ungulate. Simpson suggests calling mammals at this stage of evolution the Paenungulata, or 'near' ungulates, from the Greek *paenos*. Many of these fossil forms were huge, some as big as modern elephants, but, one by one, the lines died out leaving the remnants of only three: the sirenians, the hyraxes and the elephants. The numerous primitive features shared by these groups betray their common ancestry.

The sirenians, or sea cows, were an early offshoot of the evolutionary mainstream in the Palaeocene, over 50 million years ago. They are now highly modified for aquatic life but retain certain primitive features, such as abdominal testes and pectoral teats.

The hyrax is a furry cat-sized animal and it looks so like a rodent that the uninitiated hoot with derision when informed that it is the closest living relative of the elephant. The relationship is not very close but the signs of a common, although distant, ancestry are unmistakable. The significance of some of these characters has been discussed by Hanks (1977). Both elephants and hyraxes have primitive limbs with long upper segments and fully formed ulna and fibula. These two bones, in the lower segments of the fore and hind legs respectively, become reduced in the ungulates. The number of toes are not reduced as much as in ungulates, and elephants retain the full five on each foot. Another non-ungulate feature that they share is a pair of large upper incisors which, in the elephant, develop into the tusks.

Serological tests, which have become such a powerful tool in taxonomy, reveal a close relationship between elephants and hyraxes but the most striking resemblances between the two groups occur in the reproductive systems. Hanks (1977) lists similarities in the structure of the penis, the testes and associated ducts and in the anatomy of the foetal membranes. The position of the testes inside the abdominal cavity is also a primitive feature. Other similarities are the low level of progesterone in the blood plasma during pregnancy and the long gestation period.

From this evidence, it is apparent, that the elephants occupy a very isolated position amongst living mammals. Not only do they have no close relatives alive today, they are themselves the last couple of twigs of a once great evolutionary branch whose ramifications extended all over the globe in the geologically recent past.

The living elephants

Of the 30 species of elephant that ever existed, only two, the African and the Asian, still survive. Not only are these elephants distinct species, they belong to separate genera. The Asian elephant is sometimes called the Indian elephant but this name obscures its wide distribution throughout tropical Asia. Scientifically, it is called

Elephas maximus but even this name is inappropriate, for the maximum size amongst land mammals is reached by the African elephant, *Loxodonta africana*, so-called from the lozenge-shaped ridges of the cheek teeth, *loxos* being the Greek word for slanting.

Taxonomists have studied and revised the classification of elephants for many years and numerous subspecies have been described. Most represent no more than the normal variations to be expected in a species with a wide distribution but there is a clear division of the African species into two subspecies, *Loxodonta africana africana* and *Loxodonta africana cyclotis*, known respectively as the bush elephant and the forest elephant. The common names are not ideal because bush elephants frequently occur in forests and forest elephants in bush, but *cyclotis* is undoubtedly the elephant of the great equatorial rain forests of central Africa. As with most species that occur in both forest and grassland, the forest race is smaller, being a good 60 cm shorter at the shoulder. Other differences occur in the ears, those of *cyclotis* being more rounded, and in the tusks, which are long and straight in *cyclotis* in contrast to the stout, curved tusks of *africana*. The forest race is also said to have a darker skin than the bush elephant, as well as more hair on the trunk and around the mouth (Morrison-Scott, 1947) but such differences, if they really exist, are not obvious.

The Asian elephant has been divided into any number of subspecies but their validity is doubtful. The elephant of Sri Lanka has the best claim, perhaps, as it has several distinct features, and it is usually designated *Elephas maximus maximus*. The Sumatran elephant is often regarded as a separate type, *Elephas maximus summatranus*, but all continental Asian elephants are best assigned to a third subspecies, *Elephas maximus indicus*. There may well have been other island or isolated races deserving subspecific status but any that existed are now extinct.

African and Asian elephants are dissimilar in many ways besides size. The bulging forehead of the Asian elephant, with its paired domes, contrasts markedly with the more sloping forehead of the African species, which consequently has a triangular rather than a square outline to the head in side view. The pinnae of the ears also differ. Those of the African species are much bigger and are shaped like a map of Africa, whereas the smaller ears of the Asian elephant are shaped like a map of India. The stances of the two species are very distinctive. The African elephant stands with its head below the level of its shoulders, which is the highest point on its body, but, in the Asian species, the head is the highest point. The shape of the back is also different — convex in the Asian and sway-backed in the African. The African elephant has a leaner look about it, with a proportionately narrower body and longer legs than the rather squat Asian elephant. There are other less obvious differences, such as the two finger-like projections at the end of the trunk in the African elephant compared with the one in the Asian elephant. Both species have tusks but they are confined to the male in the Asian elephant or, more correctly, protrude beyond the lips in the male only, for small tusks are present in the female. The tusks of the female African elephant are very much smaller than those of the male but, even so, they are as big as if not bigger than the tusks of male Asian elephants.

The anatomy of elephants

The detailed anatomy of the elephant has appeared in a number of classic text-books, e.g. that by Frade (1955), which forms part of the monumental *Traité de Zoologie*, edited by P.P. Grassé. This is in French but much of the ground, at least for the African elephant, is covered by Sikes (1971). It is my intention here to concentrate on those aspects of anatomy that distinguish the elephant from other mammals.

Dentition

THE TUSKS

The tusks are the upper incisors, not canines, and they are the only incisors in the elephant. The tusks present at birth are milk teeth, which fall out after a year when they are about 5 cm long. The permanent tusks protrude beyond the lips at about 2−3 years of age and grow throughout life so that the older the elephant, the heavier the ivory, although there are individual differences, which are probably genetic, in the growth rates. The tusk growth follows a sinusoidal curve so that the tusk would be spiral in shape were it to grow long enough. The tendency towards spiral growth is very obvious in the extinct woolly mammoth, although the curve is tighter than it is in the living elephants.

A tusk is fundamentally no different from an ordinary tooth. It is composed of dentine, except for a cap of enamel that is present when the tusk first erupts but which soon wears away and is not replaced. About one quarter of the tusk is hidden within the socket and is covered with cement. The base of the tusk is hollow and contains the pulp cavity, which extends for a surprising distance up the tusk, usually reaching beyond the lip line in males. In females, the cavity tends to fill in with age and may sometimes be almost obliterated (Elder, 1970). The pulp is a highly vascular tissue with a ramification of blood vessels and nerves amongst mesenchymal connective tissue. The tusk grows from its base as fresh dentine is deposited all over the surface of the pulp cavity by odontoblast cells.

Ivory is simply dentine but the peculiar diamond pattern of the elephant's tusk in cross-section gives it a distinctive lustre that is absent from the 'ivory' of other mammals, such as the hippopotamus, warthog, walrus, narwhal and sperm whale. It is unfortunate for the elephant that its tusks are so coveted by man for the lust for ivory remains the greatest threat to the survival of the species.

Both sexes of the African elephant are tusked but there are marked differences in the size and weight. The male tusk is stouter, with a larger circumference relative to its length, and much heavier. Some elephants are born tuskless. This condition appears to be hereditary because two or more such animals are often found together in the same family group. The absence of tusks produces some profound modifications in the shape and musculature of the head and neck. Apart from the sunken, 'toothless' appearance around the upper lip, the bones at the back of the skull, to which the neck muscles are attached, are less well developed. The carriage of the head is also different. In a big tusker, the spines of the cervical vertebrae are particularly robust and serve to anchor the huge muscles of the neck, which support the weight of the tusks.

Only the males of the Asian elephant have tusks that protrude beyond the lips. Those of the females remain as small tushes, which are hardly visible in the living animal. Even so, not all males are tusked. Tuskless males are known as *makhnas* in India and, in the north-east of the country, the proportion of males without tusks is said to be 50% (Gee, 1964). The condition appears to be normal for the elephants of Sri Lanka. Possibly there has been a selection for tusklessness as a result of the persecution of tuskers by ivory hunters or it may be that the Asian elephant is in the evolutionary process of losing its tusks. Even when fully developed, the tusks of the Asian elephant never reach the size or weight of those carried by its African cousin. The lack of tusks does not seem to place the *makhna* at a disadvantage in fights with tuskers for it is said to be larger, with a stronger neck and trunk, which may make up for its deficiency.

The tusks of a male African elephant can exceed 200 kg the pair, although such weights are rare. The heaviest tusks that can be authenticated are those in the British Museum (Natural History) from an old bull shot in 1897 at the foot of Mount Kilimanjaro. These were said to weigh 209 kg when fresh, but tusks tend to lose weight in storage and the present weight of the pair is 199.8 kg. The heaviest pair of tusks collected by Laws (1966) in Uganda, during a scientific sampling exercise, weighed 109 kg but it would be very rare nowadays to find an elephant with tusks exceeding 100 kg in weight. The combined tusk weights at puberty of African elephants were reported by Laws (1966) to be 6.4–8.6 kg in the male and 2.7–3.6 kg in the female, depending on the age of maturity. Adult females rarely have tusks weighing more than 20 kg combined and the tusks of the Asian elephant weigh even less than this.

The tusks of an elephant are rarely symmetrical and often one tusk is used in preference to the other, so that the animal may be right or left 'handed'. The working tusk tends to become more worn than the other. Occasionally the tusks cross over, making feeding awkward because the elephant has to thread its trunk through the tusks in order to reach its mouth. The tusks have a variety of functions and are by no means used only as weapons. Soil at salt licks is dug up with the tusks and bark ripped off trees. One elephant that I saw had lost the tip of its trunk and could not feed properly, yet it was keeping itself in good condition by ripping up waterside vegetation with its tusks and scooping the food into its mouth with the remnant of its trunk. The elephant has the quaint habit of sometimes draping its trunk over a tusk as if to rest it.

THE MOLAR TEETH

The molar teeth of the elephant are unique in the manner of their eruption. The total number is twenty-four, six in each half jaw, but no more than two teeth, or parts of them, are in wear at the same time in each side of a jaw. The only exception occurs in young elephants in which parts of the first three molars may be in use together. There is a linear progression in their eruption, with each tooth appearing at the back of the jaw and gradually moving forwards as the preceding tooth is progressively worn down at the front. Each tooth drops out as it reaches the front of the jaw. It is as if there were a production line of teeth moving along the jaw from back to front.

It is difficult to classify the molar teeth of an elephant but, from fossil evidence, it is probable that the first three to appear in each half jaw are premolars and the others molars. Hence the dental formula for an elephant is:

$$i \frac{1}{1} \; c \; \frac{0}{0} \; pm \; \frac{3}{3} \; m \; \frac{3}{3} \;.$$

The peculiar nature of the tooth eruption may be due to the prolonged growth period of an elephant. The jaw of the young animal is so much smaller than that of the adult that a permanent tooth erupting early in life would be too small to cater for the needs of the mature animal. Most other mammals grow more quickly and can solve the problem by having small milk teeth, which last for the duration of the growing period.

The molars vary between the species but each has a series of ridges, known as *laminae* or *lamellae*, running across the tooth (Fig. 1.1). These ridges are diamond-shaped in the African elephant but, in the Asian species, the sides of the ridges are parallel. The surface of the tooth is rounded when it first erupts and the ridges are no more than smooth tubercles of dentine capped with enamel. As the surface of the cone wears down, the underlying dentine is exposed and, with the surrounding layer of enamel, forms an efficient rasping surface. Movement of the jaws during chewing is largely fore-and-aft, with little side-to-side action. The teeth in the lower jaw

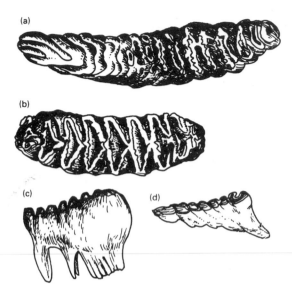

Fig. 1.1 Grinding surfaces of the molar teeth of: (a) an Asian elephant and (b) an African elephant. (c) Side view of Molar IV dissected from lower jaw showing the gap between the roots of laminae 4 and 5. (d) Similar view of Molar VI, the last tooth, towards the end of the elephant's life. Note the resorption of the anterior roots leaving a projecting shelf of worn tooth which eventually breaks off.

become more worn than those in the upper and the wear is more regular. Consequently, the lower teeth are more useful for age determination (p.28).

The molar has an open root system filled with 'pulp', each tooth having a number of 'roots' corresponding to the number of laminae. There is usually a pronounced gap between the roots of laminae 4 and 5 (Fig.1.1c). The roots are perpendicular at first but, as the tooth wears out and moves forwards, they incline backwards. The anterior roots begin to be resorbed until only a shelf of unsupported tooth is left (Fig. 1.1d). This quickly erodes from the front and soon breaks off, either dropping from the mouth or being swallowed.

8

The number of laminae in the African elephant is said by Sikes (1966) to be constant for each tooth. Laws (1966), on the other hand, considers that the number of laminae varies. Sikes (1971) believes that confusion has arisen because not all laminae erupt through the gums and she maintains that, if the jaw is split open, the number of laminary roots will be found to be constant. This could well account for fewer laminae being reported, but Laws (1966) shows the range of molar VI extending to fourteen, one more than the maximum reported by Sikes. The matter is of some significance because the method of age determination devised by Sikes (1966) assumes a constant number of laminae.

The period during which a molar remains in the mouth varies considerably. The first is shed after only 2 years but the last (molar VI) remains in place for about 30 years. According to Laws (1966), the ages at which the six teeth are lost are 2 years (molar I), 6 years (molar II), 13–15 years (molar III), 28 years (molar IV), 43 years (molar V) and life's end (some 65 years) for molar VI. The age at eruption is not clear cut. Molars I and II are present at birth and molar III is in place, but not worn, by the first birthday. The first few lamellae of molar IV appear at 6 years and molar V makes its first appearance at around 18 years. The last tooth (molar VI) begins to erupt at 30 years of age.

A consequence of its peculiar dentition is the definite limit placed on the life span of the elephant. Once the last molar is worn out, the animal cannot chew its food properly and death from starvation or malnutrition will ensue. Some elephants, about 10% of those in the older age groups, have an extra, seventh, molar but the supernumerary tooth is never as fully developed as the others (Laws, 1966).

Comparable studies have not been carried out on the Asian elephant but its dentition appears to be essentially the same as that of the African species, although details, such as the number of laminae, may well differ.

The trunk

There is no doubt that the most remarkable and distinctive organ of the elephant is the trunk. Anatomically, it is the nose and upper lip with paired nostrils running through its length. The skin covering the front (dorsal) side is annulated with deep furrows and carries a sparse covering of sensory hairs. Entirely muscular, the trunk is extremely flexible and its dexterity is illustrated by the ease with which a zoo elephant can pick up and hand a coin to its keeper. The ability to manipulate objects is enhanced by the finger-like projections at the tip of the trunk. The elephant is capable, therefore, of selecting its food with great delicacy but, curiously enough, it is unable to exploit this facility to the full because its great size requires it to eat so much that it has to shovel in the food in bulk, with little opportunity for selection. Nevertheless, the trunk is used with finesse in comfort movements and an elephant can gently scratch its ear or rub an itchy eye with the back of its trunk. The trunk is also used to caress other elephants, both in courtship and when tending calves.

Above all, the trunk is an exploratory organ. Much of the information about its surroundings comes to the elephant through its trunk. At the first sign of danger, the elephant raises its trunk aloft, periscope-like, to test the breeze. Closer to hand, the trunk may explore the food in another elephant's mouth or test an interesting smell on the ground.

The use of the nose in drinking is very curious. This is a most remarkable phenomenon, unique amongst mammals, in which the nostrils are generally used solely for the intake of air. The elephant can hold about 4 litres of water up its nose and can also suck up both mud and dust and squirt them over its body.

The trunk also has its aggressive uses. It is sometimes flicked threateningly towards a human intruder and, if the elephant lets go of an object it is holding at the time, it gives the impression of having hurled a missile. Some authors believe that elephants deliberately throw objects at each other and at human intruders, including zoo visitors (Kühme, 1963). Elephants may lash out with their trunks at a man and, in serious attacks, are said to pick up people in their trunks and to hurl them to one side. An elephant usually tries to kill a man by tusking him or crushing him with its feet. The trunk is not used in fighting except for more or less friendly wrestling matches between young bulls.

Owing to its multiplicity of uses, the trunk is essential to the survival of the elephant. Occasionally an elephant may lose its trunk as, for example, when it gets caught in a wire snare. If only the tip is lost the animal may survive but, if a substantial portion is severed, death is more likely.

The ears

No less expressive than the trunk are the ears although, because of their size, it is in the African elephant that the ears are more important as signalling organs. An example is the threat display, in which the ears are spread wide on each side of the raised head, presenting a huge frontal area. Ears are also important in the regulation of body temperature (see p.119).

The ear of the African elephant measures 183 cm by 114 cm in the bush elephant and 137 cm by 99 cm in the smaller forest race, according to measurements taken by Sikes (1971) of dried speci-mens. Approximate dimensions for Asian elephants are probably 60 cm by 30 cm.

The ear flap is essentially a cartilaginous sheet to which the relatively thin skin is closely attached. The ear skin is the only part of the hide that has much commercial value as it can be processed into a fancy leather. In mature animals, the top edge of the ear typically turns over — backwards in African elephants and forwards in the Asian species.

The skin

The skin of the elephant is not particularly thick, except over the back and sides, where it may reach 2–3 cm. The belly skin is quite thin and is the only part suitable for making leather, apart from the ear skin. The skin is much marked with ridges and creases, particularly on the trunk and forehead, where it has characteristic warty outgrowths.

The skin is dry to the touch, although soft and supple, and sweat glands are generally considered to be absent. They have not been demonstrated histologically (Smith, 1890; Spearman, 1970), but people working with tame Asian elephants find sweat under the saddle and harness at the end of a day's exertions. It is possible that such moisture is not sweat at all but condensation from the humid air, although Benedict (1936) has shown that the Asian elephant loses water vapour through the skin and it is difficult to see how this could occur without sweat glands.

The only glands that have been described in the skin are the mammary glands and the two temporal glands, one on each side of the head between the eye and the ear. The temporal gland is a huge organ, weighing up to 1.5 kg in the male, and producing a copious secretion, smelling strongly of elephant, which trickles down the side of the face. The mammary glands are about the size and shape of the breasts of a woman and are a useful aid in identifying the sex of an elephant in the field.

The natural colour of the skin is greyish black in both species but the apparent colour is determined by the nature of the soil of the surrounding country because of the habit of the animal of throwing mud over its back. Unpigmented or pinkish regions frequently occur on the ears and trunks of Asian elephants.

The hair

The elephant's skin is usually considered to be hairless but bristly hairs occur sparsely all over the body. The foetus is covered with the lanugo, i.e. a felt of long downy hair, but most of this is shed before birth. Even so, the calf is quite hairy, particularly over the head and back. Specialized hairs occur around the eyes, which sport long lashes, and in the ear orifices, where their function is probably protective. There are also long hairs on the lower lip. It is likely that some, at least, of these hairs have a sensory function but none contributes anything to the regulation of body temperature.

The largest hairs on an elephant are those on the tail. They are oval in cross section, with a curious consistency, rather like plastic wire, and form a double row along the mid-dorsal and mid-ventral lines. The longest, around the tip of the tail, may reach 100 cm in length, and the longest of all arises from the ventral tip. The tuft presumably serves to dislodge flies, for the tail is in continuous motion. These hairs are much in demand for the manufacture of plaited bracelets.

The feet

The sole of the foot is pitted and ridged, contributing no doubt to the surefootedness of the elephant on all kinds of terrain. Although all elephants have five toes on each foot, they are buried inside the flesh and the only external evidence of their existence is the toe nails, which are cornified shields in the epidermis and are not attached to the digits. Not all toes have nails, but there are usually five on each fore foot and four on each hind foot. There is no difference between the species in this feature nor between the forest and bush races of the African elephant, despite frequent assertions to the contrary in the literature (e.g. Carrington, 1958). There may, however, be deviations from these numbers and these are probably genetic.

The fore foot is circular in outline but the hind foot is more oval. The circumference of the fore foot is roughly equal to half the shoulder height, a relationship that is made use of by hunters wishing to identify a large tusker worth the effort of tracking. In forest areas, or in regions where elephants are so few as to be rarely sighted, measurements of the footprints can give a good idea of the population structure, although the size of the elephants will be overestimated because the sole of the foot spreads out somewhat when the animal's weight is put on it.

The foot narrows to a thinner 'waist' above the sole. Most of the body of the foot is composed of fatty, fibrous tissue, which acts as a cushion or shock absorber. The tissue is elastic and helps the elephant to maintain its grip on the ground. The cushion of the foot makes the elephant look plantigrade — i.e. walking flat-footed on the sole, as in man or bears — but really it is digitigrade, as it walks on the tips of its toes (Fig. 1.2). The heel is nearer to the ground in the hind foot than in the fore foot so that the former more nearly

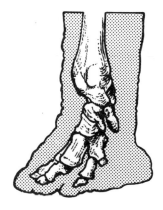

Fig. 1.2 The fore foot of an African elephant showing the position of the bones. Note that the elephant really walks on its toes but the great cushion of connective tissue causes it to be functionally flat-footed.

13

approaches the plantigrade condition. The functional gait is plantigrade and, because of its great weight, an elephant cannot jump or even run in the accepted sense since it must keep one foot on the ground at all times. An account in *Elephant Bill*, by J.H. Williams, however, describes a cow elephant jumping a deep ravine 'like a 'chaser over a brook'. The ravine is described as being wider than she could have stepped across.

Such athleticism apart, the average elephant can cover the ground remarkably quickly in a shuffling run and it also has a fast extended walk, during which it takes maximum strides. Normally, the elephant moves slowly, with short, deliberate steps, and it can be kept out of an area, such as a garden, by a trench wider than its pace. The trench must be deep enough to prevent the elephant getting into it and climbing out the other side but a width of 220 cm and a depth of 180 cm will deter it. An elephant has a remarkable ability to step over high fences, but anything above 170 cm or so tends to get pushed down rather than stepped over.

The skull

The skull differs markedly between the two species. The bulbous forehead of the Asian elephant does not denote any special intellectual prowess for the imposing domes contain sinuses, not brains. The skull of each species is richly pneumatized so that it is much lighter than its size suggests. There are many differences between the species in the proportions of the skull bones. The Asian elephant has a relatively longer and narrower face in anterior view and its skull appears to be more compressed from front to back. This is particularly obvious if the lower jaw is included with the skull, because it is almost as deep as it is long. The jaw is much longer in the African elephant and is triangular in profile. The premaxilla, or upper jaw-bone, is very much more developed in the African species, particularly in the male because of the enormous development of the tusks.

There is a prominent distinction between the sexes of the African elephant in the shape of the skull. The posterior side is flattened in both sexes to provide anchorage for the enormous neck muscles necessary to hold up the head, but the nuchal region (the nape) is extended in the female into a ridge, the nuchal eminence, along the

14

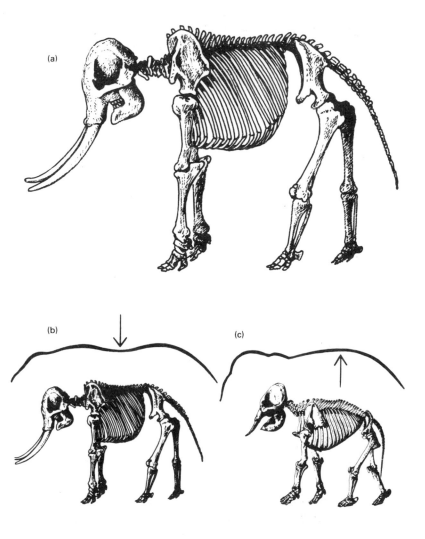

(a)

(b)

(c)

Fig. 1.3 (a) Skeleton of a bull African elephant. Note the graviportal features mentioned in the text. (b) Comparison of the skeletons of a bull African elephant (left) and a bull Asian elephant (right). Note the different angles of the neck and that the highest point of the body is the shoulder in the African species but the top of the head in the Asian species. Note also the bulbous forehead and humped back of the Asian elephant which contrast with the flatter head and sway-back of its African cousin. The profiles in life of the head and back are shown above the skeletons.

15

top of the forehead. This gives a 'square' appearance in profile, in contrast to the more rounded forehead of the male, and is a convenient way of distinguishing the sexes in the field, particularly with young animals whose tusks have not developed.

The skeleton

The elephant is the largest living land animal and its huge bulk has influenced the skeletal system, which has developed numerous graviportal features (Fig. 1.3). Thus the backbone forms a rigid girder for the suspension of the soft tissues. The vertebrae are robust with stout neural spines that are particularly high in the thoracic region. There are normally 20 ribs, extending most of the way down the backbone and forming a huge barrel-shaped rib cage.

The limbs are also graviportal, with each segment directly in line with the others, forming a rigid columnar pillar to support the great weight. Even the girdles form near-vertical extensions of the limbs, with the articulations (the glenoid cavity and acetabulum in the pectoral and pelvic girdles respectively) facing downwards. The upper segments (femur or humerus) of the limbs are long and about equal in length to the lower — another graviportal feature. All the bones are well developed, due no doubt to the need for load-bearing. The radius and ulna, the bones of the 'forearm', are permanently crossed in the position of pronation, i.e. with the palms facing downwards.

The neck is short and characterized by a massive double spine arising from the axis, the second cervical vertebra. The neck is nearly horizontal in the African elephant but is held at an angle of about 45° in the Asian species. This is why the head of the Asian elephant is the highest part of the body.

The brain

The brain of an elephant is located at the back of the skull, well away from the forehead. Although it occupies only a small part of the skull, it is nevertheless very large, being bigger in absolute terms than the brain of any other land mammal, not excluding man. Sikes (1971) gives the brain weight of a bull African elephant as 4.2–5.4 kg and of a cow as 3.6–4.3 kg. In proportion to the size of the body, it is, of course, smaller than the human brain. Brain size, however, is not directly related to intelligence. More important is the degree of brain growth after birth. Most mammals are born with brains that are around 90% of the mass of the adult brain but, in elephants, the figure is 35% (Laws, 1970). Hence, there is considerable development of the brain as the calf grows up and this is associated with the great learning ability of young elephants. A similar correlation is seen in man, in which the relative weight of the brain at birth is 26% of the adult weight.

The structure of the elephant's brain is described by Sikes (1971). The temporal lobe is the part which most increases in size during development. The cerebrum is richly convoluted, as in man, but is relatively much smaller, so that the cerebellum is exposed. Anatomical details suggest that the elephant is amongst the more intelligent animals, a conjecture readily confirmed by a study of its behaviour.

The digestive system

The digestive tract of an elephant tends to be of a fairly simple mammalian type, in keeping with the primitive evolutionary stage of the group to which the elephants belong. The mouth is small for the size of the animal and cannot be opened widely. Salivary glands are well developed and the short oesophagus is richly supplied with mucous glands, which help to lubricate the rather coarse vegetation on which the elephant feeds.

The stomach is a simple sac of an unusual cylindrical shape, oriented almost vertically. Part of the middle region is glandular but not much digestion takes place in the stomach and its main function is storage.

The intestines are very long, up to 19 m in a large African bull. At the junction of the small and large intestines, there is a huge sacculated caecum where fermentative digestion of cellulose takes place through the action of bacteria (see p.89). Products of digestion are absorbed through the relatively thin and highly vascularized walls of the caecum. The remainder of the gut is largely concerned with the consolidation of the faeces and the resorption of water. The faeces are in the form of boluses, each the shape of a short cylinder whose dimensions reflect those of the rectum. The faeces usually retain their shape after falling to the ground and may be used to

17

judge the size of the elephant producing them. The anus of the elephant is covered by a distinctive fold of skin — the anal flap — which provides a useful topographical reference point when measuring the size of elephants.

Other viscera associated with the digestive system, e.g. the pancreas and liver, are of the ordinary mammalian type, and are distinguished only by their size.

The heart and blood system

The vascular system of an elephant is unexceptional, although there are some departures from the normal mammalian condition. The heart, as might be expected, is huge, weighing up to 28 kg in an African bull, but this is only some 0.5% of body weight, a proportion normal for large mammals. The ventricles are peculiar in being slightly separated at their apex and there are paired *venae cavae* instead of the usual fused single vein. These features are found in other paenungulates and are probably primitive.

The arterial system follows the usual mammalian plan, although on a massive scale. Because of the large size, junctions between arteries are often supported by ridges of elastic fibres or muscle cells. These ridges may become calcified in older elephants. The veins are also supported by having proportionately much thicker walls than other mammalian veins. Some of the blood vessels are very long, up to 350 cm in an African bull, and veins of this size would, if they had thin walls, require an undesirably high blood pressure to prevent their collapse.

The respiratory system

The respiratory system of an elephant is exceptional in a number of ways. There is no pleural cavity and the lungs adhere directly to the walls of the chest cavity and to the diaphragm. Respiratory movements, therefore, are induced only by the chest musculature and there is no mechanism of inflating the lungs by negative pressure in the pleural cavity, as is usual in mammals. Consequently, the elephant finds it difficult to breathe if any restraint is placed on the movement of the chest and diaphragm, a point which must be borne in mind during immobilization work (p.45).

Air enters the lungs through the internal nares, which are

unusual in being high up on the forehead. Their position is indicated externally by the plate-sized circle of skin, which hunters say is the only safe frontal shot. An elephant can breathe through its mouth as well as through its trunk, so it can retain water or dust in the trunk without having to hold it breath.

The reproductive system

MALE

The reproductive system of the male elephant (Fig. 1.4a) shows important differences from that of most other mammals. The testes do not descend into a scrotum but remain in the abdomen where they are suspended from the dorsal body wall in the lumbar region by a fold of peritoneum and connective tissue. The testes are similar histologically to those of other mammals, with normal spermatogenesis taking place (Johnson and Buss, 1967a), despite the high body temperature. Although huge in absolute terms, with a weight of up to 4 kg, the testis is proportionately small relative to the condition in many other species (Johnson and Buss, 1976b). Thus the testis of the elephant is 0.1% of the body weight, a figure which, although higher than that for man (0.08%), is below those for the domestic bull (1.24%), dog (1.9%) or rat (8.9%).

The spermatozoa of the elephant are similar to those of the horse (Short et al., 1967). They are stored mainly in the Wolffian duct, for the elephant's testis has no obvious epididymis such as is found in most mammals. With an initial diameter of 1 mm, increasing gradually to 5 mm in the middle region and to over 1 cm at the distal end, this duct, which consists of a mass of coiled tubules about 100 cm long, can store a vast number of sperm. Histologically, the anterior part of the duct is quite different from that found in any other mammal. The epithelium is raised into numerous longitudinal folds whose tips contain a network of large blood vessels thought to be concerned with the metabolism of the immobile spermatozoa (Short et al., 1967). The Wolffian duct opens into the duct of the seminal vesicle through a muscular sac to form a common ejaculatory duct.

The penis has a peculiar structure, probably because of the unusual arrangement of the female genitalia. It is erected, as in other

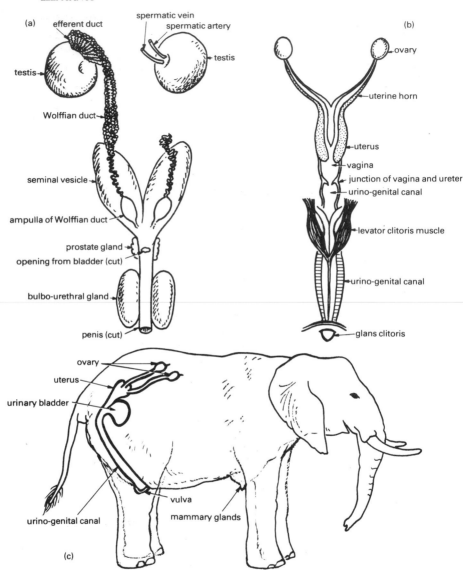

Fig. 1.4 The reproductive systems. (a) Ventral view of the reproductive system of a male African elephant. (From Short *et al.*, 1967.) (b) The reproductive system of a young female African elephant. (From Perry, 1953.) (c) Position of the reproductive organs in the female elephant. Note the long urino-genital canal, which runs anteriorly to open between the hind legs.

mammals, through the dilation of blood vessels in erectile tissue. Contraction of the musculature then throws it into an S-shaped flexure, allowing it to hook into the forwardly directed vagina of the female. There is no baculum or penis bone. The end of the penis is enclosed in the prepuce, which like much of the tip of the penis, is often devoid of pigment. The urethra opens at the tip through a Y-shaped slit.

The penis is a huge organ, pendulous in form like that of a horse. When extended, it almost touches the ground but normally it is withdrawn into a dermal sac in the perineal region. This sac faces downwards and is similar in shape to the vulva of the female. It is difficult, therefore, without practice, to sex elephants in the field from the appearance of the external genitalia.

FEMALE

The reproductive tract of the female elephant (Fig. 1.4b) conforms to the generalized mammalian plan. The most distinctive feature of the ovary is that the *corpora lutea* do not regress after pregnancy, as in other mammals, but accumulate in the ovary. The *corpus luteum* is also unique in not producing progesterone, the hormone that controls the process of pregnancy. Presumably some other hormone with the function of progesterone must occur in the elephant but its source and nature are as yet unknown.

Unlike the condition in most mammals, the vagina and urethra do not open separately into a shallow vestibule but into a very long urino-genital canal, which passes downwards and forwards to open at the vulva in front of the hind legs (Fig. 1.4c). It is this curious orientation that has necessitated the development of the equally curious penis of the male.

The clitoris is very well developed, up to 37 cm long according to Eisenberg *et al.*, (1971), with a large erectile *corpus cavernosum*. The clitoris can be extended and retracted in a similar manner to that of the penis in the male, although not to the same extent. Unlike the male organs, the retractor tendons are partly cartilaginous. The vulva is also well developed and, although it normally faces forwards, it is turned downwards, and to the rear by erection of the clitoris during copulation.

21

The sense organs

SMELL

There is no doubt that smell is the most important sense for the elephant. All strange stimuli are first investigated by testing the air for scent. Even when the elephant can see the source of the disturbance, an enquiring trunk is always extended before any action is taken.

SIGHT

Sight is generally poor, although the elephant can see well enough at close quarters. The eye of an elephant is quite large — about the same size as a human eye — and is provided with long lashes. There is only a vestigial lachrymal (tear) gland but its function is taken over by the Harderian gland, an accessory lachrymal gland associated with the nictitating membrane, or third eyelid, which is particularly well developed in elephants. There is no tear duct and 'tears' (secretions of the Harderian gland) evaporate from the eye or occasionally run down the cheek.

HEARING

The elephant is usually considered to have an acute sense of hearing, although firm data on the matter are hard to find. The large pinnae are not necessarily indicative of good hearing because their primary functions lie in temperature control and in social signalling. Elephants do not appear to communicate over long distances so perhaps there is little need for particularly good hearing, but it is difficult to be certain whether an elephant has not heard a distant sound or is simply ignoring it.

TOUCH

The sense of touch is certainly well developed in the trunk of an elephant particularly at the tip. The bristles on the trunk are probably tactile in nature and help to inform the animal of its surroundings when its head is buried in a thicket during feeding. The tongue is also well supplied with sensory nerve endings, which probably serve to identify food placed in the mouth. The whole of the skin is sensitive to touch, despite its rather corrugated appearance.

2 The study of elephants

History

Elephants have been familiar animals for millenia and much is known about their management in captivity. As a result of autopsies on specimens dying in collections, the anatomy of elephants had been thoroughly studied by the middle of the nineteenth century.

Later work on elephants, e.g. Gilchrist (1851) and Evans (1910), was of a distinctly applied nature and was concerned with the health of captive animals, most of which were of the Asian species. Much of the information given was based on hearsay or on casual observations (often misinterpreted) of captive animals and the first genuinely experimental study of the elephant was that of Benedict (1936), which was confined to the physiology of a captive female Asian elephant named 'Jap'. The conclusions, therefore, may not be generally applicable.

Apart from its anatomy, nothing was known of the biology of the African species until the late 1950s, when some field work began in Uganda. Even less was known about the ecology of wild Asian elephants and it is only very recently that any attempt has been made to study the species in its natural habitat.

Serious ecological work on elephants began in 1956 when some American Fulbright scholars were assigned to Uganda. One of the first to arrive was the late Dr Hal Buechner, whose first project was a study of the trees in Murchison (now Kabalega) Falls National Park, which were being destroyed by elephants. His visit marked the beginning of the study of elephants in Uganda, which was continued by other visiting American scientists, such as Irvine O. Buss and W. Longhurst. When, in 1961, the Nuffield Unit of Tropical Animal Ecology was established in the Queen Elizabeth (now Rwenzori) National Park in Uganda, the study of elephants became a major research interest of the Director, Dr R.M. Laws. Work on the elephant continued at the Uganda Institute of Ecology, which succeeded the Nuffield Unit in 1971, and has persisted up to the present day. Dr Laws moved to Tsavo National Park in Kenya in 1967 to direct the newly formed Tsavo Research Project, whose brief was to advise on elephant management in the national park. Although the principal investigation ceased after only a year, less intensive studies of elephants continued intermittently from the Project. Elephant research started in Tanzania soon afterwards at the Serengeti Research Institute, where a number of elephant biologists were based. The first detailed study of elephant behaviour was carried out in the nearby Lake Manyara National Park by Iain Douglas-Hamilton.

A 4-year investigation into cardiovascular disease of East African elephants was begun in 1963 by Sylvia Sikes while, at the same time, Keith McCullagh carried out a pathological study of elephants shot in a culling operation in Uganda.

Elephant research blossomed in East Africa during the 1970s. Its principal centres were in the Kabalega Falls National Park in Uganda, Tsavo and Amboseli National Parks in Kenya and the Ruaha and Serengeti National Parks in Tanzania. Some of the results of the earlier work have been published in book form (Sikes, 1971; Laws et al., 1975) while the Douglas-Hamiltons (1975) wrote a popular account of their studies in Lake Manyara National Park.

The study of elephants has not been confined to East Africa. Elephants in the Kruger National Park in South Africa have been closely monitored for many years and much knowledge has been gained of their movements and general behaviour. More recently, studies have been made in Addo National Park in South Africa, as well as in Zimbabwe (Sengwa), Malawi (Kasungu National Park) and Zambia (Luangwa Valley). Although there has been no long-term study of elephants in West Africa, incidental observations of the species have been made in the region from time to time (Merz, 1977).

The Asian species has received much less attention. A joint survey was carried out by the Smithsonian Institution and local scientists in Sri Lanka (Ceylon) from 1967 to 1976. The only other study of any size was an ecological project in Malaysia, sponsored by the country's Game Department, between 1973 and 1976.

The fate of both species has given rise to concern amongst conservation bodies. Although it is still relatively abundant the African elephant has recently suffered drastic declines in numbers throughout the continent, which have emphasized how vulnerable the species really is. The Asian elephant is in an even more precarious state and fears for its survival led to the formation, in 1976, of specialist groups within the International Union for the Conservation of Nature and Natural Resources (IUCN) to further the conservation of elephants.

Weights and measures

In many cases no particular techniques are required for the study of elephants but their large size can cause some problems. Thus an investigation into the reproductive cycle may require an inspection of the ovaries but instead of using a microtome to prepare sections the biologist may find a bacon slicer more convenient!

Direct weighing

Taking weights and measures presents difficulties because no lifting tackle available in the bush is strong enough to lift a whole elephant. The only place where wild elephants have ever been weighed whole is Kikumbi, in Zambia, where an abattoir for processing elephants was built, incorporating a 10-t gantry fitted with a 7-t crane weigher (Hanks, 1979). Tame elephants can be weighed by leading them across a weighbridge (Brownlee and Hanks, 1977; Lang, 1980). An alternative is to cut the animal up into pieces and weigh each bit separately, adding on a percentage, usually 3%, to allow for loss of blood and coelomic fluids. Such a technique is not very accurate, besides being extremely laborious and messy, and an indirect method is generally preferred. In several ungulate species, the dressed hind leg weight bears a constant relationship to the total weight (Smith and Ledger, 1965) and the same correlation was found to exist in elephants (Laws *et al.*, 1967). Hence, it is necessary to weigh only the dressed hind leg in order to estimate the total weight. To dress the leg of an elephant, the limb is skinned and separated at the acetabulum before being cut free. Finally the foot is

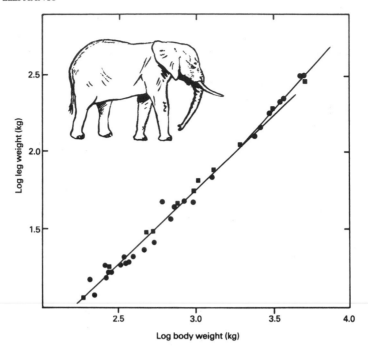

Fig. 2.1 Relationship of dressed hind leg weight to total weight of an elephant. The lower line refers to all elephants up to 1000 kg in weight and the upper line to males heavier than 1000 kg. Subsequent reappraisal of expanded data has shown that this distinction is unjustified and that all elephants conform to the relationship indicated by the upper line. (From Laws *et al.*, 1967.)

removed at the hock. The hind leg weight as a percentage of the total weight varies slightly with age (Fig. 2.1) but is within the range of 5.3–6.3%.

Shoulder height

The weight can also be estimated from the shoulder height, but the relationship is not a simple one as the shoulder height varies approximately with the cube root of the body weight. There is also a marked sex difference, unlike the relationship with the weight of the dressed hind leg (Fig. 2.2).

Shoulder height is of particular value since it is a measure of weight and, therefore, of age. The peculiar nature of the anatomy

26

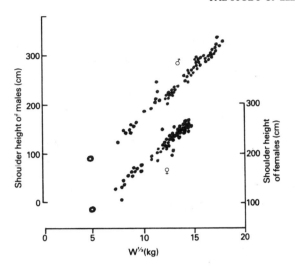

Fig. 2.2 Relationship between shoulder height and body weight in African elephants culled in Kabalega Falls National Park, south of the Nile, or its surroundings. There is no difference between the sexes up to 15 years of age. (From Laws *et al.*, 1975.)

makes the shoulder height an easy measurement to take on dead elephants. In life, the limb bones form a straight column with the pectoral girdle so that it is a simple matter to straighten the leg of a dead elephant and obtain an accurate measure of its standing height.

Standard measurements and sampling

Standard measurements are usually taken whenever the opportunity presents itself. These include overall body length along the curves, from the tip of the trunk to the end of the tail, and the straight-line distance from the mid point between the ears to the anal flap at the base of the tail. The latter is an important measure as it is the one taken from elephants photographed vertically from the air and is about the same as the shoulder height, the elephant being roughly square in profile.

Further details of routine measurements taken from dead or immobilized elephants are given by Laws *et al.* (1975). It is also usual to collect samples of parasites, blood etc, even though immediate use may not be made of them.

Age (years)

— 40

— 15
— 10
— 6
— 3

— 1
— 0

Fig. 2.3 A field guide to the ages of female African elephants based on their relative heights. (From Laws, 1966.)

Age determination

So far, techniques for estimating age are available for the African elephant only, although the principles would certainly hold for the Asian elephant. The two principal methods depend on the examination of teeth and have been described by Laws (1966) and Sikes (1966; 1968) respectively. Both can be used only with dead specimens. The age of living elephants cannot easily be estimated, although shoulder height can be used as a criterion. The annual increment after maturity is so small, however, that observations of living elephants can give only a very approximate indication of the age structure. Both Laws and Sikes give silhouettes of elephants at different ages for use under field conditions and, providing that a mature adult is present as a standard, it is possible to get a rough idea of the population structure (Fig. 2.3).

Teeth examination

The technique of determining the age of elephants from their dentition entails the identification of the molars which are in wear. This can usually be done readily enough with molars I to III from the ratio of the length to width but there is a considerable degree of overlap in this ratio with the remaining teeth. One problem is that the teeth of males are more massive than those of females and, if the molars can be separated into sexes, the overlap is reduced (Hanks, 1972a). The identity of the molar can usually be confirmed by reference to the number of lamellae and to the laminary index (Morrison-Scott, 1947). The last molar is easily recognized once it is in wear because the bony capsule becomes flattened and solid with no further tooth capsule present in the jaw.

Laws (1966) divided his sample of elephants (from Uganda) into 30 age classes defined on the basis of which tooth, or part thereof, was in use and on the degree of wear on the surface of the tooth.

Sikes' technique depends on identifying the particular lamina of the particular tooth that is directly above the *foramen mentale*, a hole in the lower jaw for the passage of nerves and blood vessels. Both methods have their faults but Laws' seems to have been used more by other workers and it has tended to become the standard. Malpas (1978) has compared the two techniques and his results (Fig. 2.4) show a very close correlation between the two, although the absolute ages assigned by Sikes are younger than those assumed by

Fig. 2.4 Comparison of two ways of estimating the ages of the same elephants. If both methods gave identical results all the points would fall on the 45° line. Note that Sikes' method allots a slightly younger age than that of Laws to most of the elephants. The upper line is the regression line fitted to the points. (From Malpas, 1978.)

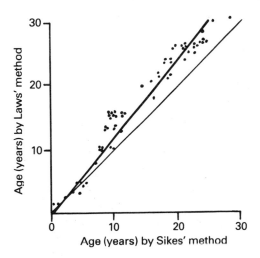

Laws. Other techniques for estimating the age of elephants from the teeth have also been published (Johnson and Buss, 1965; Krumrey and Buss, 1968).

Dried eye lens weight

An alternative indicator of age is the weight of the dried eye lens, a method first used with cottontail rabbits (Lord, 1959) but also applicable to African elephants (Laws, 1967a). When plotted against age, determined from molar characteristics, the lens dry weight shows a close correlation, which does not vary between populations, although there is a slight sex difference.

Condition

It is often imperative for management purposes to know whether elephants are in good condition. It is usually obvious when elephants are in the last stages of debility or when they are in perfect health but it is the stages in between that are of interest. The general body configuration is the best guide. The head should be held up, the sides and flanks well fleshed out, the skin smooth and supple. Older elephants, not necessarily in poor condition, have sunken hollows in the cheeks and forehead and protuberant bones along the back and girdles. The backbone is usually prominent, even in healthy elephants, but the hips and shoulder blades should not be obvious in young or middle-aged animals.

Height to weight ratio

More precise estimates of condition require the examination of the carcase. If the weight is known, the height to weight ratio gives a good indication of condition. All things being equal, an elephant which is heavier than another one of the same height is in better condition. In order to use the technique effectively, a height/weight graph, similar to that shown in Fig. 2.2, must first be constructed. Comparisons between different elephant populations must be made with caution in case there has been a seasonal difference in the times of sampling. Also the possibility of a size polymorphism must be kept in mind. The method cannot be used to compare forest and bush elephants, for example, or African and Asian elephants but, even within races, there may be size differences, e.g. elephants from the Rwenzori National Park, Uganda, are slightly smaller than those measured by Laws (1966) elsewhere.

Kidney fat index

The traditional way of assessing condition in mammals is to express the weight of fat surrounding the kidney as a percentage of the weight of the kidney. This, the kidney fat index, has been used to assess the condition of African elephants by Laws *et al.* (1970), Albl (1971), Sherry (1975), Williamson (1975) and Malpas (1977).

Fat content of bone marrow

The fat content of bone marrow taken from the femur has been used to measure condition in a number of ungulates but only Malpas (1977) has used the method with elephants. Extraction of the fat can be time-consuming and expensive, but, in a number of ungulates

Fig. 2.5 The percentage of fat in the marrow of thigh bones from Ugandan elephants plotted against the percentage of dry matter in the marrow. The close agreement between the two values means that the condition of an elephant can be determined from the dry weight of the marrow by reading off the corresponding fat content from the regression line. This is a much simpler technique than measuring the fat content directly. (From Malpas, 1978.)

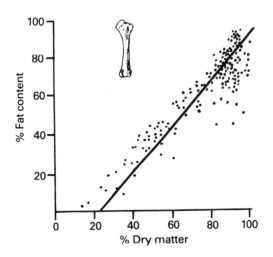

there is a close correlation between the percentage fat content and the dry weight as a percentage of wet weight and Malpas (1978) found this relationship to be applicable in the elephant (Fig 2.5). Hence the condition of elephants can be determined by simply weighing the marrow before and after drying.

The technique of assessing condition through the fat deposits should not be applied blindly for there is evidence that the kidney fat is metabolized before the marrow fat and hence is the more likely to show seasonal changes in condition. The marrow fat index is the more useful measure to determine the effects of severe nutritional stress.

Serum analysis

The level of serum protein has been used as a measure of condition in East African elephants by McCullagh (1970) and Malpas (1977), but the method is not generally considered to be very sensitive for other species in which it has been used (Franzmann, 1972).

Serum urea has been used to assess protein levels in the food as a measure of condition in a number of mammals. Brown *et al.* (1978) have used the technique to determine condition in African elephants. The ratio of albumin to globulin in the serum has been suggested as a further measure of protein intake in bighorn sheep by Franzmann (1972), but Sykes and Field (1973) question its reliability. The method has been used on elephants only by Malpas (1978) but with inconclusive results.

Food and feeding studies

Qualitative Studies

ANALYSIS OF STOMACH CONTENTS

The most obvious way of finding out the nature of the food is to examine the stomach contents and this has been done with African elephants on a number of occasions (McCullagh, 1969b; Buss, 1961; Laws and Parker, 1968; Malpas, 1978). If the sample of stomach contents is taken from the pyloric region, very little digestion will have taken place and it is usually possible to identify the food items despite a certain amount of mechanical damage. Some idea of the diet can be obtained by inspecting the droppings (Field, 1971) but differential digestion may have taken place and the most common items in the faeces are not necessarily the most common food items but rather the most indigestible. The elephant's digestion is so inefficient, however, that a lot of plant material comes out in a recognizable state.

FIELD OBSERVATION
Observation of elephants in the field gives a very good qualitative measure of the food eaten and, with care, the observations can be quantified, e.g. by recording the item selected every minute or at some other convenient time interval (Field, 1971). The method requires elephants to tolerate man or a vehicle and demands an ability on the part of the observer to identify plants as they disappear into an elephant's mouth. As the elephant frequently waves the food item around in its trunk before stuffing it into the mouth, the latter task is not too difficult. It is not essential to see the elephant in the process of eating in order to determine the food because inspection of the rangeland after an elephant troop has passed through will reveal which plants have been taken. A certain degree of judgement is required to recognize foliage torn down but not eaten, as well as plants damaged by other herbivores.

Quantitative estimates
Quantitative estimates of the food eaten are more of a problem. Two values are required for the calculation; the weight of food in the stomach and intestines and the rate of passage of food through the gut. Neither of these is known with any accuracy for elephants, although it would not be difficult to measure them. The rate of passage has been measured on a number of occasions but with varying results (p.91). The usual technique is to give the animal food stained with a coloured dye or containing a plastic marker.

The weight of the stomach contents has often been recorded but not the total weight of material within the entire gut. The weight of the stomach contents can be used, however, as a quantitative index of the food consumed, since it is likely to bear a constant ratio to the total gut contents.

33

ELEPHANTS

Using the Food Intake Index of Malpas (1978), which expresses stomach fill weight as a percentage of live weight, the relative food intake of elephants in different regions and at different seasons can be compared.

DROPPINGS

Attempts have been made to estimate the amount of food eaten by weighing the droppings. The ratio of weight of food to weight of droppings was found to be 1.78 : 1 for Jap, the tame Asian elephant (Benedict, 1936), and this ratio was used by Petrides and Swank (1966) to calculate the total food intake of a wild African bull elephant whose droppings were collected over a period of 12 hours. Obviously, there is ample room for error in such a calculation, which uses data from an elephant of a different species and of the opposite sex, feeding on dry hay rather than natural forage.

DIRECT ESTIMATION

A direct method for estimating the daily intake of food is to count the number of times a trunkful of food is placed in the mouth, having assessed the average weight of a trunkful. One cannot safely deprive an elephant of its trunkful while it is feeding but it is possible to collect and weigh an equivalent amount of vegetation. Obviously, the technique is as good as the observer's ability to estimate the quantity of each kind of food plant that the elephant picks up in its trunk.

AVAILABLE FOOD

The food available to elephants in their natural habitat often needs to be known. A straightforward botanical survey will give some idea of this but not all the plants growing in an area are available to animals — some might be out of reach for example. This is not usually a problem with elephants on grasslands but standard vegetation surveys can yield quite erroneous results in forests, where even elephants are unable to break down or reach the branches of the huge forest trees. The size of the food plant is also a consideration but the amount of food available is not necessarily directly proportional to size. Thus a clump of tall mature bamboo may contain more plant tissue than a shorter, younger clump of similar area but the amount of food available to elephants would be the same in each case. Attempts to allow for such variations must be largely subjective but, provided the same observer is used, the results from different areas will at least be comparable and, given an experienced investigator, the degree of error will probably be small.

Growth estimation

Growth may be defined as the amount of tissue formed in the body over a given time and may be measured by weight gain or by some linear measurement. In the case of weight measurement, unassimilated food and water in the gut are rarely excluded and hence most measures of live weight gain include an inherent error, although this can be allowed for. The level of hydration of an animal is a problem in assessing weight gain and really accurate measures can be made only on a dry weight basis. Because it is not easy to oven-dry an elephant, wet weights are normally used but probably without much significant loss in accuracy.

Weight
Growth in weight can be determined by successive weighings of the same animal or by weighing a large number of elephants of known but varying ages. In either case, a growth curve of weight against age is plotted. Each method has its advantages and disadvantages; the individual's growth may not be typical of the species, particularly if the animal concerned is a captive feeding on unnatural food. On the other hand, the larger sample may not be put into accurate age classes. Another disadvantage, at least with elephants, is that wild animals have to be killed before they can be weighed and their age estimated. We have seen earlier how the weight of an elephant can be determined and how the weight bears a constant ratio to a linear measurement, the shoulder height. Once this relationship is known, and this can come about only by killing at least some elephants, it is necessary only to measure the shoulder height to produce a growth curve.

Shoulder height
It is not essential to kill an elephant, or even to immobilize it, in

order to measure its shoulder height. Various techniques exist for measuring the shoulder height of living elephants in the field. The crudest is simply to guestimate the height but more accurate measurements are made by photography. If a large number of elephants are photographed, at least one will be full-sized and, if the shoulder height of an adult elephant is known, the largest elephant on the photograph can be used as a reference. There are bound to be inaccuracies, however, for there are always some individual variations and there is really no 'adult size' for an elephant because growth continues throughout life, albeit very slowly once the animal becomes mature. An alternative, but rather more time-consuming, technique is to measure a nearby tree or other object on the photo-graph after the elephants have moved on. If no suitable object is available, a surveyor's pole may be placed in the footprint of the elephant and a second photograph taken. Alternatively, the shoulder height can be calculated from the focal length of the camera lens, without the necessity of taking a further photograph, if the distance between the elephant and camera is measured.

Aerial photography

An extension of the photogrammetric technique is to photograph elephants from an aircraft flying vertically above them and to measure, on the prints, the lengths of the backs from a point between the hind border of the ears and the anal flap (Fig. 2.6). This measurement approximates to the shoulder height and, hence, bears a constant ratio to the weight. The method was first used by Laws (1969b), with photographs taken from a helicopter equipped with a radar altimeter, so that the height above the elephant was known, and it was a simple matter to convert the measurement from the photographic image to the real length. A second set of photographs was taken without the benefit of such an altimeter but the sizes of the elephants were estimated by using the largest and smallest animals as the scale. These animals were assumed to be an adult male and a new-born calf respectively and their average lengths were known. Croze (1972) describes a refinement of this technique and gives an equation for correcting the slight errors which arise.

The great advantage of photogrammetric techniques is that elephants can be measured without killing them or harassing them

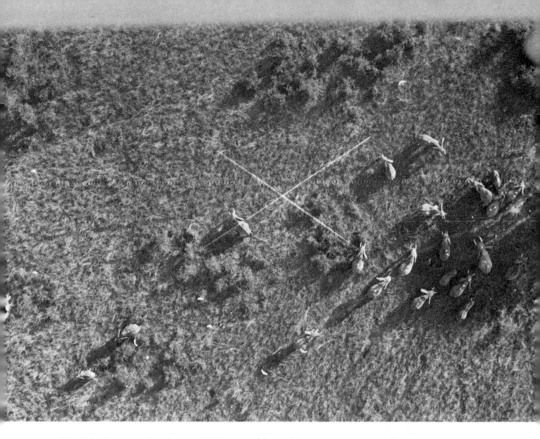

Fig. 2.6 An example of an aerial photograph used in assessing the age distribution of an elephant population. The cross marks the exact centre of the negative, the only point at which the photograph is absolutely vertical. Measurements of elephants away from the centre have to be corrected to allow for the slightly oblique angle at which the photograph was taken. Note the cattle egrets fluttering away as the aircraft passes over.

in any way. The method also allows for much bigger samples to be taken and taken more quickly than is the case with culling.

Instantaneous growth rate

Any estimate of growth rate of an elephant based on successive weights or measures is really only an historical record and tells one nothing about the current growth rate, or even if the animal is still growing. It is very likely that the growth rate has varied throughout life, depending on the level of nutrition or other factors, but such changes will not be apparent from weight measurements. It is,

37

however, possible to estimate the instantaneous growth rate by carrying out a biochemical test on the urine. The method was developed by Whitehead (1965) for use with children and is based on the fact that the rate at which collagen turns over in the body is a measure of the growth rate. Hydroxyproline is a breakdown product of collagen metabolism and so its presence is an indication of growth. It is secreted in the urine but a direct measure of its concentration is of no value because urine varies so much in dilution. The amount of hydroxyproline is, therefore, measured against a standard, in this case, the concentration of creatinine in the urine. The excretion of creatinine is known to be related directly to muscle mass, i.e. to size, in man and is presumably so in elephants. The ratio of hydroxyproline to creatinine, therefore, is a measure of instantaneous growth. The technique has been used on elephants by McCullagh (1969a) and Malpas (1977).

Reproduction

Information on sexual behaviour can be obtained by observation but examination of the reproductive organs is necessary for a more detailed knowledge of reproduction.

Female

MATURITY

Using the presence or absence of *corpora albicantia*, *corpora lutea* and follicles in sectioned ovaries as criteria, Laws and Parker (1968) classed female elephants as mature, pubertal or immature. If the ages of the elephants are assessed from the condition of the molars, the age at which females become mature can be determined. There is bound to be some individual variation but Laws *et al.* (1975) give a method whereby the mean age at sexual maturity can be calculated from a simple formula. If the elephant is pregnant or has placental scars in the uterus, it is obviously mature and there is no need to examine the ovary. The elephant is one of the few mammals in which the placenta leaves a permanent scar on the uterus (Laws, 1967b) and the number of scars indicates directly how many calves the elephant has produced.

INTER-CALVING PERIOD

If the age of maturity for the population has been determined, the interval between births, or the inter-calving period, can be easily calculated. This is an important variable in elephant populations which can also be calculated from the percentage of pregnant females in the population, according to the expression given by Perry (1953):

$$\frac{\text{number pregnant}}{\text{number non-pregnant}} = \frac{\text{gestation period}}{\text{lactation anoestrus.}}$$

The mean calving interval for the population can be obtained by adding the gestation period (22 months) to the lactation anoestrus. Malpas (1978) points out that this expression converts to another, from which the mean calving interval (MCI) can be estimated directly:

$$\frac{\text{number pregnant}}{\text{total mature females}} = \frac{\text{gestation period}}{\text{MCI.}}$$

There is a difference in the two calving intervals so derived. In the case of the value obtained by counting placental scars, variations in the reproductive rate over the life histories of the elephants concerned will influence the result so that the mean calving interval may not correspond to any one period. The MCI calculated from the pregnancy rate, on the other hand, has a real meaning and reflects the current status of the population. Hence it is called the instantaneous mean calving interval.

LACTATION

Lactating females can be recognized by whether or not it is possible to express milk from the nipples immediately after death.

SEASONALITY OF REPRODUCTION

The presence or absence of a breeding season can be detected by recording the dates of births of all calves but this is time-consuming and subject to inaccuracies. In the case of large populations, many births are likely to be overlooked and, while most births will probably be detected in small groups, the sample size may not be significant. A quicker technique is to measure the weight of foetuses from a sample of pregnant females. The age of the foetus can be determined from its weight by means of a growth equation derived by Huggett and Widdas (1951) for mammalian foetuses in general. The date of conception can then be calculated. By plotting these dates as histograms, in the form of monthly frequencies of conception, the presence or absence of any seasonality is clearly revealed. This method has been used for African elephants by Perry (1953), Buss and Smith (1966), Laws and Parker (1968) and Malpas (1978).

Male

Carcase examination reveals relatively little about reproduction in the male. Measurements and other observations show only the age of sexual maturity and the degree of seasonality.

MATURITY

Laws and Parker (1968) describe a method for assessing sexual maturity in male elephants, based on smears of fluid from the *vas deferens*. They found that smears from immature elephants lack sperm, whereas those from mature animals show a dense mass of spermatozoa, which become mobile on the addition of fluid from the seminal vesicles. They also recognized a third category of 'pubertal' animals, smears from which reveal a mass of cellular debris and spermatogonia with a few spermatozoa, which usually become mobile on the addition of seminal fluid. The mean age of sexual maturity is calculated by the same method used for females.

EXAMINATION OF REPRODUCTIVE ORGANS

Testes, seminal vesicles, prostate and bulbo-urethral glands are usually weighed. The testis is preferred for histological examination and the diameters of samples of tubules are measured. Evidence for seasonality in reproduction is sought principally from testes weights and tubule diameters.

TEMPORAL GLAND

Although not a sexual organ, the temporal gland can be mentioned here because of its alleged association with sexual activity in the male Asian elephant. The presence or absence of secretions is recorded and the gland is usually removed from a shot animal and weighed to see if there is any seasonal variation in size.

Physiology

There has been only one comprehensive study of the physiology of living elephants, that of the Asiatic female elephant Jap (Benedict, 1936). Heat production was calculated by housing her in a barn with an open circuit respiratory chamber in one corner, through which

Fig. 2.7 The apparatus used to measure the metabolism of Jap, the female Asian elephant studied by Benedict. The respiration chamber was a large metal box in the corner of the elephant's stable. (Benedict, 1936.)

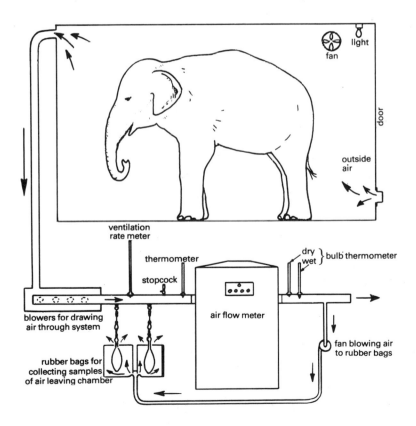

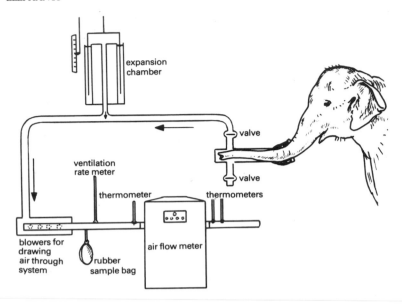

Fig. 2.8 The apparatus used in the trunk breathing experiments with Jap. (Benedict, 1936.)

air was drawn by blowers and analysed to determine the gaseous exchange (Fig. 2.7). A more refined experiment was carried out with a trunk breathing apparatus (Fig. 2.8). Jap actually allowed the tip of her trunk to be sealed within a tube through which air was drawn. The technique was not as accurate as that with the respiratory chamber, because of the mouth breathing that took place, and the results showed an apparent reduction of 29% in metabolic rate compared with those from the other experiment. Various other physiological measurements were also made with Jap (see p.118).

Pathology

Little work has been carried out on the diseases of wild elephants although Sikes (1969) and McCullagh (McCullagh, 1970; McCullagh and Lewis, 1967) have each studied cardiovascular disease in the African species. Pathological and parasitological surveys are standard with all elephants collected for any reason. Certain studies, such as measuring the level of gut parasites, can be made by examining the droppings.

Behavioural studies

Studies of behaviour can be made with no more than a pencil, notebook and well developed powers of observation, but methods of recording data are continually evolving so that ethology, the science of animal behaviour, is becoming more objective and less anecdotal. There has been a general tendency to quantify observations, rather than simply to describe behaviour, and numerous sampling methods have been devised (Altmann, 1974). No special techniques have been developed for elephants but one long-term study of the activity of elephants used the method, originally designed for cattle, of recording the type of activity being indulged in at 4-minute intervals (Wyatt and Eltringham, 1974).

Marking

The observations are usually made on individual animals and it is useful if the selected specimen can be easily recognized. Marking the animal in some conspicuous way is helpful, but not essential, as individuals can often be easily identified from such idiosyncracies as irregularly shaped tusks or holes in the ears. Elephants are particularly convenient subjects for marking, however, because their dry hairless skin can be painted without causing harm. I used this method extensively in Uganda, painting numbers on the ears, forehead and rump of immobilized animals (Fig. 2.9). Those regions of the body were chosen because they are the least likely to get plastered with mud. In order that the subject should show up from the air, in the event of it being lost and having to be located from an aeroplane, three chevrons were painted across its back. The finished product looked very garish but the paint soon faded and, within a few months, the elephant was indistinguishable from its neighbours. Such paint marks proved invaluable at night when often only part of an elephant was visible inside a bush. Curiously enough, the other elephants showed no reaction at all to the marked animal, although the smell of fresh paint must have been very strong in their sensitive nostrils.

Fig. 2.9 The author painting a number on the forehead of an immobilized elephant before carrying out a behavioural study.

Marked animals are also useful for recording the movements of herds. Plots of the sightings of marked elephants reveal seasonal migrations or individual home ranges but reliance on chance observations is unsatisfactory and greater progress can be made by the use of radio-marked elephants. Small radio-transmitters can be fixed to some durable material, such as machine belting, and fixed around the neck of an immobilized animal. With the use of a directional aerial, the position of the elephant can be rapidly located. The range of such transmitters is variable and, along the ground, may be no

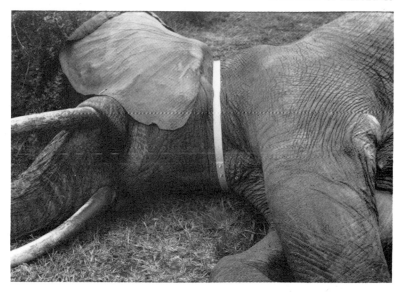

Fig. 2.10 An immobilized elephant fitted with a collar made of plastic normally used for marking cattle.

more than a few hundred metres but it is greatly increased if the receiver is carried in an aircraft. Elephants are very tolerant of collars and other objects attached to their persons and leave them in position, although they could easily rip them off (Fig. 2.10).

Radio transmitters sensitive to temperature and movement have been implanted beneath the skin of some species, but not elephants as far as I know, to transmit physiological data.

Immobilization

In order to handle elephants, it is first necessary to restrain them. The simplest way is to inject them with an anaesthetic contained in a dart fired from a modified shot gun. The most suitable drug for elephants is the synthetic morphine derivative etorphine hydrochloride, also known as M99, developed by Reckitt & Sons, Hull. It is an extremely powerful drug and I have known a full-grown African elephant to collapse after an injection of as little as 1.5 mg. The drug has a wide safety margin and, because of various defects in

45

the delivery system (Woodford *et al.*, 1972), it was our practice in Uganda to use 5 mg as the dose, so as to ensure the success of the operation.

The narcotic is often mixed with a tranquillizer although this seemed to make little difference to our elephants which were docile on recovery even when M99 was used alone. There are antidotes to M99 and the one normally used in wildlife work is another synthetic morphine derivative, cyprenorphine or M285, which acts by competing with M99 for the active sites on the brain. An overdose of antidote will, therefore, send the animal off to sleep again.

The actual placing of the dart in the elephant is an art with all the excitement of big game hunting. The shot has to be made from a distance of no more than 35–40 m, so it is necessary to stalk the animal first, either on foot or from a vehicle. The latter is probably preferable, not only from the safety angle but also because elephants, particularly those in national parks, are used to vehicles and allow them to approach more closely than a man on foot. It is little use simply driving up to an elephant, for it will move away long before it is within range and an indirect approach is usually more rewarding. It is sometimes possible to remain on one spot and wait until the elephant approaches closely enough. One ploy, which I found could be exploited with obstreperous elephants, was to wait for them to charge. Most vehicles move off at high speed under such circumstances, but the elephant is really just having a bit of fun and, when it finds to its dismay that its mock charge is not being taken seriously, it frightens itself into turning round and dashing off. The point at which its broad backside swings into view is the time to loose off the shot. The injection should be made into a mass of muscle and the rump is one of the best target areas. The shoulder is another, but it tends to be obstructed by the ears.

The elephant usually takes 10 to 20 minutes to collapse and it must be kept under constant surveillance during this time for, if it falls over and is not found, it will die. An elephant which falls down on its brisket, suffers severe respiratory problems because the heavy mass of viscera presses onto the diaphragm. Any elephant that collapses in this position should be pulled over onto its side by means of a rope thrown around its neck. Even though lying on the side is the natural position of a resting elephant, it should not be left down for long because of the danger of congestion in the lower lung. An elephant which lies down voluntarily can always change its position should it become uncomfortable, but the immobilized subject obviously cannot. The effect of the antidote is very rapid and the elephant is on its feet about 3 minutes after receiving the injection, which is usually made into one of the large veins on the back of the ear (Fig. 2.11).

Sometimes the elephants have difficulty rising to their feet on recovering from the drug, particularly if they have fallen awkwardly. In trying to rise, the elephant may swing its hind leg to give it sufficient momentum to shift its centre of gravity. This can be very

Fig. 2.11 Administering the antidote to a drugged elephant. The antidote, which is injected into a vein on the back of the ear, brings the elephant to its feet within 3 minutes.

tiring and an elephant would soon become exhausted if it struggled to rise for very long. Sometimes we found it necessary to drive the Land-Rover up to a recumbent animal and nudge it behind the shoulder with the bumper. This assistance makes all the difference, allowing the elephant to rise gratefully to its feet. It is at such times that the lack of aggression is particularly welcome.

Sometimes the other elephants in the group will attempt to lift an immobilized animal with their tusks and sometimes they succeed, probably because the level of anaesthesia is not very deep.

Counting elephants

Most ecological or management problems with elephants sooner or later require that the animals should be counted. Except in the case of very small populations, it is almost impossible to record the number of animals exactly. All sorts of factors operate to prevent this, e.g. some animals may be hidden in bushes or perhaps the observer is not very good at spotting elephants, even if they are not completely out of sight. Such factors are called *biases*. Some biases, such as the weather, are uncontrollable, but others can be standardized. Thus, if the same observer is used each time, any errors he makes are likely to be constant — if he sees three quarters of the elephants today he is likely to see the same proportion next week. If we substitute another observer, however, he may see only half the elephants and the difference in observer bias will appear as a decline in the number of elephants.

This example illustrates an important point in counting. Sometimes it is essential to obtain as accurate an estimate of numbers as possible. Thus, if we wish to keep the density of elephants at a particular figure, we must know how many are present. If, on the other hand, we are simply interested in whether or not the elephants are increasing or decreasing in numbers, we do not need to know the actual total but merely some constant measure of the population which can be used as an index.

Sample counts
An alternative approach is not to attempt to assess the actual number but merely to sample the population. We could, for

example, count only a tenth of the area involved and multiply the answer by ten to obtain the true total. This technique involves less work and is, therefore, cheaper and quicker. It is also possible, by sampling a number of discrete areas and using an appropriate statistical technique, to calculate the degree of error in our answer, e.g. we may arrive at a total of, say, 9366 with 95% confidence limits of ± 1201. This means that, even though our estimate may not be correct, we can be reasonably certain (with a chance of being right 95 times out of 100) that the true total lies somewhere between 8165 and 10567. This may not seem to be much of an achievement (in fact it is better than the accuracy usually obtained) but at least we are not working in the dark, as with the solitary figure of unknown accuracy from a total count.

Total counts
Total counts of elephants can be made from a vehicle, or on foot for that matter, but this is generally impracticable. Ground counts are used nowadays only in small study areas where it is essential to find every animal present, perhaps because the area is also being counted from the air and a factor for converting aerial counts to true totals is required. Ground counts can also be used as an index of numbers but the total area that can be covered is often so small that the errors are unacceptably high. Such counts are often made from roads, but this practice introduces a host of biases because elephants are attracted to roads, which in any case rarely follow the random course required of a true sample.

Elephants are ideal subjects for aerial survey and most counts are made from light aircraft, which can conveniently cover the huge areas over which the elephants roam. The animals, being big and black, stand out against the background better than most other species. Total counts from the air are made while flying over a regular pattern of flight lines at a convenient height, usually 150 m.

Droppings counts
Elephants in forests cannot be counted from the air or from the ground. As most Asian elephants occur in forests, aerial counts are of little use in recording their numbers. An alternative approach is to count some object produced by elephants, such as a pile of

droppings or a footprint. There is an obvious correlation and a large number of droppings indicates a large number of elephants. The problem is to quantify matters more accurately. In theory, one simply needs to know the number of times a day an elephant produces a pile of droppings and the length of time the dung persists before decaying. Thus, supposing an elephant defaecates 12 times a day and the droppings are recognizable as such as for some 2 months (60 days), to find out the number of elephants, we would divide the total number of droppings by 720 (12 × 60). Not surprisingly, matters are not that simple as many errors can arise. In the first place, the frequency of defaecation has not been determined with certainty. Possibly the rate fluctuates from place to place, depending on the diet. Secondly, the rate of decay of a pile of droppings can vary widely and, thirdly, the elephant is often walking while defaecating so that the droppings are spread out and may be classed as several piles instead of one. Finally it is very difficult to be certain of finding every pile of droppings that is produced, particularly in forests. Consequently, attempts to census elephants by counting droppings can yield some wildly fluctuating results, depending on the technique used to analyse the counts (Wing and Buss, 1970).

Droppings counts can be more safely used as an index of population size. Thus, if a road or track alongside a forest is cleared of droppings and a record is kept of the number that accumulates over the next day or week, we have a measure of the movement of elephants to and from the forests. This could yield valuable information on seasonal use. The technique has been used successfully in East Africa by Laws *et al.* (1975), Afolayan (1975) and Malpas (1978) and with the Asian elephant by Mueller-Dombois (1972), Eisenberg and Lockhart (1972), Seidensticker (1976) and Olivier (1978a). In all these cases, the counts were used as indices of occupancy and not to estimate actual numbers.

Tracks and trails

Tracks and trails left by elephants can be taken as a measure of their use of an area. Agnew (1966) described a technique for assessing habitat utilization of a region by large mammals by estimating the percentage cover of game trails, but the method is not suitable for a single species. Elephant tracks, however, are usually distinct from those of other mammals, particularly in Asia, so the method has some applicability.

Informed estimation

A biologist trying to count elephants in forests tends to become desperate and will grasp at any piece of information. In time, he will probably acquire a fair idea of the number present but such random estimates are rarely considered reliable. Olivier (1978a) has tried to regularize the use of diverse pieces of information and has devised a technique which he describes as 'Informed Estimation'. The cynical may smile at this fancy term for guestimation but the method does try to be objective. Olivier considers that the most important sources of information on which to build an informed estimation are: direct evidence, previously published data, aboriginal estimates and personal estimates.

Informed estimates are inevitably subjective and often cannot be checked. In addition, no measure of accuracy can be applied to them. Hence, they are thoroughly unsatisfactory but, unfortunately, there is often no alternative. They are most useful in comparing estimates over a wide area, provided the same person makes the estimates. Errors are likely to increase with the area surveyed and, for small regions, the estimates are probably reasonably accurate.

3 The social life of elephants

In the last few years, there have been some excellent studies of the social behaviour of the African elephant and, from the more limited observations on Asian elephants (e.g. McKay 1973), it seems that the two species have almost identical social structures. Hence the following discussion can be assumed to apply to both species.

The family unit

Elephant society is fundamentally matrilineal and the old female has a status far higher than is usual in most animal species. The unit of society is the family, which consists of a number of mature females and their calves. The adults are closely related to each other, being either mother and daughters, or sisters, half-sisters and cousins. Sometimes one female, the matriarch, is very much older than the rest. She is probably the mother, or grandmother, of the others and she is very much the leader. In times of trouble she will defend the group and the rest look to her for guidance. If she runs away, they will follow her but, if she turns around and attacks, they will charge with her. This was often brought home very forcibly to me during immobilization programmes. If one darts a young female in the group, it is extremely difficult to chase off the matriarch. She will stand guard over the stricken animal, trumpeting loudly and attempting to lift it to its feet. The others follow her example and one is then faced with a milling mass of furious beasts. One tries to avoid this debacle by waiting for a female to wander off a little way before darting her and hoping that the matriarch will not have noticed. An alternative is to dart the matriarch herself. The difference in the reaction of the elephants is striking. In this situation, they seem to have no idea of what to do and rarely make any show of resistance as they are shooed away to stand in a forlorn group,

Fig. 3.1 A family group in Samburu Game Reserve, Kenya.

anxiously watching the proceedings. Their first reaction when the matriarch falls is to run to her, and this is put to use in culling operations in which whole family groups are usually taken out.

The matriarch also plays a positive role in more peaceful times. It is she who decides where to go, when to move and when to sleep. Her leadership is unobtrusive and depends on her taking the initiative while the others follow. The seasonal movements of elephants are presumably instigated by the matriarch. As a young calf, she has accompanied her group to choice feeding grounds or to water in the dry season and this information is retained and used when she takes over leadership of the group. The younger animals learn from her and so a local tradition is built up, enabling elephants to survive when times are difficult. If the females are killed by poachers before the youngsters have absorbed this lore, the chain is broken and the collective wisdom of the community, built up over

ELEPHANTS

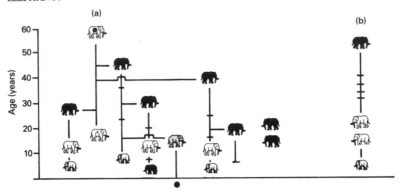

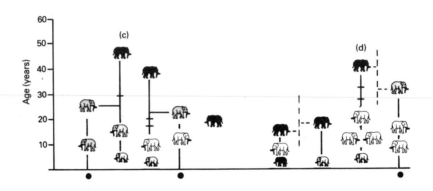

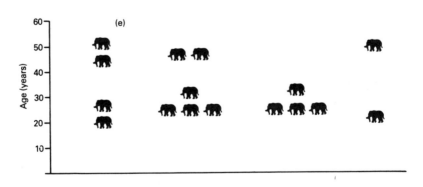

Key:

● foetus or embryo	✚ pregnancy	🐘 sucking ♂ calf
🐘 sucking ♀ calf	🐘 pregnant ♀	🐘 sexually immature ♂
🐘 sexually immature ♀	🐘 lactating ♀	🐘 pubertal or sexually mature ♂
🐘 anoestrous mature ♀	🐘 pubertal ♀	🐘 mature bull

54

the centuries, is lost. Tradition plays an important role in the lives of many mammals and even birds, but probably never to a greater degree than in the case of elephants. The widespread illegal killing of elephants which has taken place recently in East Africa is particularly disturbing for this reason. That the numbers should be so reduced is bad enough but far worse is the fact that the survivors, which tend to be young because they have the smallest tusks and are, therefore, less attractive to poachers, are left as leaderless mobs with no one to look after them when times are difficult.

Leaderless elephants tend to join up with others and extra-large groups are a sure sign that something is amiss. Douglas-Hamilton (1973) found that elephants tended to bunch together into larger units as soon as they were disturbed and I have found in Uganda that, in areas where they are hunted or heavily poached, the mean group size is higher than usual (Eltringham, 1977). Such bunching is thought by Douglas-Hamilton to be defensive and to have evolved particularly as a reaction to hunting by primitive man. Against this tendency to aggregate for mutual protection, competition within the group for limited resources, such as water-holes during the dry season, probably results in low-ranking females splitting away and forming their own groups. Douglas-Hamilton suggests that these conflicting tendencies of defensive grouping and competitive dispersion are instrumental in determining the optimal group size of a band of elephants.

Not all family units are matriarchal in the sense of being led by

Fig. 3.2 The composition of some family groups and bull herds culled in Kabalega Falls National Park, Uganda. Presumed relationships are shown by continuous lines. A broken line indicates a presumed relationship through a matriarch that had died some time previously. A horizontal line indicates the age at which a female produced a calf, based on the evidence of placental scars. (These scars are not distinguishable in females that are pregnant.) (a) A typical matriarchal group, i.e. with one old female and her descendants. Two bulls were in attendance when the group was shot. (b) A mother/offspring group, the fundamental unit of elephant society. (c) A group with two matriarchs, possibly sisters which stayed together after their mother had died. One mature bull was in attendance. (d) A sibling group with four mature females, none of which is obviously matriarchal although the oldest may have taken on a leadership role. (e) Four bull herds. Membership is temporary and made up of unrelated elephants of all mature age groups. (After Laws et al., 1975.)

one old female and the group may consist of several females of about the same age. These are probably families which have lost their matriarchs. It is likely that each female will eventually wander off, taking her calves with her, and become the founding matriarch of a new group, although non-matriarchal groups can retain their identity for considerable periods.

Laws *et al.* (1975) found that nearly one quarter of 57 family units culled in the southern part of the Kabalega Falls National Park consisted of one old female and several younger females but, in other cases, the group contained more than one matriarch. Such groups (17% of the total) are similar to sibling groups except that the animals are older and they possibly represent several family units that have come together temporarily. Extended studies of living elephants by Douglas-Hamilton (1973) have revealed that certain family units regularly mingle together and form part of a larger association known as a *kinship group* (p.62). Examples of some types of group structure are shown in Fig. 3.2.

Subsequent studies by Moss (1977) and Martin (1978) suggest that the family units in other parts of Africa are less stable than they are at Manyara. Moss found that the family units in the Amboseli National Park in Kenya sometimes split up into sub-units — usually during the dry season and often after the birth of a calf — but the elephants soon came together again. Membership of a family unit is for life and a female from one unit never leaves it to become a member of another.

Perhaps the fundamental unit of elephant society is the adult female and her own immature offspring. 6% of the groups examined by Laws *et al.* (1975) were in this category. As they grow older, such females become matriarchs as their daughters mature and produce calves of their own. All groupings of females are really various combinations of the mother/offspring unit.

It is not clear how leadership is exercised in family groups lacking a clear matriarch or in those with more than one matriarch. Possibly one animal becomes dominant over the others or perhaps no overt leadership is necessary. Under normal conditions, decisions over when to make seasonal movements and where to go do not need to be taken by any one individual, since all the matriarchs are equally knowledgeable and would be in general agreement. It was found, during cropping, that, if one matriarch was shot in a group consisting of two or more family units, her followers would abandon her and run off with a new leader (Laws *et al.*, 1975).

Bull herds

Male calves leave the family group on reaching sexual maturity and join up with other males to form bull herds. These herds are very unstable and no two animals remain together for more than a few days at a time. The Douglas-Hamiltons (1975) believe that they are driven out by the females and those they watched were indeed bullied and chivvied by the cows before leaving but it is likely that some young bulls leave of their own volition. The break with their families is not abrupt and the youngsters may return periodically, forming a loose association with the females. Laws *et al.* (1975) found that nearly half the family units they examined in Kabalega Falls National Park and almost three quarters of those in Tsavo National Park and Mkomazi Game Reserve had sexually mature bulls in attendance. Some of these may have been present because one or more of the females were in season, but it is likely that the majority of them once belonged to these groups.

Evidence for this comes from the average age of these males which, at about 24 years, is very significantly less than that of males in bull herds (nearly 31 years), showing that it is the younger bulls that hang around the female groups. Bulls over 40 years old spend very little time with the family units. Alternatively, perhaps it is only the young bulls which breed and are, therefore, attracted to the family units. Martin (1978) noticed that certain large males in Zimbabwe keep apart from the other bulls and do not share the latter's dry/wet season movements but remain all year round in certain prime riverine habitats. These bulls seem to have no interest in the cows and may be reproductively senescent.

The young males do not spend a period as solitary animals on leaving home but quickly link up with other bulls. This is clear from an examination of elephants shot during culling operations. The average ages of solitary bulls and bulls in groups were the same. If the youngsters remained alone for any great length of time, the average ages of solitary bulls would be lower than that of the others.

Size of elephant groupings

The average size of the family unit in East Africa was found by Laws *et al.* (1975) to vary from 7.8 to 12.3 (Table 3.1). These figures are derived from shot animals but the size of the 48 living families studied by Douglas-Hamilton (1973) averaged 10, which is of the same order. The average group size of the elephants that I counted from the air in western Uganda was 6.3 (Eltringham, 1977) but these groups included bull herds, which are generally smaller. Hence the true size of the female unit would be rather higher than this figure. As mentioned earlier, the fundamental unit of elephant society is the adult female and her offspring and the size of such a

Table 3.1 Average size of family units and group structure in some elephant populations from East Africa*

	Kabalega Falls National Park, South	Kabalega Falls National Park, North	Tsavo National Park	Mkomasi Reserve East
Number of groups examined	59	129	25	23
Number with attached bulls	27 (45.8%)	52 (40.3%)	18 (72%)	17 (73.9%)
Average number of attached bulls	2.15	1.77	1.56	1.35
Average group size	11.61	7.80	11.28	12.26
Group structures				
Average number of adult males	0.98	0.71	1.12	1.69
Average number of adult females	4.75	2.76	3.72	4.00
Average number of immature elephants	5.88	4.33	6.44	6.57

*From Laws *et al.*, 1975

grouping was found by Laws *et al.* to average 2.8. This figure is based on a sample of only four groups but, if it is accurate, we might expect the mean family size to be a multiple of 3. The average size of matriarchal groups was 6, in keeping with this assumption.

The average size of the 110 bull herds culled by Laws *et al.* in Uganda was 3.1 south of the Nile and 2.4 north of the river, with a range of from 1 to 11. Similar results were obtained from an aerial survey of elephants in Tsavo National Park, Kenya, where the mean group size of 427 bull herds was 2.4 (range 1–14).

The average group size of Asian elephants is less well known but some details are given by McKay (1973) and Kurt (1974) for elephants living in Sri Lanka. They did not calculate a mean group size, presumably because they do not consider the groups to be stable units. McKay maintains that the data merely reflect the relative amounts of time that an elephant will spend in groups of various sizes. It is, however, unlikely that the Asian elephant differs from the African species in its social structure and, judging from the much more detailed studies in Africa, it is probable that the apparent instability of the group sizes noted by McKay and Kurt is due to the temporary mingling of family units. Details of the group sizes recorded by McKay are given in Table 3.2, from which the mean group size of bulls can be calculated as 1.46. A similar calculation cannot be made for the females because the data are grouped, but the mean size is likely to be small since over 70% of the groups contained 10 or fewer elephants. Olivier (1978a) estimated the mean size of 62 elephant groups from the rain forests of Malaya and Sumatra to be 5.6, with the most frequently observed group sizes being 3 and 5. These observations agree well with Laws' assumption that the basic unit of elephant society is a family unit containing an average of 2.8 animals.

McKay maintains that there is a significant difference between his study areas in the size of elephant groups but his samples are too small for the statistical methods used to be valid. There is also no statistical support for his suggestion that there may be a seasonal variation in group size. Such differences as were found are quite insignificant.

McKay looked at the age distribution of elephants in 53 small groups and concluded that there were two classes of female

Table 3.2 Composition of elephant groups in Sri Lanka. Data combined from several areas (regions around Gal Oya National Park, Lahugala Tank and Yala in Ruhunu National Park)*

Males only		Mixed groups	
Number in group	Number of groups	Number in group	Number of groups
1	284	1-5	72
2	71	6-10	54
3	21	11-15	22
4	6	16-20	8
5	4	21-25	5
6	1	>25	16
7	5		
>7	0		

*After McKay, 1973

groupings, the nursing unit and the juvenile-care unit, but I find his arguments unconvincing. There is no reason to think that the behavioural ecology of the Asian elephant is any different from that of the African species (Olivier, 1978a), in which the fundamental unit of society is the female with her offspring.

Implications of elephant groupings

Bull herds are very different, socially, from family groups because the members are only loosely attached to one another. One or other of the bulls may wander off on its own or join up with another passing group. This lack of cohesion is very obvious when one darts a bull from a group during immobilization work. Unlike females, bulls pay little attention when one of their number collapses and they move off, on being chivvied, without so much as a backward glance.

This difference in reaction is explicable on theoretical grounds. Recent developments in evolutionary thinking have centred on the concept of 'kin selection'. There has been a tendency in the past to consider that animal behaviour has evolved 'for the good of the species' but animals do not found dynasties and have no conception of 'species', or any other taxonomic category for that matter. It is not even the individual that is most important in evolution, for natural selection acts on the genes. Animals are certainly interested in self-preservation but what is good for the body is good for the genes. Evolution, therefore, selects for gene complexes, which may exist in more than one body. Closely related animals have many genes in common — 50% on average in the case of parent and child or brother and sister. There is, therefore, genetic advantage in assisting a near relative and any gene which causes animals to do so will spread in the population, provided that the cost to the helper does not exceed the benefit to the receiver by more than a certain amount, which varies with the degree of relatedness. Such assistance is said to improve the 'inclusive fitness' of the individual.

We have seen that female elephants in a family unit are as closely related as it is possible to be. Mutual assistance, therefore, would greatly increase the inclusive fitness of all members. The members of a bull herd, on the other hand, are likely to be completely unrelated and no genetic advantage whatsoever would accrue to them if they helped one another. It could be said that it benefits bulls *not* to aid each other for they are in reproductive competition and, in genetic terms, it would pay a male elephant to be the only breeding bull in the population. Against this, there are certain advantages in co-operation. Bulls which group together afford themselves a certain degree of mutual protection and, although nowadays their only enemy is man, they may have been subject to predation in Pleistocene times, when large sabre-toothed cats and outsized lions were prevalent. There is also the advantage of sharing pooled knowledge concerning feeding grounds etc., which could be very important to a young inexperienced male which had just left his family. Possibly, also, bulls associate because they like company. They certainly appear to know each other and they sort themselves out into a pecking order, which is of significance when females come into heat. Unless bulls spent a lot of time in each other's company, it would not be possible for a dominant animal to become recognized as such and due deference paid to his exalted rank.

An example of the age composition of some bull herds culled in the southern part of Kabalega Falls National Park is given in Fig. 3.2. From this it can be seen that males of all ages may associate together and there is certainly no question of peer-groups isolating themselves. Some of the groups consist of an old bull accompanied by a youngster and such pairs are probably responsible for the old belief that an elderly bull, towards the end of his life, recruits a young squire to look after him. Young elephants will certainly attach themselves to an old bull but it is in their own interests to do so and such associations are only short-lived.

Kinship groups

There is good evidence from Douglas-Hamilton's studies, amongst others, that elephants are organized into units higher than the family group. All elephants within a particular region know each other and form a society. Contacts between certain groups are more frequent than one would expect from chance and it is likely that members of these groups are quite closely related. When an old matriarch dies and her adult daughters break away to establish family units of their own, it seems that they remain in touch with each other and may even join up again temporarily. The actual process of parting is likely to be a long drawn-out affair, with each female separating for a day or two and then for a few weeks before making the final break, if indeed such a final break ever occurs. The groups found by Laws *et al.* (1975), with two or more matriarchs, may be examples of such temporary associations of sisters who once lived together permanently.

Most of these conclusions are conjectural and further study of the social organization of elephants at this community level is obviously desirable. Douglas-Hamilton calls such an assemblage a *kinship group*, although he restricts the term to an association comprising some three or four family units numbering up to 50 elephants. An example of the relationships within a kinship group that he studied is given in Fig. 3.3. Douglas-Hamilton thinks that, for a group to have reached this size, it must have existed as a distinct entity for at least a century and perhaps for very much longer. The family units of the kinship groups in Lake Manyara National Park keep close

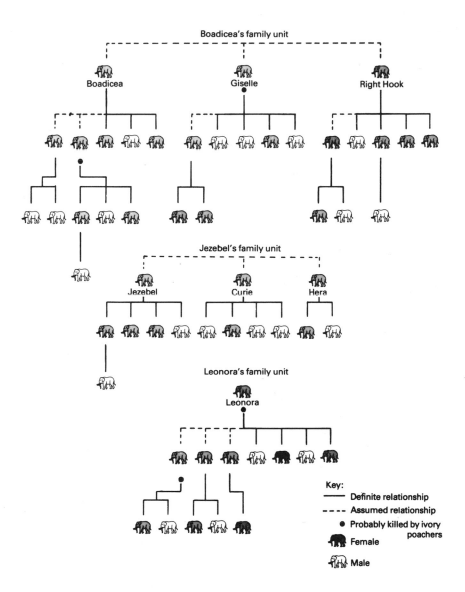

Fig. 3.3 Family tree of the kinship group of the matriarch Boadicea in Lake Manyara National Park between 1966 and 1972. The three family units were usually within a few hundred metres of each other. (After Douglas-Hamilton and Douglas-Hamilton, 1975.)

together for most of the time but, occasionally, they separate for several days and may even go to opposite ends of the Park.

The evidence for the existence of kinship groups, at least at Lake Manyara National Park where Douglas-Hamilton worked, seems incontrovertible but it is probable that such groups form part of a bigger association, which has been called a 'clan'. Such a unit is common in animal society and the term 'deme' has been coined to describe it. A deme is a group of interbreeding animals which live in a particular area. It is doubtful that a deme is completely self-contained and individuals may leave and others join from outside. Such interchange is desirable to avoid the deleterious effects of inbreeding.

Martin (1978), from radio-tracking studies, found good evidence of the existence of clans in the Sengwa Wildlife Research Area in Zimbabwe. The elephants in a clan are all females, apart from the prepubertal males, and share a common home range. Animals within the clan intermingle freely and sometimes come together for a short time, resulting in the large herds of 100 or more elephants that are occasionally reported in the literature. The home ranges of clans overlap to some extent but it is rare for herds from adjacent clans to be in the overlap area at the same time. The home range of a clan is not a territory since it appears not to be defended, at least not by the females, which show no hostility to elephants from neighbouring clans on the rare occasions that they meet. Possibly clan areas are defended by males (see p.70) but the home ranges of the bulls do not coincide with those of the females.

Communication

Elephants are very communicative animals. Despite their short-sightedness, much of their communication is visual. The carriage of the ears and trunk can be very expressive, even to human eyes, and no doubt messages are passed by a flick of an ear or curl of a trunk. Even the tail appears to have a signalling function because, when an elephant is frightened and runs away, it raises the tail almost in the fashion of a warthog. The black rhino also has this habit.

The ears are the most visually expressive organs possessed by the elephant. Normal flapping of the ears is no more than a cooling device but, when an elephant is angry or otherwise stimulated, the ears are held out sideways from the head. When the ears are fully extended, the apparent size of the elephant increases enormously, especially in the African species, and this display probably serves to intimidate rivals. A charge is generally no more than a gigantic bluff, for the elephant usually stops short and then proceeds to use its ears for another impressive display. It gives a vigorous shake of its massive head and the ears crack like whips as they flap against the body (Plate 4). The whole demonstration is accompanied by shrieks and trumpeting that would not disgrace a steam locomotive. A serious attack is not preceded by such antics. On the few occasions that Douglas-Hamilton (1975) was attacked in his Land-Rover, the elephant simply walked up and stuck its tusks into the vehicle.

The carriage of the head is also an indication of the psychological state of an elephant; the higher it is raised, the more excited is the elephant. A low intensity threat consists of pointing the head towards the object threatened. As the threat develops, the head is lifted higher and higher until the elephant is glaring balefully over its raised tusks.

The trunk is no less expressive. Apart from feeding and scenting, it is used in a number of displays. As a gesture of irritation, it is lashed out towards a transgressor but it is not used in an actual attack and, when charging, the elephant carries its trunk rather floppily.

The more common use of the trunk is in social intercourse. In greeting each other, for example, the trunks are extended and the tips touch, rather like two people shaking hands except that more information, in the form of scents, is exchanged than is the case with a handshake. Elephants are very demonstrative creatures and the trunk is used to caress their companions. Much of the touching seems to be a form of reassurance, for it is particularly common under mildly threatening conditions.

Elephants frequently put their trunks into each other's mouths, possibly as a gesture of affection but more probably to exchange information. A young calf, for example, learns what to eat partly by sampling food items in its mother's mouth. Elephants of all ages, and of both sexes, indulge indiscriminately in such trunk-to-trunk or trunk-to-mouth contacts.

65

Communication by smell is probably very important for elephants. The discharge from the temporal gland smells very strongly of elephant and, while the animal feeds, the secretion, known as temporin, must be liberally coated over the vegetation, so providing other elephants with much information about the identity and activity of their neighbour. African elephants probably smear the temporin deliberately onto trees and bushes, for broken pieces of stick and other objects are often lodged in the duct of the gland (Short *et al.*, 1967).

Vocalization

Elephants are noisy creatures and make extensive use of sound in communication. They have a wide repertoire of calls, although there is some disagreement over how some of them are produced. Elephants have well developed vocal cords and many of the noises are clearly vocalizations but there is dissension over two calls, the trumpeting and the 'tummy rumble'. Trumpeting, or screaming, is the loudest call and is thought by most authors to be produced by blowing air through the trunk but McKay (1973) maintains that, at least in the Asian elephant, it is modified from a vocalization, the squeak, which is emitted as a single protracted sound of extremely high amplitude and resonated through the trunk. Trumpeting appears to be directed more at other species than at fellow elephants. Excited elephants often run through the bush trumpeting loudly but others in nearby groups rarely pay any attention to them.

The tummy rumble is more of a puzzle. Elephants certainly have noisy digestive systems but it is doubtful that intestinal churnings have any direct function in communication. It is alleged that elephants can switch off the tummy rumble at will but this seems unlikely on physiological grounds and it is probable that such reports have confused digestive noises with the low growl.

Sounds that are certainly made with the vocal cords include growls and soft roars. There is great variety in the intensity of these vocalizations, although the circumstances under which some of the sounds are produced are not always clear. Peaceful elephants frequently utter soft growls, which appear to be a means of communication, possibly between elephants that are out of sight of each other in thick vegetation. Elephants may also growl when startled, particularly if surprised on a road by a vehicle. These growls seem to have a different quality from those produced by undisturbed groups. Growling may also have aggressive overtones for it is sometimes heard when elephants appear to be angry, as when demonstrating before making a bluff charge, but it may be as much a form of reassurance as an offensive signal.

Elephants emit a variety of squeaks and squeals and Sikes (1971) maintains that the Asian species makes, as a form of greeting, a particular kind of squeak with its trunk that the African species cannot produce. She quotes a report of an anatomical difference in the nasal passages that makes this possible. McKay (1973) recognizes only three basic sounds in the Asian species, the growl, the squeak and the snort. The first can be developed by resonance and increased amplitude respectively into the rumble and roar. Multiple short squeaks produce a chirping sound and McKay believes that the trumpet is also derived from the squeak as mentioned above. The snort is said not to be a vocal sound but to be produced by exhaling rapidly through the trunk. If the trunk is bounced on the ground at the time of exhalation, a loud, booming sound, audible for a kilometre or so, is produced.

Home range

Not much is known about home range in elephants. Home range is a concept in biology which refers to the area covered by an individual animal throughout its entire life (Jewell, 1966). Within this region, all of which will be visited at some time or another, there is often a core area where the animal spends the great majority of its time. In order to determine the home range, one has to record the movements of an individual animal throughout its lifetime but this is clearly impossible in the case of elephants. Repeated observations over a long period will probably give a good idea of the home range but this term should be avoided in studies of limited duration.

The most prolonged series of observations is probably that carried out by Douglas-Hamilton (1973) in the Lake Manyara National Park. From more than 15 000 records of 48 family units and 80 independent bulls, he found that the elephants ranged over areas varying from 14 km² to 52 km². These are quite small ranges, considering the large size of elephants, but fragmentary evidence from other sources suggests that they are typical. In the Rwenzori National Park, John Wyatt and I recorded the sightings of 33 marked elephants during an 18-month period and none was found more than 22 km from the initial point of capture.

Leuthold and Sale (1973) observed the movements of individually recognizable elephants between December 1971 and March 1973, as well as following radio-marked animals, in the Tsavo National Park, Kenya. The average range of four elephants in Tsavo West was 350 km², with extremes of 294 km² and 441 km². The maximum distance between any two sightings of the same animal was 60 km for one of the males. Ranges were rather bigger in Tsavo East, with a mean area of 1580 km² and lower and upper limits of 525 km² and 3120 km² respectively. The maximum distance between sightings was 112 km. In this part of the Park, it was a female that moved furthest but it is likely that ecological factors, such as the availability of food, rather than sex, are responsible for differences in ranging behaviour. It is known that Tsavo West provides better elephant habitat than Tsavo East and hence one would expect the range to be smaller there.

In the Luangwa Valley, Zambia, thirty-seven marked bull elephants were followed by Rodgers and Elder (1971), using mainly tourists to record the sightings. The results showed that the elephants were extremely sedentary during the dry season and kept close to the Luangwa River, with only one animal straying more than 3 km from water. Movements up and down river were more extensive but the maximum distance between sightings for any elephant in the dry season was only 25 km. Few sightings were made during the wet season but from these, and from observations of unmarked elephants, it seems that widespread dispersal takes place at this time of the year.

Martin (1978) reports that very few sightings of marked elephants in the Sengwa Wildlife Research Area, Zimbabwe, were made more than 30 km from the point of capture. Fairall (1979) found a similar tendency to stay put in two groups of young elephants translocated to the Sabi Sand Game Reserve, next to the Kruger National Park. Their average monthly range was only 3.9 km² but, as the elephants had been artificially brought together and had had no previous experience of the region, their behaviour is not necessarily representative.

Olivier (1978a) studied the home range of Asian elephants in the rain forests of Malaysia by means of radio-tracking. His observations were too few and extended over too short a time for him to be able to determine true home ranges but, over periods lasting from 114 to 303 days, the elephants roamed over areas varying from 32.4 to 166.9 km². Interestingly, the range of family units in primary forest was found to be about twice as big as that in secondary forest. This difference is likely to be related to the different amounts of food available in the two types of forest (see p.105). Such a difference was not found in the males, probably because only a single bull was tracked in the primary forest whereas a group of two or three was followed in secondary forest. The latter would obviously require more food and, one would suppose, a larger foraging area. The sample studied by Olivier was too small for any general conclusions to be drawn but his operation suggests that the Asian elephant resembles the African in having a small home range.

It is clear that many elephant populations undertake seasonal movements. These do not necessarily, or even usually, involve a migration in the sense that the whole population moves from one region to another. Thus, in the Rwenzori National Park, Uganda, I found that the number of elephants in the grasslands fell during the dry season and it was obvious that many had moved into the nearby forest (Eltringham, 1977). Yet there were always some elephants in the grasslands and some in the forest at all times of the year.

Seasonal movements are dictated by rainfall not because the elephants need to find drinking water, but because of food availability, which, in tropical grasslands, is directly related to rainfall (Coe et al., 1976). Weir (1972) found that the seasonal movements of elephants in Wankie National Park, Zimbabwe, were governed by the distribution of water-holes that were rich in salt. Elephants have a precarious sodium balance, particularly in the harsh dry season in Wankie, which lies in the Kalahari Sands. Sodium demand rises in the dry season, because more is required for the digestion of the desiccated vegetation, and so elephants tend to remain within easy reach of these water-holes, despite the suitable browse elsewhere.

The finding that elephants have a small home range is surprising, because it is generally assumed that they move over huge areas. Such a belief is largely based on the stories of hunters and the early explorers, who write of vast elephant migrations, but the longest proven straight-line distance between sightings of an individual elephant is no more than 112 km (Leuthold and Sale, 1973) and the longest regular seasonal migration extends over only 30 km (Laws *et al.*, 1975). This does not necessarily mean that large-scale movements never took place in the past and it would certainly be unwise to rule them out completely over Africa and Asia as a whole (see p.157).

Territoriality and aggression

The question of territoriality in elephants has sometimes arisen. In a territorial species, one or more individuals guard all or part of their home range against others of their species. There need be no actual defence but the essence of territoriality is control over a piece of land. Usually, this involves exclusive use but, in some cases, the presence of other animals is tolerated, provided the dominance of the territory holder is respected.

The only recent authors seriously to propose the existence of territoriality in elephants are Sikes (1971) and Martin (1978). The evidence advanced in support of the suggestion by Sikes is circumstantial and capable of other interpretations, e.g. fighting amongst bulls and marking with secretions from the temporal gland. Martin's evidence rests on the behaviour of a radio-tagged bull, which was followed for over a year in the Sengwa Wildlife Research Area in Zimbabwe. One day, this elephant left his normal home range and, with a group of bulls with which he associated, was observed to indulge in a 'major battle' with another group of males occupying the area into which he had moved. He was chased back into his home region and subsequent tagging of the bulls on each side of the battle line showed that the large bulls always remained on their own side, although small bulls, and, to a lesser extent, medium-sized ones, readily crossed the boundary. Martin speculates that the large males hold territories which are visited by females for mating purposes. From the information given, it would appear that such territories, if they exist, are more in the nature of group territories since, in the observed case, there was a communal defence. It may be that elephant society is organized in a similar way to that found in the black rhinoceros, in which there is mutual tolerance between animals living in the same region but aggression towards strange beasts (Goddard, 1967).

The Douglas-Hamiltons (1975) specifically looked for evidence of territoriality in the Lake Manyara elephants but were unable to find any trace of such behaviour. In fact, all their evidence suggested the contrary. Wyatt and Eltringham (1974) came to the same conclusion from detailed observations of elephants in western Uganda. Admittedly, most of these elephants were females and it may be that territoriality, if it exists in elephants, is confined to the males. No sign of territoriality was found in any of the recent behavioural studies of Asian elephants and, in view of the similarity between the social habits of the two species, it would be surprising if one were territorial and the other not. In the great majority of cases, all observed contacts between elephants of both species have been peaceful, apart from those between bulls in the presence of oestrous females or the occasional aggressive reaction from a cow.

Aggression between bulls occurs, even in the absence of females, and such contests probably decide positions in the pecking order. Male elephants belong to a social hierarchy, which tends to reflect the age structure, since older elephants are bigger and contests are usually decided by weight. Very old bulls appear not to compete for status. Fighting between elephants takes the form of trunk wrestling but it is not easy to distinguish between play-fighting and the real thing. There is probably no hard and fast distinction and most incidents may start as a friendly tussle but develop into something more serious if the dominant animal finds itself being roughly handled. Most encounters take the form of a shoving match in which the tusks are not used. Tusk wounds do occur, however, and there are records of bulls being killed by others. Most of such fatalities presumably result from well matched pairs disputing mating rights. An elephant which is losing a dominance contest will break away before the fight becomes serious.

Play-fighting between elephants of both sexes occurs during calfhood and adolescence. Some of the younger cows may wrestle

Fig. 3.4 Two young bulls sparring. Such fights are seldom serious but they are important in sorting out the pecking order amongst males.

with each other but female elephants rarely show any animosity at all towards each other. There is apparently a social hierarchy amongst the females but again this is based on age and the old matriarch does not have to assert dominance over the others because her supremacy is never challenged. It appears from the work of the Douglas-Hamiltons (1975), that the matriarchs in the kinship group are ranked socially, with the oldest being the dominant animal. It is not clear whether the females in a sibling group have equal status or whether one is dominant. For the most part, elephant society is a model of friendly cooperation.

Aggression towards other species is not unknown. Elephants tend to ignore other herbivores, which in any case get out of the way. I have often seen elephants march up to a wallow containing resting buffaloes and with a lordly wave of the trunk see them off. On the other hand, I have seen instances at Treetops and at Mountain Lodge, on Mount Kenya, of a bull buffalo standing up to an elephant at the salt lick and even driving it away. Black rhinos defer to elephants but the supposed animosity between the species, which is often alluded to in the natural history literature, is rarely in evidence. One case is known, again at Treetops, of a group of elephants killing a rhino which had attacked one of their calves. The tables are sometimes turned with the Asian species and Laurie (1978) reports a number of instances of rhinos killing elephants. The species concerned is the great Indian rhino, which is much bigger than the black rhino of Africa. It often charges tame elephants but, if the elephant stands firm, the attack is not pressed home but, should the elephant turn and run, the rhino may chase after it and disembowel it with a slash of its razor-sharp tushes. Hippos and elephants appear to be mutually tolerant of each other but, as in the case of buffaloes, hippos move out of the way if directly approached by elephants.

Most antelopes, warthogs and zebras are treated as neutral objects by elephants although occasionally a youngster will charge one, apparently out of mischief. With predators it is a different story. The usual reaction of an African elephant towards a lion is to chase it and elephants will go to considerable trouble to seek out lions in their vicinity. They have some cause to do so because young elephants are at risk from predation. Adult elephants are invulnerable, although a hearsay report was quoted by Mgaah (1979) of a mature male elephant which was killed in 1975 by eleven adult lions at Mzima Springs in Tsavo National Park, Kenya. Such an occurrence must be very rare, if only because of the danger of injury to the attackers. There are numerous reports of Asian elephants being clawed by tigers but, in most cases, the elephants were carrying hunters. Sometimes the wounds are inflicted on females going to the aid of their calves. As the Asian elephant is smaller than the African elephant, and the tiger bigger than the lion, there is presumably less inhibition in making such an attack. The main danger to the elephant is that the wound may turn septic.

4 *Reproduction in elephants*

Elephants are slow breeders, producing only one calf at intervals, generally, of at least 4 years. There are records of twin foetuses in African elephants at a frequency of 1.35% (Laws, 1969a), and sometimes two infants will be seen with one female, but one can never be certain that one of them has not been adopted. Twinning in the Asian elephant is also known.

Courtship and copulation

The sexes live apart mostly and, if a mature male elephant is found in attendance on a family unit, it is likely that one of the females is in oestrus, unless it is a bull maintaining a friendly relation with its natal group. Females come on heat for a short period only, perhaps as little as 48 hours according to Short (1966). Each oestrous cycle takes about 2–3 weeks to complete and, if fertilization does not take place, further cycles occur over the next 2 months or so. Only one egg is released from the ovary at each cycle. In technical terms, therefore, the elephant is monovular and polyoestrous. The elephant does not conceive until late on in the oestrous period and the first three or four cycles are sterile.

From the few observations of mating in wild elephants, there appears to be little in the way of courtship. Kühme (1963) describes in detail the mating of captive African elephants at Kronberg Zoo. The female showed no obvious signs of being on heat but her condition was detected by the bull, probably from smelling her genital region, for Kühme noticed that the bull frequently touched the female's vulva with his trunk. The female moved away from the male on his first approach and there followed a short chase, very similar to the 'driving' seen in many ungulate species. This is a mutual activity in which the female encourages the male to follow

74

her. Periodically the cow turned to face the bull and trunks were entwined. Mounting was preceded by the bull laying his trunk and tusks along the back of the cow.

Observations on wild elephants suggest that their sexual behaviour is very similar. Sometimes a precopulatory chase is clearly described but, at other times, it seems that the bull simply walks up to the cow and mounts her (Buss and Smith, 1966). Short (1966) observed a young cow of about 18 or 19 years of age over much of her oestrous cycle and found that she was sometimes, but not always, chased before mating. There was certainly no attempt to solicit the male under any circumstances and the female remained completely passive during all copulations. Mounting was immediately preceded by the bull laying his trunk and tusks along the back of the female. Copulation lasted for less than a minute and some mountings were of only 5 or 10 seconds duration, but it is unlikely that penetration took place during such brief encounters. The bull stands almost upright during copulation and does not make any pelvic thrusts. These would be very difficult to execute in such a heavily built animal but, to compensate, the penis is particularly mobile and is moved up and down inside the urino-genital canal during copulation.

Copulation in the Asian elephant has often been observed and appears to be identical to that in the African species (Slade, 1903; Eisenberg et al., 1971; Ferrier, 1948).

Eisenberg and his colleagues recorded fourteen copulations by tame elephants in Sri Lanka and the average duration of the mount was 23.6 seconds (range 14–36 seconds). Successful mating was achieved on eight occasions with an average period of intromission of 9.2 seconds (range 6–15 seconds), although some of this time was spent probing for the vulva and the actual intromission lasted for less than 6 seconds. Precopulatory behaviour is very similar to that described by Kühme for the captive African elephants but Eisenberg et al. stress the frequency with which the male places his trunk in his mouth after touching the female's genitalia. It is likely that the elephant possesses a Jacobson's organ since one is present in the newborn calf. This is an organ in the roof of the mouth of many male mammals and it is used to detect oestrus by testing for the presence of hormones in the female's secretions. Most male mammals show *flehmen*, the curled lip grimace, when carrying out the test and Eisenberg *et al.* suggest that putting the trunk in the mouth is the equivalent of *flehmen*.

All aspects of reproductive behaviour are so much alike in the two species that the following account applies to both although most work on the physiology of reproduction has been carried out with the African elephant.

No detailed studies of the behaviour of bull elephants in the presence of oestrous females in the wild has ever been published and most of our information comes from casual observations. Some reports are conflicting but the recorded differences in behaviour may be explained by the observations of Short (1966), made over most of the oestrous period of one female. He found that, early in the oestrous cycle, mating was promiscuous and no antagonism was observed between any of the bulls. On the second day, however, there was much excitement, with several more bulls in attendance and much fighting between them. Usually this consisted of a large bull putting to flight a smaller rival but some of the fights were more serious and at least one bull had drawn blood, which had stained its tusks. At the end of the day, one of the large males had asserted its dominance and thereafter remained close to the cow, threatening any other male which approached. It is of interest that this bull did not show any discharge from its temporal gland.

The explanation of this pattern of behaviour may be that actual ovulation does not take place until late in the oestrous period. Hence early matings may not be fertile and there would be no point in the dominant bull competing for the cow at this stage. On the contrary, it is probably sound tactics to allow others to copulate for, having satisfied their sexual urges, they are more likely to wander off. When it really matters, i.e. when the egg has been released from the ovary, the dominant bull makes sure that he is the only one to mate with the cow. This explanation assumes that the sperm from earlier matings does not long survive in the genital tract of the female.

Kühme (1963) mentions that captive male elephants whose copulation attempts are frustrated roll in damp hollows. Buss and Smith (1966) observed wild males rolling in mud or taking a dust bath after failing to find a cow in oestrus or if they had been driven away by a larger bull. Perhaps this is the elephant equivalent of a cold shower!

A lot of ink has been spilled over whether or not the male elephant comes into season. Evidence for this was thought to come from the periodic appearance of musth in Asian bulls, when the temporal gland discharges continuously and working animals become truculent and unmanageable. Eisenberg *et al.* (1971) believe that musth is a rutting period, which, in Sri Lanka, tends to coincide with the wet seasons. The gland is not active in the female Asian elephant, nor in the male outside the period of musth, although Gee (1964) mentions that he has heard of cows producing a secretion and he further suggests that it is only captive bulls which become aggressive while on musth. Eisenberg *et al.* (1971) certainly found no evidence of aggression by wild bulls on musth towards cows. Whatever the explanation may be for the state of musth, it is not a condition directly associated with sexual activity, for elephants with quiescent glands are frequently observed copulating and bulls on musth do not necessarily show an interest in females.

There is, nevertheless, a marked increase in the level of testosterone, the male sex hormone, in the blood of elephants on musth (Jainudeen *et al.*, 1972). There is no relationship between testosterone in the blood and secretion of the temporal gland in African elephants, however, and low serum levels of the hormone have been recorded in males showing active spermatogenesis (Buss and Johnson, 1967; Short *et al.*, 1967).

Both sexes of the African elephant may produce a copious discharge from the temporal gland without showing any obvious change in behaviour and, consequently, it has always been assumed that the African elephant, like the female of the Asian species, does not experience musth. Recent work by Cynthia Moss and her colleagues (Poole and Moss, 1981), however, has revealed behaviour in bull elephants from the Amboseli National Park, Kenya, that has all the characteristics of musth. Certain bulls in Amboseli monopolize the matings and are easily recognizable from their aggressiveness and from changes in the penis, which becomes greenish in colour and dribbles a continuous mucous discharge. All the elephants in the park are known individually and these bulls were once as placid as the others. The symptoms develop suddenly, just like the onset of musth in Asiatic elephants. It would not be surprising if the two species, so alike in many ways, did not also share the phenomenon of musth but, so far, the condition has not been reported in elephants from other parts of Africa. This may not necessarily be significant because most previous studies of elephant behaviour have concentrated on cows and it is quite likely that musth, now that it has been recognized in Amboseli bulls, will soon be identified in other populations. It would be extremely interesting to examine the testosterone levels in the Amboseli elephants to see if they show the same variations as those found in Asiatic bulls.

Breeding seasons

The question of seasonality in reproduction is separate from that of the significance of musth. The elephant is perhaps the only large tropical mammal for which male seasonality has been suggested but, before discussing this aspect, we will consider first whether or not there are breeding seasons in elephant populations. 'Breeding season' is a vague term and, to avoid confusion, the period of copulation and conception will be called the mating season and that of births the calving season.

Conflicting statements appear in the literature on the subject of seasonality in the reproduction of elephants with Perry (1953) and Buss and Smith (1966) maintaining that conceptions and births can take place in any month. More recent studies have revealed clear-cut seasons of reproduction. It is true that breeding can occur throughout the year in certain regions, particularly on the Equator, but even so, there are certain months in which breeding is intensified. The general picture seems to be that the elephant is indeed a seasonal breeder but that it will calve throughout the year, wherever conditions make it possible. These conditions include adequate rainfall, such as is likely to be found in equatorial regions (Fig. 4.1).

A population near the Equator, whose reproductive behaviour has been studied in detail, is that in the Kabalega Falls National Park, Uganda, (Laws et al., 1975). The peak of the mating season in the area north of the Nile more or less coincides with the wettest month of the year. Most births, therefore, occur some 2 months before peak rainfall, given the 22-month gestation period. Curiously enough, the population south of the Nile shows a different pattern. There is no obvious peak, but the month with most conceptions

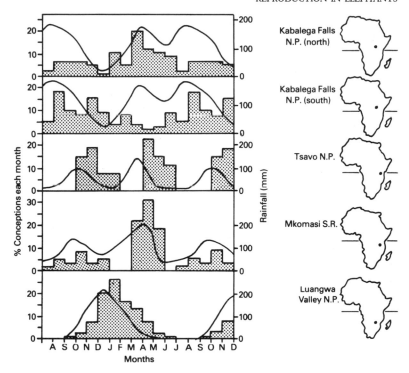

Fig. 4.1 Times of conceptions related to rainfall in African elephants. Note that there are breeding peaks in all populations but that the peaks tend to separate out into more definite breeding seasons with increasing distance from the equator. (From Laws *et al.*, 1975.)

occurs some 6 months earlier, at a time when the rainfall is beginning to decline. It is thought that this reproductive cycle is aberrant, due, possibly, to the overcrowding that used to occur there. This assumption is supported by the fact that, elsewhere in Africa, the reproductive seasons are similar to that found north of the Nile, i.e. with peak conception taking place at the time of greatest rainfall and births occurring when rainfall is rising. Besides Kabalega Falls National Park, this breeding pattern has been recorded in many other national parks. Malpas (1978) was unable to demonstrate seasonal breeding in the elephants of Rwenzori National Park, Uganda, but his sample was rather small. The breeding cycles recorded were by no means identical but had in common the association between conceptions and rainfall. In some parks, such as Luangwa Valley (Smith and Buss, 1973) and, in certain years, Kruger National Park (Smuts, 1975), peak conceptions occurred towards the end of the rainy season, i.e. a couple of months after the wettest period.

In regions with two wet seasons a year, such as those on or near the Equator, peak conceptions seem to occur during the first of the two rainy seasons, i.e. during the long rains, according to the results of Laws *et al.* (1975) in Kabalega Falls National Park, although, in a subsequent but less intensive study, Malpas (1978) detected a further peak in conceptions during the second wet season.

Rainfall is clearly the trigger that stimulates mating in elephants and, consequently, births tend to occur soon after the beginning of the rains at a time when rainfall is increasing. Being born at this time of the year is highly advantageous, for the grass is growing vigorously and is highly nutritious, being rich in proteins and sugars. The excellent grazing ensures that the mother elephant has an abundant flow of good quality milk with which to rear her calf at the most critical stage of its life.

Male seasonality

In theory, it would seem to be non-adaptive for a bull elephant to enter a period of sexual quiescence for the elephant is not an annual breeder and, although there are mating seasons, some females may come into oestrus in most months of the year. It would be highly disadvantageous for a male if it were to run the risk of meeting an oestrous female at a time when its testes were non-functioning. In those mammal species that experience periodic regression of the testes, such as deer or rodents, there is a definite mating season when all males are fertile. Conversely, there are no females at all on heat during the time that the males are sexually inactive. Nevertheless, there is evidence of a seasonal variation in reproductive activity in bull elephants. Thus the mean diameter of the seminiferous tubules in the testes of elephants culled in Uganda varied from 180μ, during a month of peak conception, to 163μ when conception was low (Laws, 1969a). It has not been established, however, that bulls with narrow seminiferous tubules are infertile. It

Fig. 4.2 A young bull sniffs another. Such small animals would be unlikely to breed in the presence of fully adult bulls, which would soon chase them away if they attempted to mate with an oestrous female.

is possible that the variation is not a seasonal one at all but is rather the reflection of a difference in the reproductive status of the males, similar to that found by Cynthia Moss in the Amboseli bulls.

The general picture of elephant society that is beginning to emerge is that of a number of bulls loosely associated with a kinship group of females and their young and living within a defined area, which is possibly a group territory. The bulls know each other and often keep company but only on a most casual basis. There is almost certainly a social hierarchy amongst the bulls but perhaps no one bull is dominant over all the others. When a female comes into oestrus, she is taken over by the nearest high-ranking male but he does not necessarily prevent copulations by other bulls, although such matings are unlikely to lead to conception. At least in the Amboseli, and probably elsewhere, only a proportion of the bulls are reproductively active at any one time but, even there, a bull not on musth will copulate if the opportunity arises.

This is the pattern that can be deduced for the African species and, while it is likely to apply to the Asian species as well, we cannot be so confident because there have been fewer field studies on the Asian elephant.

81

Birth

The birth of a wild elephant has been witnessed on a number of occasions but no particular sequence emerges from the published accounts. The most detailed and best-illustrated account of an elephant birth is that given by the Leutholds (1975). Sometimes the female separates from her group but there are plenty of examples of births taking place within the family unit. No particular arrangements are made and the infant falls wherever the mother happens to be standing. Birth sometimes appears to be an exhausting process, understandably, perhaps. with a baby bouncing at 120 kg, and the mother may rest for several hours afterwards. The other elephants in the group take a great interest in the new arrival, feeling it all over with their trunks. One case has been reported by the Douglas-Hamiltons (1975) of another adult female in the group acting aggressively towards a newborn calf that happened to approach her, but the elephant had a young calf of her own and may have been particularly edgy in her protective zeal. By contrast, a 9-year-old female in the same group was particularly solicitous of the calf's welfare and such 'baby-sitting' is a common trait in adolescent female elephants. The care provided by 'auntie' is probably an important factor in calf survival and is compatible with modern ideas on kin selection because of the close degree of relatedness between members of a family unit. It is not surprising, therefore, to find frequent reports of mutual suckling of calves by females within a group. In the case of virgin females, the helpers themselves derive benefit from baby-sitting because they gain experience in the rearing of calves which they can put to good use when they themselves become mothers.

Maternal care

The degree of maternal care is exceptionally high in elephants and is certainly no less than that found in the human species. Such care extends beyond protection from predators or the mere provision of milk, for the mother's watchful presence ensures that the baby does not get lost or meet with an accident. I have often seen a mother fall back and offer a calf a helping trunk to enable it to scramble up a

Fig. 4.3 A threat, even one as mild as that posed by the photographer, drives the baby elephant to sanctuary between its mother's front legs. Note that the cow is scenting the air to see if there is any real cause for concern.

steep bank. As the calf grows older, the mother's attention wanders and it is left more to its own devices but she will always come to its aid should real trouble threaten. She is probably quite aware of the fact that the younger females will look after it anyway. The Douglas-Hamiltons tell of a young elephant who fell asleep and did not notice his mother's departure. He was roused by his elder sister.

The easy tolerance of calves by all the females within the group led Woodford and Trevor (1970) to attempt to foster an abandoned infant onto another family unit. Baby elephants are extremely difficult to hand-rear, particularly with the limited resources usually available in the bush, and most soon succumb to digestive upsets. The young elephant found by Woodford and Trevor was lucky. Its first approach to the wild herd was met by a bull, who knocked it over, but its second rush brought it to a nursing cow with a calf of her own, only a little bigger than the orphan. She immediately suckled it, and the rest of the herd, after showing the same interest in it as in a newborn calf, accepted the newcomer, which was seen alive and well over a week later. An attempt by Douglas-Hamilton at a similar fostering had a less happy ending for, although the orphan was accepted, it was not suckled and grew steadily weaker and died. I had even less luck with a fostering attempt. The group I had chosen as the new family for an abandoned calf would have nothing to do with it and the matriarch marched towards the young creature and tossed it through the air with her tusks.

The mother will suckle the calf for years and older siblings will also try to feed, even those as old as 9 years. Such large calves do not need their mother's milk and the experience of suckling an offspring with well developed tusks is probably a painful one which is not encouraged. Weaning begins at a few months of age but it is a gradual process and the calf is not fully independent of milk until it is around 2 years old. The calf sucks with its mouth, not with its trunk, and newborn elephants have to stretch to reach the breast.

Puberty

The age at which elephants become sexually mature varies with locality and appears to be dependent on the environmental resources. Variation in the age of puberty is one of the mechanisms controlling the birth-rate in elephants. The normal age of sexual maturity for African elephants is about 11 to 12 years but, in Kabalega Falls National Park in Uganda, it was found to be between 17 and 18 years (Laws *et al*., 1975). Females in the Budongo Forest, Uganda, were even older, with an average age of over 22 years. One 34-year-old female in Budongo was still not sexually mature but the condition was probably pathological. Despite statements to the contrary, there is no significant difference between the sexes in the age at which they become sexually mature (Table 4.1). There is however a considerable difference in the age at which they begin to breed. Mature females are soon mated and produce their first calf some 2 or 3 years after their first ovulation. The males, on the other hand, do not reach social maturity for many years and have no hope of fathering calves until long after they have passed puberty. As we have seen, there is keen competition amongst bulls for oestrous females and an 11-year-old youngster would not stand a chance.

Table 4.1   Mean age of African elephants at sexual maturity

Locality	Year of study	Age (years)		Authority
		Male	Female	
Budongo Forest, Uganda	1966	—	22.4	Laws et al., 1975
Gonarezhou Game Reserve, Zimbabwe	1971–72	12	12–13	Sherry, 1975
Kabalega Falls National Park, North, Uganda	1966	15.6	16.3	Laws et al., 1975
,,	1974	13.2	9.6	Malpas, 1978
Kabalega Falls National Park, South, Uganda	1957–64	—	7–15	Buss and Smith, 1966
,,	1967	17.2	17.8	Laws et al., 1975
,,	1974	14.8	9.0	Malpas, 1978
Kruger National Park, South Africa	1970–74	—	12	Smuts, 1975
Luangwa Valley National Park, Zambia	1964–69	15	14	Hanks, 1973
Lake Manyara National Park, Tanzania	1966–70	—	11	Douglas-Hamilton, 1973
Mkomasi Reserve, Central, Tanzania	1968–69	10.8	12.2	Laws et al., 1975
Mkomasi Reserve, East, Tanzania	1968–69	12.5	12.2	Laws et al., 1975
Rwenzori National Park, Uganda	1974	18.3	12.3	Malpas, 1978
Tsavo National Park, Kenya	1966	14.9	11.7	Laws et al., 1975
Wankie National Park, Zimbabwe	1972	—	11	Williamson, 1976

Detailed figures for Asian elephants are not available. Williams (1950) maintains that the average female is first mated between the ages of 17 and 20 years. This seems rather on the late side but presumably he was referring to captive elephants. Nevertheless, this is well within the range noted for African elephant and it is likely that in this, as in so many other features, the two species are very similar.

Calving interval

The gestation period in both species is about 22 months (*c*. 660 days) so that, theoretically, it would be possible for a female to produce a calf every 2 years. Sikes (1971) believes that this is normal in African elephants and cites the case of a second birth, to a zoo elephant, 124 weeks (about 2 years 5 months) after the first. Her evidence that wild elephants also breed every 2 years is less convincing and depends on the assumed difference in ages between calves seen with the same female. The only information I can find on wild Asian elephants comes from similar evidence. Gee (1964) measured three calves in a family of wild elephants caught in a stockade and, from their shoulder heights, estimated their ages as 1, 3 and 7 years, i.e. an average calving interval of 3 years with one as little as 2 years. The shortest interval estimated for African elephants is 2.9 years for the population in the eastern sector of the Mkomasi Game Reserve in north-eastern Tanzania but, elsewhere in the reserve, the period was 4.9 years. Data for other regions of Africa show that the calving interval can extend for up to 9 years but, more usually, it is between 4 and 5 years (Table 4.2). most of these are instantaneous calving intervals (p.39), based on the percentage of pregnant females, but some refer to estimates derived from placental scars.

Perry (1953) showed that the elephants which he studied in Uganda undergo a lactational anoestrus of 2 years following birth, i.e. the female does not come into season during the 2 years that she is suckling a calf. This would result in a minimum of 4 years between births.

All the evidence points to 4 years as the optimum calving interval. A 2-year period would probably place too great a strain on the cow if continued throughout her lifetime. The food resources in Mkomasi East are particularly good and probably account for the short inter-calving period there, but Laws *et al*. (1975) point out that

Table 4.2. Calving intervals in African elephants estimated by two methods: a) from the percentage of pregnant adult females (the instantaneous calving interval) and b) from the number of placental scars.

Locality	Elephant density* per km²	Year of study	Calving interval (years)		Authority
			From % pregnant	From placental scars	
Budongo Forest	2.12–4.12	1966	7.7		Laws *et al.*, 1975
Gonarezhou Game Reserve	1.85	1971–72	3.7	4.3	Sherry, 1975
Kabalega Falls National Park, North	1.16	1966	9.1		Laws *et al.*, 1975
Kabalega Falls National Park, North	1.10	1974	5.1	4.6	Malpas, 1978
Kabalega Falls National Park, South	1.00	1958–64	8.6		Buss and Smith, 1966
Kabalega Falls National Park, South	2.70	1967	5.6	4.9	Laws *et al.*, 1975
Kabalega Falls National Park, South	1.22	1974	3.5	5.1	Malpas, 1978
Kruger National Park	0.41	1970–74	4.5	4.5	Smuts, 1975
Luangwa Valley National Park	2.17	1965-69	3.5**	3.4	Hanks, 1972b
Lake Manyara National Park	5.00	1966–70		4.7***	Douglas-Hamilton, 1973
Mkomasi Reserve, Central	0.82	1969	4.2		Laws *et al.*, 1975
Mkomasi Reserve, East	0.82	1968	2.9		Laws *et al.*, 1975
Rwenzori National Park	2.14	1973	4.5	4.2	Malpas, 1978
Tsavo National Park	0.88–1.11	1966	6.8		Laws *et al.*, 1975
Wankie National Park	0.62	1972	4.0	4.3	Williamson, 1976

*Elephant density figures are derived from various sources in the literature.
**According to Malpas (1978) this figure is more correctly calculated as 3.8 years.
***The calving interval for Lake Manyara National Park is based on observed births in a population of individually known elephants.

the 63% pregnancy rate (on which the estimate is based) could not be maintained for long because, once the pregnant females had given birth and entered lactational anoestrous, only 37% of the cows would be available to become pregnant. Even if all of these conceived right away, the instantaneous calving interval would rise to nearly 5 years. This would literally be true only if the births were synchronized but, as they almost certainly are not, a period considerably shorter than 5 years is possible.

Density and fecundity

Marked deviations from the ideal 4-year calving interval are thought to be due to nutritional factors. Variation in the calving interval is the most potent way of altering recruitment to an elephant population (Hanks and McIntosh, 1973) and it appears to work on a density dependent basis, the higher the density of elephants, the longer the calving interval. Table 4.2 is not very convincing on this point but some of the density figures are not very accurate and the population counts were not necessarily made at the same time as the calving intervals were estimated. If, as seems likely, there is a density dependent relationship, the connecting factor is presumably food. Because elephants destroy their habitats at high density, the amount of food available to them is reduced, causing a lowered fertility in the females. The principal anomalies in the relation between density and fecundity in those elephant populations included in Table 4.2 are the high density in Lake Manyara National Park and the 'wrong' difference between the elephants north and south of the Nile in Kabalega Falls National Park. The latter is probably due to short-term fluctuations in the pregnancy rates (Laws *et al.*, 1975), since the populations were sampled in different years and at different seasons. In the case of Lake Manyara, the likely explanation is that, despite their high density, the elephants there have not damaged their habitat to an extent whereby they suffer from food shortage. Lake Manyara National Park is particularly productive, with rich volcanic soil and an abundant supply of water from a high water table and numerous permanent streams cascading down the Rift wall. The park and the nearby Marang Forest represent a nutritional 'hot spot' for elephants, where densities may reach levels that would prove disastrous in less favoured localities.

5 Food and feeding habits

Digestion

The elephant's diet contains a high proportion of cellulose, a carbohydrate which mammals are unable to digest. Herbivores have, in their digestive systems, millions of protozoans and bacteria that produce cellulase, an enzyme capable of breaking down cellulose. These organisms digest the food and the herbivore simply absorbs the products of digestion, as well as digesting the protozoans and bacteria when they die. The process of digestion is a form of fermentation and, therefore, the herbivore must carry around a fermentation chamber inside it. In the case of the ruminants (animals that chew the cud), the fermentation chamber, or rumen, lies in front of the gastric part of the stomach. Such mammals are called *pregastric digesters*.

In non-ruminants, which besides elephants include horses, rhinoceroses, rabbits and rodents, digestion takes place in the greatly expanded caecum and in the colon. These parts of the gut are anatomically behind the stomach, so non-ruminants are called *postgastric digesters.*

The main fermentation vat in the elephant is the caecum, although fermentation also takes place in the duodenum and colon. Eloff and van Hoven (1980) took samples of the intestinal fluid from fifteen elephants shot on control in Kruger National Park and from two elephants in Zaire. The concentration of protozoans was highest in the colon, due to the absorption of water, but, although on a unit volume basis fermentation may be greater there than in the caecum, the caecum is more important in respect of the total amount of fermentation that takes place. All the protozoans were ciliates, one of the most advanced groups in the phylum. Some examples from elephants are shown in Fig. 5.1.

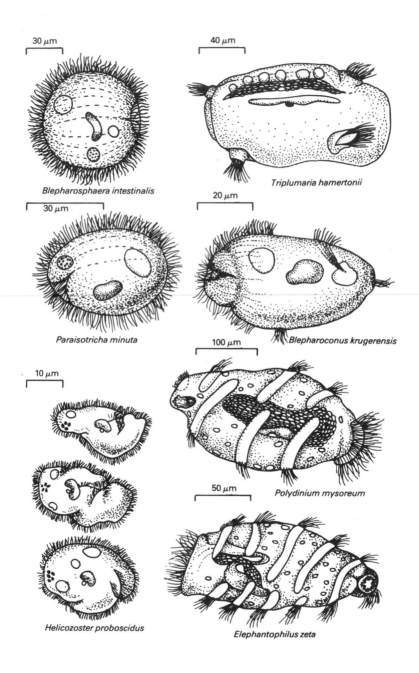

30 μm
Blepharosphaera intestinalis

40 μm
Triplumaria hamertonii

30 μm
Paraisotricha minuta

20 μm
Blepharoconus krugerensis

10 μm
Helicozoster proboscidus

100 μm
Polydinium mysoreum

50 μm
Elephantophilus zeta

The possession of micro-organisms in the gut is essential to the herbivore but it is not born with them and must be 'infected' after birth. In the case of ruminants, the young calf acquires the protozoans during mutual licking with its mother or by feeding on plants contaminated by saliva. Because ruminants are continually bringing up boluses of cud from the rumen, drops of rumen fluid are bound to be distributed liberally over the pasture. This does not happen with the postgastric digesters and 'infection' must take place through the droppings. Although most of the ciliates and bacteria in the rectum are dead, a few must survive and pass out with the faeces. Contamination of food by the droppings is quite likely but instances are known of deliberate coprophagy (eating faeces) in young elephants (Guy, 1977). Such a practice could be widespread and have as the principal function the introduction of fermentative bacteria and protozoans into the gut. It is known that such micro-organisms can survive passage through the stomach in rabbits without being digested and this is probably also the case in elephants.

In general, ruminants are more efficient at extracting protein from their food than non-ruminants, but the latter compensate for this by passing the food more rapidly through the gut. As a result, they are more efficient than ruminants at dealing with low-quality food. Although the ruminant extracts a higher proportion of the protein from inferior forage, the non-ruminant, because of the rapid passage of food, processes a greater quantity in a given time and so, in the long run, it obtains more nourishment.

The time taken for food to pass through the gut of elephants has rarely been measured but, for the African species, it is given as 11 to 14 hours by Bax and Sheldrick (1963) and 21.4 to 46 hours by Rees (in press). Benedict (1936) suggests an average figure of about 24 hours for the Asian elephant. There is probably no specific difference and the rate is likely to vary with the nature of the food,

Fig. 5.1 Examples of some ciliates from the intestines of African elephants. These organisms are responsible for breaking down the cellulose in the food, which the elephant itself cannot digest. (From Eloff and van Hoven, 1980.)

but any of these passage times is much faster than those òf ruminants.

Food passage is relatively slow in ruminants because the food has to be broken down into particles small enough to pass through a sieve-like opening between two of the four 'stomachs'. Freed of this necessity, the non-ruminant can increase food intake at times when the quality falls off (as in winter or during the dry season) and so maintain a constant nutritional level (Janis, 1976). The elephant, therefore, is adapted to feeding on low-grade food that is abundant and varies seasonally in quality, i.e. grass, and so, on theoretical grounds, one would expect the elephant to be a grazer.

The food of elephants

Many of the investigations made of the feeding behaviour of elephants do indeed show that grass figures prominently in the diet. Buss (1961) considers that grass is so important that open grassland must be the natural habitat for the African elephant. This is not entirely logical for animals need more than food from their environment. The most detailed study of feeding in the African elephant is that of Field (1971), who worked in two contrasting regions of the Rwenzori National Park. His results confirm the predominance of grass in the diet but also show that elephants tend to take plant types in the proportions in which they are available. He

Table 5.1 Food types taken by elephants in the Rwenzori National Park, Uganda, expressed as percentages of the total feeding time spent eating each type*

| Food type | Short grass study area | | Tall grass study area | |
	Monthly mean (August-May)	Monthly range	Monthly mean (August-May)	Monthly range
Grass	54.8	31.0–74.0	71.1	45.0–92.5
Browse	20.6	8.0–45.0	6.4	1.0–11.5
Forbs	24.6	9.0–42.0	22.9	1.5–49.0

*After Field, 1971

divided the food items into grass (including sedges), forbs (non-woody dicotyledons) and browse, the latter consisting of woody vegetation from thickets or trees.

There was considerable seasonal variation. In the long grass area, where there were few woody plants, nearly three quarters of the diet consisted of grass whereas, in the short grass region, with numerous thickets, the proportion fell to little more than half (Table 5.1). There was not much difference in the proportion of forbs but there was a very marked increase in the consumption of browse in the area where it was plentiful. There were notable seasonal changes in the diet. In the short grass area, browse was very important in the dry season and consumption rose markedly when the total monthly rainfall fell below 50 mm. In the long grass area, there was also a tendency for browse to increase in the dry season but in neither region did browse become a dominant food item at any time of the year.

The two study areas concerned were close enough together for

Fig. 5.2 A grazing elephant. Without its long trunk, the tall elephant would be unable to reach the ground and, therefore, would be unable to be a grazer.

Fig. 5.3 A browsing elephant. The long trunk enables the elephant to reach high up in the trees. Occasionally, an elephant will rear up onto its hind legs to extend its reach even further.

the same animals to occur in both, so the differences recorded cannot be ascribed to population preferences but suggest that elephants eat whatever is available. Field's conclusions were supported by Wyatt and Eltringham (1974) who worked in the same park.

Comparable studies by Field and Ross (1976) in the Kidepo Valley National Park, which lies in the semi-arid north-east corner of Uganda, showed that the diet of the elephants comprised 46% grass, 17% forbs, 29% trees and 9% shrubs (i.e. 55% browse). There was considerable seasonal variation (Table 5.2), with a significantly smaller amount of grass (28.6%) taken in the dry months compared with the wetter periods (57.2%). Seasonal rainfall averages are shown in Table 5.2.

Elephants probably take more browse in the dry periods because, firstly, the grass is usually withered and unpalatable and, secondly, the browse is often green for, with their deeper root systems, bushes

Table 5.2   The average percentage composition of the diet of elephants from the Kidepo Valley National Park, Uganda, 1969–72*

Food type	Dry seasons		Wet seasons		Intermediate seasons	
	% Taken	Range	% Taken	Range	% Taken	Range
Trees	41.0	35.4–46.3	17.3	1.0–37.2	23.9	20.1–27.7
Shrubs	17.6	14.7–20.7	3.5	1.9–4.9	3.6	3.0–4.2
Forbs	12.8	8.6–17.7	22.2	4.6–40.9	14.7	14.0–15.4
Grasses	28.6	26.1–32.0	57.2	53.5–61.7	57.8	55.3–60.3
Average rainfall	28.3 mm		134.7 mm		56.0 mm	

*After Field and Ross, 1976

and trees can find water even at the driest time of the year. Many savanna trees are deciduous and lose their leaves during the dry season but some, bushes particularly, retain their leaves throughout the year.

Forbs are important food items because they contain a higher proportion of protein and sugars and a reduced fibre content compared with grass. Their consumption by elephants seems to vary inversely with that of grass and is highest during the rains. Again this reflects the tendency of elephants to eat whatever is most available.

The feeding habits of the African elephants away from equatorial regions were studied by Guy (1976) in Zimbabwe. There, the seasons tend towards summer and winter rather than wet and dry but ecologically there are three seasons, cold (May — July), hot (August — October) and wet (November — April). Thus the cold season falls in the winter and the wet season in the summer and autumn. The elephants, 48 in all, were followed on foot and their feeding habits recorded by direct observation of the species of plant eaten and an attempt was made to quantify the data by counting the number of trunksful passed to the mouth.

Guy's results show distinct seasonal differences. Over the whole year, the elephants took more browse than grass in the proportion of 1:1.8. The greatest difference occurred in the hot season (1:7.5) but in the wet season more time was spent grazing than browsing (1:0.4). This is presumably because grass grows actively in the wet season and is rich in proteins and sugars. In the hot season, when the grass is withered and of little food value, the elephants, as in East Africa, turn more to browse. The very marked seasonal differences recorded contrasts with results from East Africa but may in part be due to inadequate sampling, for Guy's observations extended on average for less than one third of each 24-hour period and none was made at night.

The food of elephants does not correlate mathematically with what is on offer and a considerable degree of choice occurs. The elephant cannot subsist solely on grass and, even in Field's tall grass area, where the animals had to go to some trouble to find woody forage, browse made up a significant proportion of the food in most months of the year. Conversely, in the short grass area, where the

Fig. 5.4 The percentage of browse taken by elephants in Zimbabwe at five levels, the lower four of which are roughly equal in extent. Note that most of the food is taken from the lower levels. (After Guy, 1976.)

% of browse eaten

c. 280 cm   V 8.5

IV 9.6

III 24.4

II 30.1

I 27.4

elephants could have eaten nothing but browse had they so wished, grass remained the dominant food in all but one (anomalous) month.

Guy found that his elephants did not make full use of their reach but tended to feed on vegetation growing within 6 m of the ground (Fig. 5.4).

It is of interest to see what elephants that live in forests eat. Grass is a rare plant on the forest floor and grassy pastures are found only along river banks or in open glades. An elephant that wants to feed on grass in a forest, therefore, has to go out of its way to find it. One of the very few studies made of the feeding habits of the forest race of the African elephant (*Loxodonta africana cyclotis*) is that of Merz (1977), who worked in the Ivory Coast. He found that seeds figured notably in the diet during the fruiting season, which extends from December to February, and could make up to 35% of the dry weight of elephant droppings. A wide variety of fruits was eaten, with 29 species being recorded in January. After February (26 species), the number of species found in the dung fell off rapidly with 12 in March, 11 in April and only 3 in May. The seeds themselves mostly pass through the gut undamaged.

At other times of the year, the forest elephants fed on a wide variety of plants — 67 species were identified. The parts eaten included leaves, twigs, whole branches and bark. Trees from 41 species were found to have been knocked over and mostly eaten. The plants were not consumed indiscriminately and, although a precise quantification was not possible, it is clear from Merz's studies that certain species were particularly favoured as food.

Secondary forest proved especially attractive (see p. 105). Foliage was the principal food taken but some grass from open spaces was eaten by forest elephants, although its proportion in the diet was extremely low.

Studies by Alexandre (1978) in the same rain forest in the Ivory Coast showed the importance of elephants as seed dispersers. Of the 71 species of tree in the Tai Forest whose seed dispersal mechanism was known, 21 (29.6%) were dispersed by elephants. Altogether, seeds from 37 tree species were identified in elephant droppings and, of these, only 7 were known to be dispersed by monkeys or birds. At certain times of the year seeds from only 2 tree species could make up half the dry weight of the droppings.

It is interesting to compare these results with the much more detailed study made by Olivier (1978a) of the Asian elephant living in the forests of Malaysia. Olivier compared the percentage of the various food items in the diet of tame elephants feeding freely in the forest with the percentages on offer to the elephant in its environment. His results show that there was considerable selection by the elephants of certain food types, particularly grass (Table 5.3). Thus, although grass comprised only 1% of the available food, it constituted one third of the elephants' diet. Although these elephants were tame, it does appear that the Asian elephant differs from the African forest elephant in seeking out grass. Despite forming such a high proportion of the diet of Asian elephants, grass is not the most important food item. Palms make up nearly half of the food — a proportion not greatly different from that on offer. Tree material tended to be unpopular as food but there was a certain preference for forbs.

McKay's study (1973) in Sri Lanka, where grassland and savanna are much more abundant than in Malaya, confirms the importance of grass in the diet of the Asian elephant. A typical set of observations in the Ruhunu National Park shows that over 88% of the time was spent feeding on grasses. This pattern is much more

Table 5.3 Food preferences of elephants from Malaysian forests calculated from the amounts of different types on offer and the amounts eaten* (A preference index greater than 1.0 means that the food is actively selected)

Food type	% Available	% Eaten	Preference index % in diet/% available
Trees	33.6	14.9	0.44
Palms	58.6	43.9	0.75
Forbs	6.8	8.1	1.20
Grasses	1.0	33.1	33.10

*From Olivier, 1978a

like that of the African bush elephant and provides further evidence that, in similar vegetation types, the ecologies of the two species are alike.

Food quantities

Various techniques are available for determining the intake of food (see p. 33) and estimates for wild African elephants have varied from 120–300 kg fresh weight (Guy, 1975). Those based on droppings weights include figures of 120 kg and 270 kg. Estimates derived from the weight of stomach contents are liable to error, depending on the allowances made for the amount of water that may have been drunk and the accuracy in determining the rate of passage through the gut.

In order to measure the daily intake of elephants in Zimbabwe, Guy (1975) counted the number of trunksful taken by an individual and multiplied this by the estimated weight of a single trunkful of food (75 gm). The amount varied from season to season and between the sexes but the daily consumption averaged 170 kg for males and 150 kg for females. The highest values were found in the wet season, with figures for males and females of 225 kg and 200 kg respectively.

There is little information on the amounts of food eaten by Asian elephants, apart from those in captivity, which are usually fed on concentrates. Olivier (1978) does not give a figure, contenting himself with a consideration of relative quantities as being the more reliable method of comparing elephant diets, but McKay (1973) estimates the daily intake to be 150 kg in Sri Lanka.

All these values refer to wet weights, i.e. fresh forage. The dry weight of green foods is about one quarter of the wet weight but this value is rather higher for twigs and other woody foods taken by elephants.

Feeding rates

The technique of counting the number of trunksful of food taken in a given time was used by Wyatt and Eltringham (1974) with Ugandan elephants. They showed that the feeding rate varied considerably during the day and also found some evidence to suggest that differences occurred between the sexes and between elephants feeding in different habitats. There was a very significant tendency for the feeding rate to increase from morning to evening. The minimum rate recorded was 3.5 trunksful per minute between 0800 and 0900 hours and the maximum was 8.5 per minute between 1900 and 2000 hours. These figures were for females in grassland; a male feeding on bush vegetation by a lake shore had a much higher feeding rate of 14 trunksful per minute.

Guy (1975) examined the feeding rates in greater detail during his studies of Rhodesian elephants but he did not detect any increase during the course of the day. He did, however, find a higher feeding rate in males compared with females but the difference was slight and not statistically significant. Seasonal trends were also apparent, with increased rates during the periods when food was not readily available. The overall feeding rate was about half that of the Ugandan elephants (5.9 per minute) with means for males and females of about 2.7 and 2.4 trunksful per minute respectively. In Serengeti, Croze (1974 a) gives a figure of 2.4 trunksful per minute for tree-feeding and one of 5.3 trunksful a minute for grass, much the same rate as those for Ugandan elephants.

The feeding rates of Asian elephants from Sri Lanka were found by McKay (1973) to be rather lower than those observed for the African species (Table 5.4). There were some variations, depending on the type of food eaten and the sex of the elephant, but the differences are not significant. Vancuylenberg (1977) studied the same elephants and his data reveal even lower feeding rates. He reports that the elephants ate 8 kg of food in 1 hour and, using his figure of 150 gm per trunkful, the feeding rate can be calculated as 0.89 trunksful per minute. Olivier (1978a) recorded similar rates with elephants from Assam (0.87 per minute) and Malaya (0.88 per minute) but his results may not be strictly comparable because he studied tame, hobbled elephants, although they were allowed to wander freely in the forest and to select natural vegetation.

The rate at which elephants stuff food into their mouths obviously depends on a number of factors, not least their degree of hunger. It was obvious to me that elephants feed in real earnest on rising from their night's rest, when they presumably have empty stomachs.

Table 5.4   Feeding rates of elephants in Sri Lanka*

Type of food	Number of elephants observed	Sex of elephants	Observation period (minutes)	Number of trunksful taken	Rate (trunksful per minute)
Grass	14	Male	141.75	131	0.92
Grass	11	Female	52.0	71	1.37
Shrubs	5	Male	27.5	39	1.42
Shrubs and grass	2	Male	29.0	35	1.21
Fruit	1	Male	10.0	30	3.00
All types (totals)	33	Both	260.25	306	1.18

After McKay, 1973

Towards the end of a feeding bout, they are much more fastidious, picking over possible food items and almost playing with their food. The other important factor that determines how long it takes an elephant to eat a mouthful is the amount of preparation that is necessary. This is usually much greater in the forest than in open grasslands. An elephant feeding on grass has an easy time. Grass is plentiful and readily gathered, the elephant doing little more than wrapping its trunk round a tuft and pulling, perhaps pausing only to knock off any soil from the roots before popping the bunch into its mouth. In the forest, on the other hand, food has to be searched for. The edible parts of lianas are high up in the forest canopy and out of sight. The elephant has to spend a lot of time and effort in pulling down the stems in order to reach the leaves. Many woody plants have strong thorns or other mechanical defences which have to be gingerly negotiated if the elephant is not to hurt itself while collecting food. Some plants may have only small portions that are edible, e.g. the pith, and their extraction can be particularly time-consuming. Twigs and small branches have to be broken up into suitable lengths and properly oriented in the trunk before being

101

placed in the mouth. Sometimes food selection takes place in the mouth, with unwanted items being passed to the side of the jaws and discarded. All this takes time.

Some foods, such as fruits, are particularly time-consuming to eat because of their small size and scattered distribution and the elephant feeds on these only if they are abundant and can be rapidly popped into the mouth one after the other. Despite its great dexterity, the trunk can rarely be used as a precision instrument in this way because the time involved in dealing with small food items is excessive in terms of rewards.

We can only conclude that both species have similar requirements and are mainly non-selective bulk feeders on poor quality food. A certain amount of high quality food is taken but the quantity is limited by the time taken to prepare it before it can be put into the mouth. For this reason, the elephant is principally a grazer. Grass is easily gathered, has few mechanical or chemical defences and is usually abundant. Only in the forest is it scarce but forest-dwelling elephants go to great lengths to find it. The preponderance of grass in the diet does not mean that elephants can survive on grass alone. Woody material is essential, for apart from providing important nutrients absent from grass, a certain amount of fibrous bulk is necessary to ensure adequate digestion. There is little woody or other structural matter in succulent young grass and an elephant feeding exclusively on it would be liable to constant colic and other digestive upsets. The feeding strategy is a rapid passage of food through the gut and perhaps the worst fate that could befall an elephant is constipation. Roughage ensures that this does not happen. This may well be the reason why elephants tend to strip the bark off trees more in the wet season than at other times of the year. Suggestions that bark-eating satisfies nutrient requirements are less probable. Anderson and Walker (1974) found no correlation between the chemical composition of the bark and leaves from 16 species of trees in Zimbabwe and the likelihood of such trees being attacked by elephants.

Food diversity

A few species of grass make up the bulk of the food plants taken by most elephants but a great variety of other species is eaten, albeit in small amounts. The first detailed examination of stomach contents was made by Buss (1961), who found at least 7 grass and 18 other plant species in 71 elephants collected in western Uganda during the dry season. From direct observations of feeding elephants, Field (1971) recorded 19 grasses, 3 sedges, 16 woody species and at least 4 forbs in the short grass region of Rwenzori National Park in Uganda. Comparable figures for the long grass area were 17 grasses and at least 10 browse species. (The imprecision is due to some unidentified forbs and browse species.) An analysis of the stomach contents of elephants shot on control in the Wankie National Park, Zimbabwe, revealed a minimum of 60 plant species in the diet (Williamson, 1975). As mentioned earlier, the food of the forest subspecies of the African elephant was found to consist largely of fruits, of which 53 were identified as coming from trees and 5 from herbaceous plants (Alexandre, 1978).

There is less information on the Asian elephant, but up to 400 food plants were identified by Olivier (1978a) for elephants in Malaya and Sumatra. Not all of these species would be eaten by any one group of elephants and the figure represents the variety of food plants that might be taken throughout the whole range. McKay (1973) recorded the species of plants eaten by elephants in Gal Oya National Park in Sri Lanka and his list comprises 18 herbs, (including 14 grasses), 3 vines and 67 trees or shrubs.

Elephant food and plant defences

Grasses respond to grazing primarily by increasing their growth rate and can soon replace lost leaves. They grow continuously from the base, so that a cropped leaf easily regrows, with only a square tip to show that it was once nipped off by a grazer. The leaf of a dicotyledonous plant, however, grows from a bud and once lost cannot be replaced until the next spring or equivalent season. Such leaves are 'expensive' to produce and, under the uniform conditions of the tropical rain forest, there is no physiological reason why trees and shrubs should ever drop their leaves and indeed some leaves are very durable, living for up to 7 years before being shed. If the leaf is to last for that length of time, it must have some protection from the attentions of herbivores. Defences may be mechanical or chemical.

Many plants are protected by spines or thorns, as well as by a thick cuticle. A thick corky bark is another mechanical protection and it certainly limits the damage caused when an elephant uses a tree as a rubbing post. There has been no study of the effectiveness of thorns against mammalian browsers but certainly elephants do not seem to be much inconvenienced by them. There is only one reference in the literature to a large mammal (impala) being deterred by thorns (Dunham, 1980), although a · thorough investigation would probably reveal many more because it is difficult to see what other function such thorns have. They are unlikely to be a deterrent to invertebrate herbivores, although other mechanical defences, such as a thick cuticle, are effective.

Chemical protection of a plant is indicated when certain so-called secondary compounds, which play no part in the metabolism, are present in the leaf or stem. The principal function of secondary compounds is presumably to deter animals from feeding on the foliage, although some, such as fruit flavours and floral scents, are attractive to animals. Chemical defences include acrid latex, tannins, cyanogenic glucosides, alkaloids, saponins and aromatic oils. Some of these are poisonous but others are merely distasteful.

Vegetation containing toxins can be eaten only if the animal is capable of detoxifying the poison in its liver. Most invertebrate herbivores and some mammals, such as the koala, feed nearly exclusively on one species of plant and have evolved an enzyme that permits them to neutralize any poison that the plant may contain. Most mammalian herbivores, and certainly a generalist feeder like the elephant, could not easily evolve an enzyme to deal with every poison that might be present in the wide range of food plants taken. One solution is to avoid eating poisonous plants and, indeed, most of the food plants of the elephant are low in chemical defences. Another ploy is to eat only a little of each poisonous plant, because the liver is capable of detoxifying small quantities of any poison, although it would be overwhelmed by a single massive dose. This strategy has also been adopted by elephants, which take a wide range of plant species when feeding in forests.

Other chemical defences act not by poisoning the animal but by reducing the digestibility of the food. Tannins do this by binding

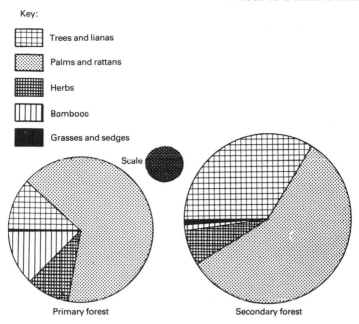

Key:

Trees and lianas

Palms and rattans

Herbs

Bamboo

Grasses and sedges

Scale

Primary forest   Secondary forest

Fig. 5.5 Pie diagram showing that the food available to elephants in the Malaysian secondary forests is both more abundant and more suitable than that in primary forests. The scale represents 10 trunksful per 400 m². (From Olivier, 1978a.)

with proteins, rendering them indigestible so that the animal has to eat much more of the plant in order to obtain sufficient nourishment. The animal is deterred, not because it has an insight into the biochemistry of its own digestive processes, but because a plant high in tannins is distasteful.

Plants of the tropical rain forests, where many elephants live, are particularly well endowed with chemical defences. This is to be expected because rain forest vegetation is at the extreme of three gradients of plant defences (Janzen, 1975), i.e. it is a climax vegetation, growing in a region of poor resources with little or no seasonal influence. It is not, therefore, an ideal habitat for herbivores and the animal biomass is generally low. This is certainly true of elephants, which much prefer secondary forest because of the greater amount of food available (Fig. 5.5). In the early stages of a secondary forest, many of the plants are colonizing species, with few chemical

Table 5.5 Direct and indirect estimates of the relative densities of Asian elephants in primary and secondary rain forests*

Estimate	Forest type		Ratio Secondary/Primary
	Primary	Secondary	
Maximum density in plotted home ranges per km^2	0.12	0.27	2.3
Crude ecological density in adjusted home ranges per km^2	0.12	0.65	5.4
% Presence of faeces in sample plots	6.0	16.0	2.6
% Presence of tracks in sample plots	31.0	42.0	1.4
% Number of days in each habitat on which elephants were encountered	7.1	15.2	2.1

*From Olivier, 1978a

defences, and hence, are very palatable to elephants.

Evidence that elephants are more abundant in secondary forests comes from the work of Olivier (1978a), who used a variety of techniques to compare the abundance of elephants in the two forest types in Malaya (Table 5.5). In every case, the index was higher for the secondary forest. In one case, the results suggest that there were over five times as many elephants in the secondary forest. Further evidence is provided by the differences in the sizes of the home ranges that Olivier found between primary and secondary forests (see p.69). Since the resources are better in the secondary forests, one would expect the home range to be smaller and this proved to be the case. The difference was particularly noticeable with female groups, whose home range in primary forest was 166.9 km^2 compared with only 59.3 km^2 in secondary forest.

6 *The daily round*

During its long life, an elephant experiences many vicissitudes. Droughts are followed by floods, men cut down forests or settle in once virgin bush but, for long periods, conditions remain much the same and the elephant lives out its life on an even tenor in which days come and go, each much the same as any other, with only such rare highlights as matings or births. It has no predators and there is little in the way of intraspecific strife. Even seasonal changes are so gradual that one phase merges imperceptibly into the next. This gentle pace of an elephant's life is not apparent to the hunter, or even to the national park visitor intent on an arresting picture, and the high proportion of photographs in wildlife books showing elephants charging or threatening the photographer gives a false impression of elephants at home.

Very little is known about the daily round of an elephant in the wild because most observations have been made for no more than a few hours at a time and usually only during the day. When I was studying elephants in Uganda with John Wyatt (Wyatt and Eltringham, 1974), we found that we needed to know how elephants filled the 24 hours in order to put our other observations on movements and numbers into perspective and we decided to take it in turns to follow elephants during the period of full moon, so that we could see the animals at night. Binoculars are excellent light-gatherers and, with their help, one can see very clearly what elephants are doing once one's sight has adjusted to the dim illumination. Our observation period was limited to a day or so on either side of the full moon because, outside of this period, the time of moonrise falls too long after sunset for elephants to be kept in view during the dark period. Continuous watches have been maintained on elephants during the day but I think that ours is still the only published study of night-time activity in the wild. Fig. 6.1 shows in graphical form a summary of our conclusions.

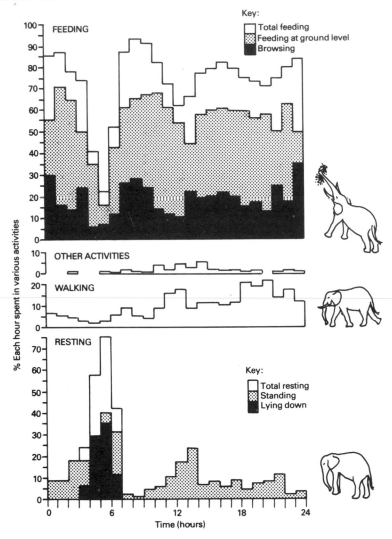

Fig. 6.1 The activity pattern of eighteen female elephants in Rwenzori National Park, Uganda, over an average 24-hour period. (After Wyatt and Eltringham, 1974.)

Feeding

The first thing that became clear to us was that elephants spend most of their time eating. About three quarters of the day and night are spent feeding, but not in one continuous session because some time is needed for digestion. We found that there were three main feeding bouts: one in the morning, another in the afternoon and the third around midnight. These peaks were not clear-cut and there were always some elephant groups feeding whatever the hour but each family has definite resting periods during which none of them feeds.

Eating is also the preoccupation of Asian elephants, judging from some studies in Sri Lanka. McKay (1973) found that the bulls spent nearly 94% of the daylight hours in feeding and the cows nearly 91%. He estimated that over the 24 hours, feeding occupied 80% of the time (19 hours), but he allowed only 2 hours for sleeping, which seems a little on the low side. Later on in the same area, Vancuylenberg (1977) found that about 75% of his day-time observations were of feeding elephants and, from this, he concludes that 17 to 19 hours a day are spent eating, without, it seems, making any

Fig. 6.2 Elephants often wander into swamps to feed on the aquatic vegetation.

allowance for night-time sleeping. Neither worker made any observations at night.

Sleeping

The main resting period for the Ugandan elephants was in the small hours of the morning, usually some time between 0300 and 0700 hours, although the period was extremely variable. The elephants fell sound asleep, often snoring loudly and contentedly. This was the only time we saw any of our study group lie down. It is often said that elephants never lie down to sleep but this is far from the case. It is true that very large elephants appear reluctant to lie down and most sleep standing up, probably because a heavy animal finds it an effort to raise its huge bulk from the ground. It is also true that elephants rarely lie down during the day, even those that habitually do so at night. The grass is flattened by the great weight of an elephant when it lies down to sleep and characteristically shaped 'elephant-beds' are left in the morning. Lying down has a marked effect on the ecology of the rangeland for long, unpalatable grasses, such as cotton grass (*Imperator cylindrica*) or blue grass (*Cymbopogon afronardus*), sprout after they have been flattened and the tender young shoots are much appreciated by grazing antelopes. The action of the elephants is very similar to that of fire in causing tough old grass to be replaced by nutritious young growth.

The Asian elephant also appears to have special sleeping sites. McKay (1973) noticed open clearings in the jungles of Sri Lanka, some 50–100 m² in area, often at the confluence of two game trails, and he believes that these are used as 'rest rooms' by elephants, who break down the vegetation to form room-like enclosures. Abundant piles of dung show that elephants remain in these 'rooms' for long periods and it is reasonable to assume that they spend the time sleeping or resting. The very fact that they stay in one place for any length of time would tend to create the conditions described, for resting elephants will often while away the time by pulling the vegetation apart.

It is fairly easy to predict when a group is going to stop eating and go to sleep. The feeding rate slows down until the elephants are merely toying with their food, taking an inordinate amount of time in slapping a tuft of grass against a foot or twisting a thicket shoot round and round in the trunk before popping it into the mouth. No one individual appears to decide when bed-time has arrived but all lie down or stand still within a few minutes, even if they appear to be out of sight of one another. I could not resist the conclusion that, in some way that I could not detect, they were able to communicate their intentions to each other.

To be within a few feet of a group of sleeping elephants at night is a profoundly moving and peaceful experience. The great shadowy hulks with moonlight-dappled hides present no danger to the observer, whose presence is accepted as part of the landscape, no different from the gleaming mounds that are the damp backs of hippos or the vague shapes that are antelopes, alert and less secure than the elephants. The background noise of the African night with the chirping of crickets and frogs, the various grunts and squeals of buffalo, and perhaps the distant roar of lions, add to the peace and tranquillity of the scene. Few other animals would dare to abandon themselves to such luxuriously profound slumber in the dangerous African bush. Clearly, the elephant is the king of beasts.

The night-time sleep can last for anything from 1 to 4 hours but it is not always continuous. Sometimes the elephants wake up and even move a few metres before settling down to sleep again. Waking up is as synchronized as going to sleep and it is an impressive sight as one huge hulk after another rears from the long grass, almost as if they had sprung out of the earth itself.

Elephants also rest during the day, usually in the early afternoon. The purpose of this rest period is probably not so much to sleep as to avoid the heat of the day, since the elephants usually move to the shade of a tree. All the elephants we watched remained standing and appeared only to be dozing. Some elephants do lie down by day and I have often seen them stretched out in the shade apparently sound asleep. Many of these were males but I never made any systematic records and there may not be a sex difference in the sleeping behaviour. It can be seen from Fig. 6.1 that resting can occur at any time during daylight hours but that there is a gradual build-up during the morning which reaches a peak between 1300 and 1400 hours.

McKay (1973) reports a decline in elephant sightings around

noon in Sri Lanka, which suggests that Asian elephants also like to shelter from the midday heat.

Drinking and bathing

Drinking in both species usually takes place once a day when water is readily available. Our elephants in Uganda drank, on average, 1.3 times in the 24 hours. On 7 of 15 days for which we obtained detailed records, the elephants drank only once. No drinking at all took place on 3 days while, at the other extreme, they drank 3 times on each of 3 other days. In arid areas, elephants may go for several days without drinking but their maximum endurance in the absence of water is not known. Heath and Field (1974) observed a group of thirty-four Kenyan elephants that became accidentally incarcerated in a 14.2 ha paddock where no water at all was available. Although they became very emaciated, the elephants survived for 14 days before most of them broke out. Of the four remaining, two escaped and one died on the following day, while the remaining animal died on the seventeenth day. Both victims were young animals, aged between 2 and 3 years. Although no free water was available, the elephants would have obtained some moisture from the dew which formed in the grass at night and some further water would have been available in the vegetation. The elephants suffered from more than water shortage, since the quality of the food was well below that necessary for health, but these observations show that elephants can survive for long periods without free drinking water.

The elephant is not very fussy about the quality of the water it drinks. I have seen an elephant stop within a few metres of the edge of a lake with crystal clear water and drink from a small muddy wallow. It was my impression that elephants do not go out of their way to find water but drink at the nearest available source when they happened to come across it. In the area where I carried out my observations, there was an abundance of wallows so that the elephants could have drunk frequently had they so wished, yet they appeared to ration themselves to only an occasional drink.

Elephants use water for more than drinking, since they frequently bathe. I was unable to determine what factors induce an elephant to immerse itself in water. The animals we were watching in Uganda could have bathed at any time, for they were never more than a few kilometres from a lake or river, yet none of them took the opportunity of doing so during the study periods. When they do bathe, elephants give every sign of thoroughly enjoying the experience, thrashing around in the water and often completely submerging themselves. The youngsters, in particular, show great high spirits, tussling with each other and climbing over the recumbent bodies of their elders.

Elephants usually anoint themselves with mud after drinking. It is said that they do this to protect themselves from the sun or from insect bites but the body is only patchily covered and I think that the main function of such daubing is to lose heat through evaporative cooling, with the mud performing the function of sweat, which the elephant does not seem to produce. Elephants will also cover themselves with dust, which cannot have the same cooling effect. The 'dust' usually contains sand and gravel and Spearman (1970) suggests that these particles act as abrasives and promote the shedding of the hard keratinized flakes in the skin. He also thinks that bathing by elephants is concerned with skin care as it prevents the horny layers from becoming too dry and brittle. Elephants appear to lack sebaceous glands as well as sweat glands and so produce no sebum, which, in other mammals, serves to keep the skin soft and flexible.

Walking

The elephants we watched did not move very far in the 24 hours and some typical wanderings are illustrated in Fig. 6.3, from which it can be seen that the animals often moved in a circle. We found it impossible to divert the elephants from their direction of movement. We wished to do this sometimes when the elephants were heading for thick bush country in which we expected (correctly as it often turned out) to lose them. Not wishing to disturb them unduly we merely parked the Land-Rover in their way but the elephants were not to be put off and simply walked round the vehicle when they came to it. We could not see any reason why the elephants chose to go in a particular direction but Barnes (1979), who followed elephants on foot and who was, therefore, in more intimate contact

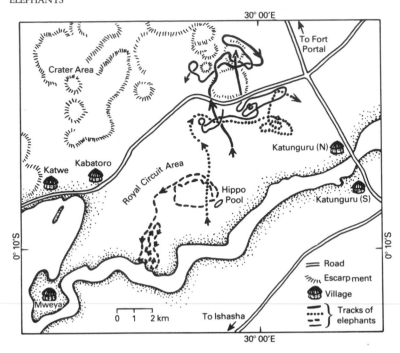

Fig. 6.3 Map of the Royal Circuit Area of Rwenzori National Park, Uganda, showing typical wanderings of four female elephants followed over 3-day periods. Note that the elephants never moved far and often returned to places which they had visited earlier. (After Wyatt and Eltringham, 1974.)

with them, found that they tended to move into the prevailing wind, particularly in hot weather. The reason, presumably, is that by so doing they ensure that a cooling current of air constantly passes over both ears.

The distances covered by our elephants were quite small (the furthest was 38.6 km — in 67 hours) and the average speed at which the elephants moved was about 0.5 km an hour. Their actual walking speed is much greater but the figure reflects the leisurely way in which elephants move through the bush, stopping to feed at thickets for up to 15 minutes at a time. Asian elephants are even slower, according to McKay (1973), who recorded the distances moved by feeding groups. There was no difference between the sexes and the average speed for all elephants can be calculated from his data as 0.129 km per hour, with a range of 0.01 to 1.5 km per hour.

The elephants often completely hide themselves in the centre of a bush when feeding. Occasionally we did not notice them leaving, particularly at night if the sky was overcast, and this was one of the ways in which we sometimes lost them. Usually the elephants alternate browsing with grazing but, in the dry season, when they spend long periods browsing, they walk directly from bush to bush without stopping to graze.

Walking was one of the activities we measured. We did not count movements from bush to bush during feeding as 'walking' but only continuous pacing at a smart rate. Such deliberate walking tended to occur soon after dusk and often resulted in a greater change of location within a few minutes than during the preceding 12 hours or so. Such walking was always in single file along the well marked game trails. I used to fall in behind the elephants to keep them in sight and one evening I found that I had been rather quick off the mark because three others suddenly appeared behind me and

Fig. 6.4 A family group, with the matriarch in the centre, moving through thornbush to better pasture. The matriarch's knowledge, accumulated over the years, is important for the survival of the group when conditions deteriorate.

brought up the rear. The little procession of half a dozen elephants with my Land-Rover in the middle continued across the bush for a kilometre or two, apparently without the elephants seeing anything untoward in the arrangement. I could never see the point of this sudden locomotion because the elephants did not appear to be going anywhere. They moved off from featureless bush and stopped in similar country where they began to feed, the activity that they were usually carrying out before moving off. The total time spent walking amounted to 9.3% of the time for elephants followed for at least 24 continuous hours. This compares with the 5.4% and 16.1% obtained by McKay (1973) and Vancuylenberg (1977) respectively, from their intermittent day-time observations of Asian elephants in Sri Lanka.

Defaecation

Another factor in which we were interested was the defaecation rate of the elephants. This information is useful for a number of reasons, e.g. dropping counts are a measure of the number of elephants in a region — but only if the number of droppings produced in a given period is known. A knowledge of dung production is also necessary for a proper understanding of the feeding ecology of a species. Several people had made such observations before us. Benedict (1936) found that Jap, his tame Asian elephant, defaecated 14–18 times a day. This is close to the figure of 17 times a day found by Wing and Buss (1970) for African elephants in the same park as the one in which we studied them. Coe (1972) followed four tame African elephants which were allowed to wander freely through Tsavo National Park, Kenya, during the day, but which were shut up at night and provided with lucerne and natural browse. The mean defaecation rate was found to be about 17 times every 24 hours. Dougall and Sheldrick (1964) followed another tame elephant, a male, in the Tsavo National Park for 11½ hours, during which time it defaecated 14 times, i.e. over 29 times a day. Our mean figure was about 7 defaecations a day for cows, a figure which is much lower than previously published data. A subsequent study by Guy (1975) in Zimbabwe gave a rate of 14 times a day for bulls and 10 times a day for cows. The only recent figure for the Asian species that I can find is that given by Vancuylenberg (1977), who made sporadic observations, totalling 129 hours, of 37 elephants from Gal Oya National Park and Lahugala Tank in Sri Lanka. The average interval between defaecations was found to be about 2 hours (128 minutes), equivalent to a rate of 12 defaecations in 24 hours.

There is clearly considerable variation in these figures. Some of the differences may be due to errors in extrapolation, for only Coe and ourselves actually recorded the number of night-time defaecations. Coe studied immature elephants, whose defaecation rate might be different from those of adults, and it is possible that our data were inaccurate because we could not be certain that we witnessed every evacuation that took place. This uncertainty, of course, also applies to the other studies. When our data were analysed on the basis of the interval between observed defaecations, i.e. ignoring the periods before and after the first and last defaecations, the results showed an average interval of 127 minutes or a rate of about 11 defaecations a day, a figure which is close to that found by Guy for cow elephants.

Another reason for the discrepancies may be seasonal differences in the frequency of defaecation. Such differences were clearly demonstrated by Barnes (1979) in his study of elephants in Ruaha National Park, Tanzania. He found that the frequency was significantly higher in the wet season and that the differences could be correlated with the amount of green matter in the diet. An analysis of the data given by Wyatt and Eltringham (1974) also shows more frequent defaecation in the wet season — once every 3 hours compared with once every 6.6 hours in the dry season.

Defaecation is a regular phenomenon for elephants because of their continuous feeding habits, but peaks do occur. We found a bimodal distribution with peaks between 0900 and 1200 hours and between 1500 and 1800 hours, while Coe (1972) found several peaks with maxima at 0900–1000 hours and 1600–1700 hours. Dougall and Sheldrick (1974) observed an increase in the frequency of defaecation during the afternoon. There is a cessation of defaecation during the few hours spent asleep at night but faeces are produced soon after waking and are typically found near the elephant 'beds'.

7 *Physiology and growth*

Many aspects of the physiology of elephants have already been considered in earlier chapters. The first detailed physiological investigation was carried out by Benedict with the Asian elephant, Jap (see p.41). Many of the 'physiological facts' reported were more anatomical than physiological but the data included heart-rate (28 per minute standing, 35 per minute lying), respiratory rate (10 per minute standing, 4–5 per minute lying), body temperature (35.9°C), faecal production (110 kg per day) and urine output (50 litres per day). Benedict examined the urine in some detail. It was turbid rather than clear and slightly acidic, with a mean specific gravity of 1.019 (range 1.004–1.033). The average volume discharged at one time was 5 litres, with a maximum of roughly twice that amount. The weight of dissolved solids passed in the urine amounted to over 2 kg a day, of which 160 g were common salt. The nitrogen content of the urine was 5 mg per ml and the carbon content varied from 5–20 mg per ml, depending on the diet. In addition to water lost in the urine, about 22 kg of water were evaporated from the lungs and skin in equal proportions. Up to 310 litres of air were respired per minute.

Few of these findings have been tested with wild elephants for obvious reasons. Measurements of heart or respiratory rates can be made with immobilized elephants, although one cannot be sure that the drug used does not affect these variables. Several workers have taken such recordings but very few have published their data.

Body temperature

The body temperature of wild elephants was measured by Buss and Wallner (1965) from recently shot animals and from recently passed droppings. The average rectal temperature of nine elephants taken from 3 to 35 minutes after death was 36.4°C, with a range of 36.1 to 36.8°C. The mean of measurements taken from the droppings of 20 elephants was also 36.4°C, with a range of 36.0 to 36.8°C. The temperatures were taken from 1 to 8 minutes from defaecation. These temperatures are only slightly lower than the body temperature of man (36.9°C) and certainly not low enough to justify the contention of Buss and Wallner (1965) that a reduced body temperature in the elephant could be of significance in the location of the testes within the abdomen instead of in a thermoregulatory scrotum as in most mammals.

Benedict (1936) measured the temperature of the urine of the Asian elephant, Jap, and found it to be 35.9°C. The temperature inside a ball of faeces was 36.6°C. He also measured the temperature of the skin at various points on the body and found that it varied from 26–30°C. Sikes (1971) gives a diagram of an African elephant, showing temperatures as low as 21°C on the ear at an ambient shade temperature of 19.5°C. One would expect the body extremities to be at a low temperature, particularly the ear of the African elephant, because this organ is used as a heat radiator. This is possible because of the large arteries and veins close to the skin on the back of the ear. Hot blood in the arteries is cooled as it filters through the network of capillaries into the veins before being returned to the body. Wright (in Buss and Estes, 1971) found a difference of up to 19°C between the temperatures of the arterial and venous blood. It is likely that the elephant can vary the diameter of the arteries and so regulate the blood flow but the cooling effect is achieved in two principal ways (Buss and Estes, 1971). The elephant either extends its ears and faces down wind, so that the cooling air blows across the back of the ear, or actively flaps its ears to generate the current of air; this technique is particularly common when there is little wind. Ear flapping in little or no wind increases significantly when the air temperature rises above 25°C or thereabouts (Fig. 7.1) and the rate increases directly with the ambient temperature. If the ears are spread out, the flapping rate is low and independent of temperature because the elephant relies on the wind to dissipate the heat radiated from the ear. At night, or when it is cold or raining, the ears are held closely against the body and are not flapped at all.

McKay (1973) found that the Asian elephant also uses its ears in

119

ELEPHANTS

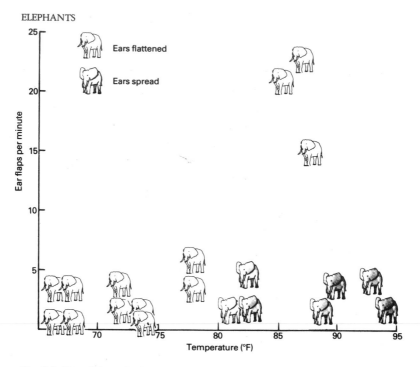

Fig. 7.1 Pictorial graph showing the rate of ear flapping amd the position of the ears of Ugandan elephants at various environmental temperatures. Note that in hot weather (over 80°F) the ears are either spread out or flapped vigorously. (After Buss and Estes, 1971.)

thermoregulation. The intensity of ear flapping increased when clouds cleared away or when the wind dropped, changes that would result in an increase in heat stress. On hot windy days, the ears were not flapped but were extended sideways, as in the African species, to catch the cooling breezes. It is interesting that extension of the ears occurred only in adult males and McKay suggests that a sub-adult male might be chary of using such a cooling technique in case it were mistaken for an aggressive gesture by older elephants.

Temperature control is a constant problem for an animal as large as an elephant. It has a low surface-to-volume ratio, so that little body heat can be lost by radiation, and it is as likely to gain heat from its surroundings as to lose it, because its dry, black skin readily absorbs the sun's rays. If, as it is thought, it has no sweat glands, it cannot lose heat by the evaporation of sweat. Its usual strategy is to

120

avoid getting too hot by sheltering from the sun in the middle of the day. Another ploy is to souse itself with water.

The differing sizes of the ears of the two species might suggest that temperature control is less of a problem for the Asian elephant. The ambient temperatures in Asia are probably no lower than those in Africa but water for cooling is generally more readily available and the predominantly forest habitat means that the Asian elephant is less likely to absorb heat from the direct rays of the sun. It is perhaps significant that the forest race of the African species has distinctly smaller ears than those of the bush elephant.

A few African elephants suffer from 'lop ear', which may affect one or both organs. The cause is not clear. Sikes (1971) believes that the condition is associated with the arterial disease known as medial sclerosis, which reduces the flow of blood to the ear musculature. I have noticed that there may be two such 'lop ears' in a family unit and wonder if the condition is hereditary.

Blood chemistry

Brown and White (1980) have recently reviewed our knowledge of elephant blood. The red blood cells of the two species are the same size but are much bigger than those of any other mammal examined, except for the giant anteater of South America, whose blood cells are of similar proportions. The mean diameter of a red blood cell of an elephant is 9.25 μm, compared with 6.7 to 7.7 μm in man. Probably because of the large size of the corpuscles, cell counts tend to be lower in elephants than in other mammals.

The amount of haemoglobin in the blood, which is a measure of the efficiency of the blood in transporting oxygen, is slightly higher for the African elephant than for the Asian species and about the same as that found in man. Abnormally low values have been recorded in wild African elephants (Debbie and Clausen, 1975; White and Brown, 1978) and may indicate anaemia, although the possibility of sampling error cannot be ruled out, especially as abnormally high values have also been reported.

Elephant haemoglobin has a higher oxygen affinity than that of most other mammals, in keeping with the size of the animal. It is slightly lower in the smaller Indian elephant. An increase in the concentration of carbon dioxide in the blood, which in most mammals causes the haemoglobin to release more oxygen (the Bohr effect), has only a slight effect in elephants.

Blood clotting, which depends on platelets in the blood, is much more rapid than in man and is slightly faster in the Asian than in the African elephant. This may be due to differences in the numbers of the blood platelets, which range from 540 to 637 $\times$ 10^9 per litre in the Asian elephant, and from 294 to 455 $\times$ 10^9 per litre in the African species. The human range is 150 to 400 $\times$ 10^9 per litre.

Various environmental factors can affect these properties of the blood. White and Brown (1978) found seasonal differences in wild African elephants, with significantly higher values in the dry season for red blood cell counts and for amounts of haemoglobin than during the wet season. On the other hand, mean cell volume was significantly lower. They attributed these differences to the effects of dehydration. These authors found no difference between the haematology of pregnant and non-pregnant animals, although such differences have been noted in the Asian species, in which there was a significantly lowered red blood cell count and packed cell volume and a correspondingly higher erythrocyte sedimentation rate in pregnant animals (Nirmalan et al., 1967). Nirmalan et al. also found differences between pregnant and non-pregnant Asian elephants in the white blood cell count, but again White and Brown (1978) could detect no such differences in the case of African elephants. In both species, however, the white blood cell count was higher in young calves than in older animals. Most authors have found white blood cell counts to be similar in both species.

The possibility that stress can alter the normal characteristics of the blood must be taken into consideration. Even shooting has been thought to have an effect, while some extreme values obtained from immobilized animals suggest that it may be unwise to rely on samples from drugged animals. Despite this, it must be admitted that results from wild elephants that have been shot and from presumably unstressed elephants in zoos do not differ appreciably.

The total amounts of protein and other nitrogenous compounds in the blood serum of African elephants from Uganda have been measured by Brown et al. (1978). Compared with other mammals, elephants appear to have a higher content of total protein in the serum but a lower amount of albumin. Much of the high protein levels is due to the quantity of γ-globulin present.

Diet and condition in elephants

Only the quality of the diet will be considered here. This can be measured in a number of ways but the protein content of the food is perhaps most important. A detailed comparative study of three elephant populations in Uganda was made by Malpas (1977), who compared diet and condition in relation to various ecological factors. Some of the details are rather technical but the general principles emerge clearly enough.

Malpas measured the quality of the diet by analysing the stomach contents of elephants shot in three regions of western Uganda. One was the Rwenzori National Park, where elephants appeared to be in good condition and living in harmony with their environment. They were considered to be the 'control' in the experiment and to represent a healthy elephant population. The other elephants were shot in the Kabalega Falls National Park, where there has been a history of overpopulation by elephants, which have destroyed the tree cover and degraded their habitat. The elephants hardest hit were those south of the Nile, which divides the park in two, so separate samples were taken from the two sides of the river.

The results of stomach analyses confirmed that the diet of elephants in Rwenzori National Park had a higher protein content than that of elephants in either region of the Kabalega Falls National Park. There was also a seasonal difference, with protein levels being higher in the wet season than in the dry season (Fig. 7.2a). Levels in the dry season in Kabalega Falls National Park fell consistently below the 6% value considered necessary for health in a young growing elephant (McCullagh, 1969b). Thus the diet of elephants during the dry season is inadequate in the Kabalega Falls National Park whereas, in the Rwenzori National Park, the quality of the food is good all year round.

This difference in food quality is not reflected in the condition of the elephants based on the kidney fat index (Fig. 7.2b). There was no seasonal difference in the kidney fat index in Rwenzori elephants

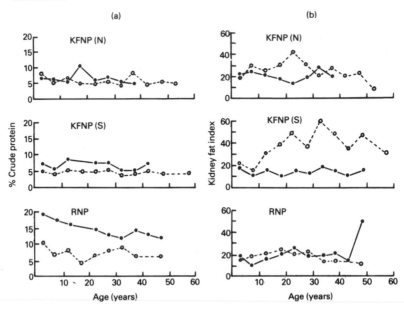

Fig. 7.2 Diet and condition of Ugandan elephants in relation to age and to the time of year. (a) Quality (in terms of crude protein content) of the food eaten. Note that in Rwenzori National Park (RNP), the protein is usually above the 6% level considered necessary for health, but that it often falls below that level, particularly in the dry season, in Kabalega Falls National Park (KFNP). (b) There is a marked seasonal difference in the amounts of kidney fat in elephants from Kabalega Falls National Park but not in Rwenzori elephants. (From Malpas, 1977.)

whereas there were highly significant seasonal differences in both populations from the Kabalega Falls National Park, with higher values, surprisingly, in the dry season. Furthermore, the kidney fat values in the dry season were significantly lower in elephants from Rwenzori National Park than in those from the less favourable Kabalega Falls. Malpas measured the hydroxyproline-creatinine ratio to determine the instantaneous growth rate. The results showed that the growth rates of Kabalega elephants were higher in the wet season than in the dry season, as might be expected, but that there was no seasonal difference in the growth rates in elephants from Rwenzori National Park. Also, growth rates in the dry season were higher in Rwenzori.

Malpas interpreted these observations on the assumption that

124

elephants with a high kidney fat index during the dry season in Kabalega Falls National Park had laid down the fat during the previous wet season and had not used it all up before being sampled. Elephants in the Rwenzori National Park had little kidney fat in the dry season because conditions were not severe at that time of year. With an adequate diet available throughout the dry season, there was no need to lay down fat. Instead, the elephants used any surplus food, over that required for normal metabolism, for growth. It is significant that growth continued throughout the year in Rwenzori National Park whereas in the Kabalega Falls National Park it ceased, or continued only at a very low level, during the dry season when the food quality dropped below the critical value.

Malpas (1978) suggested a model of the relationship between growth and fat deposition in elephants living in the Kabalega Falls National Park, or in any other region where the dry season brings deprivation in the food supply. The idea is shown diagrammatically in Fig. 7.3. Improvement in the forage quality lags some 3 or 4 weeks behind the start of the rains because it takes that long for plant growth to occur. The vegetation is at its best about 1 month into the rains and declines gradually to its lowest value towards the end of the dry season. Malpas suggests that the elephants use this period of plenty for growth and not for laying down fat. Later on in the wet season the elephants anticipate the poor conditions to come by ceasing to grow and instead use surplus food for putting on fat. This fat is not used in the dry season until conditions become really bad — usually towards the end. Hence, an elephant sampled in the wet season will have few or no reserves while one examined in the middle of the dry season will have maximum fat deposits. This is probably the explanation of the apparent anomaly noted in the samples taken by Malpas. A larger sample might have evened things out more.

Elephants from the Rwenzori National Park, which show no seasonal difference in kidney fat and which have a generally low fat reserve relative to the Kabalega elephants, are not in poor condition, as might at first be supposed. The true explanation is probably that conditions in the park are good all the year round and, consequently, there is no need to store fat. This model is oversimplified but it is likely to illustrate the physiological processes accurately enough.

125

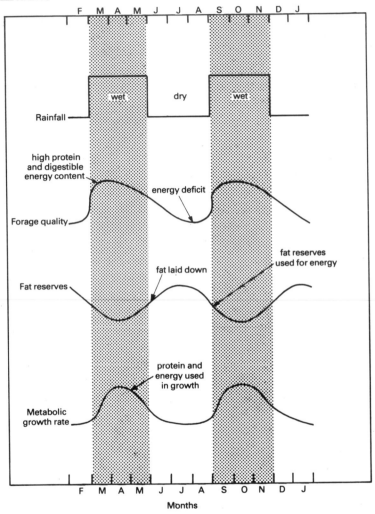

Fig. 7.3 A hypothetical model explaining the timing of observed seasonal changes in food quality, fat deposition and growth in Ugandan elephants. (Malpas, 1978.)

Growth

Elephants are peculiar in that they continue to grow long after they have reached sexual maturity. Perhaps growth never stops completely although, by middle age, it has become imperceptible. Lang (1980) measured five African elephants at Basle Zoo at regular intervals for periods of up to 18 years after their arrival as 1-year-old calves. Growth was linear, i.e. increased uniformly with time, but both weight and shoulder height tended to level off in the females between 15 and 16 years of age. The males were still growing when they had to be shot as a safety measure. The monthly increment in weight of two of the males averaged 22.6 kg and 21.0 kg respectively over the whole period. Brownlee and Hanks (1977) studied the growth rates of five young males captured in the Wankie National Park, Zimbabwe, and found a distinct increase in the growth rate with age as far as weight was concerned, although increase in height was more or less linear. The monthly increase in weight over 3½ years averaged only 14.4 kg for all five combined.

Although this seems low compared with Lang's results, the elephants were of course very young and there is probably not much difference between the growth rates of the two groups at equivalent ages. In any case, there were great individual variations in the Zimbabwe elephants, with monthly increases varying from 9.0 to 20.7 kg. There were some significant seasonal variations but no obvious correlation between growth and rainfall. The elephants were being artificially fed, however, in addition to foraging for natural vegetation and the supplementary diet might well have masked the effects of seasonal changes.

The sexes start to diverge in size from about 4 years of age so that, by puberty, the male is some 300 kg heavier and perhaps 15 cm higher at the shoulder. These and subsequent measurements refer to the African bush elephant. The differences between the sexes at puberty are hardly noticeable to the casual observer but growth in the male then seems to slip into a higher gear and the rate increases substantially while that of the female continues to level off. 'Increase' is really too mild a word and 'growth spurt' more accurately describes the phenomenon, which results in the male becoming almost twice as heavy as the female and 20% higher at the shoulder. It is not possible to give precise figures, because differences exist between populations, but, in the southern part of the Kabalega Falls National Park, Uganda, Laws et al. (1975) refer to an average weight difference of 2006 kg at 60 years of age. The difference is said to be 73.3% so that the weight of a male must be 4743 kg and that of the female, 2737 kg. Comparable figures for shoulder height are 307 cm and 252 cm for males and females respectively, a difference in this case of 21.8%. Such a large disparity between the sexes suggests that there has been an intense evolutionary selection for large size in male elephants and, in other species where a similar sexual dimorphism occurs, there is usually marked competition between males for access to females. Such observations as have been made on courtship in wild elephants (p.76) suggest that competition does indeed occur between males.

The tusks of African elephants continue to grow throughout life, despite a statement by Perry (1954) that the tusks of females, and sometimes of males, cease to grow after puberty. Laws (1966) showed that this was not so. Female tusks grow continuously and at a regular rate throughout life but male tusks show a progressively increasing growth rate and may reach a combined weight of 100 kg, about five times the weight of female tusks. Tusk weight is not a very good measure of age, however, for, apart from considerable individual variation in growth, there is a tendency for the tips to become worn away as fast as they grow. The tusks of a young (4–5-year-old) African elephant increase in weight by about 2 g per day (Laws *et al.*, 1975).

There have not been any comparable detailed analyses of growth in the Asian elephant but some growth data, derived from a variety of sources, are plotted by McKay (1973). These data show that the difference between the sexes is not as extreme as that found in the African elephant due, it would seem, to the absence of a post-pubertal growth spurt in the male. The growth rates of the sexes begin to diverge at about the same age in the two species and the male Asian elephant simply continues to grow faster than the female. It appears never to stop growing but growth in the female levels off somewhere between 15 and 30 years of age and at a shoulder height of 230–240 cm. This is about 20 cm less than the shoulder height of the female African elephants reported by Laws *et al.* (1975). Hanks (1972c) confirmed the size difference between the two species by fitting growth curves to the measurements reported for the Asian elephants and to his own data taken from Zambian elephants.

The persistent reports of a race of pygmy elephants in the central equatorial African forests may be due to precocious tusk growth. There is individual variation in the rate of tusk growth and a youngish, and therefore small, elephant may possess quite well developed tusks, giving the overall impression of pygmy proportions. Such 'pygmies' have often been reported in zoos but, invariably, the newly arrived pygmy eventually grows into a normal-sized elephant. It is also possible that poor nutrition early in life can lead to a stunted size in adulthood without affecting tusk growth too much so that, when mature, a little tusker might well be taken for a pygmy. It should also be remembered that the forest elephant is in any case considerably smaller than the bush elephant and an under-sized member of the forest race is going to look particularly small against its larger relative.

Energy budget

An animal can be likened to a machine which requires energy in the form of fuel to make it work. An animal's fuel, of course, is its food but the animal differs from a machine in the use to which the food is put. Both require fuel for conversion into mechanical work but the animal has the additional need of fuel for growth. Neither system is perfectly efficient and much of the energy taken in is wasted. Accurate measurements can be made of the efficiency of a machine and similar calculations can be carried out with animals, although with much less precision.

An elephant probably ingests 150–200 kg of fresh food a day but much of this is indigestible; Benedict (1936), for example, found that Jap digested only 43.8% of the dry matter in her food. Most of the energy derived from the food is used for the various physiological processes and only some 1% is available for growth. The digestive efficiency is low compared with that of many other herbivores but the proportion of assimilated food that is devoted to growth is about the same.

Waste is eliminated in a number of ways. Nitrogenous waste and salts are excreted in solution as urine while carbon dioxide and more water are lost through the lungs. There is also an appreciable loss of energy through the production of methane, which amounts to about

4% of the volume of carbon dioxide eliminated. About three quarters of this methane is passed out through the anus and the remainder is exhaled through the trunk (Benedict, 1936).

Heat production has been measured in only one animal, the Asian elephant, Jap. Benedict calculated her basal heat production to be 2.06 kilocalories per m^2 of skin area, or 0.013 kilocalories per kg body weight, per 24 hours. During normal activity, such as standing and feeding, but not walking, the total heat given out in a day would be higher — about 65 kilocalories for 'Jap'.

Carrying capacity

Calculation of the energy budget of a single elephant is more than an intellectual game, for the results can be used to estimate if (or to what extent) the elephant population is over-using its habitat. Any region is able to accommodate only a finite number of animals. The precise number depends on what they eat and, ultimately, the limit is determined by the amount of vegetation growing there. Plant growth is known as the primary production but not all of it is edible and it is the amount of available vegetation which is important. The total biomass of animals that a region can support without suffering a loss of energy from the system is called the *carrying capacity* but it should be clear by now that no simple definition can be given to this concept, because of annual variations in the primary production and in the numbers of other animals in the region. Carrying capacity, therefore, will fluctuate and, rather than trying to calculate its value, it is better, as an aid to management, to estimate how much of the available production is being consumed by the various herbivores, which, besides elephants and other large mammals, include rodents, birds and a whole host of insects. Ideally, one should estimate the consumption of all species and, if the total is less than the primary production, all is well.

Such an approach is rewarding in giving a rough idea of the workings of an ecosystem but, in practice, it is extremely difficult to calculate the consumption of even one species.

Petrides and Swank (1965) estimated that the amount of vegetation available to the elephants in the Rwenzori National Park, Uganda, was, in dry weight terms, 186 740 kg per km^2 per year.

They calculated the food consumption of the elephants by applying the method described earlier (p.34) to the weight of dung produced by a bull in the park and they concluded that the elephant population was taking 9.5% of the available forage. Phillipson (1975) made a similar calculation for Tsavo National Park in Kenya, using rainfall as a measure of primary production, and he found a percentage offtake varying from 4.0 to 11.8%, with the higher rates occurring in drought years. Coe (1972) had earlier made his own estimate for the Tsavo elephants, based on rather better measures of dung production, although he did not measure the primary production. He calculated that if the latter was as high as that in the Rwenzori National Park, the consumption by elephants would amount to 11.8% of the available forage, a figure identical to Phillipson's highest value. The assumption about the primary production, however, is clearly not valid, because Tsavo is a much more arid region than western Uganda, so Coe used instead production data from the Serengeti. On this basis, the offtake by elephants becomes 22% of the total available vegetation.

Such exercises make interesting reading but it is obvious that they are subject to gross errors. A glaring example is the figure for the efficiency with which food is assimilated into the body. The value of 43.8% used in all these calculations is derived from one experiment by Benedict nearly 50 years ago on a single captive elephant of a different species feeding on an artificial diet. Further doubt is cast on the validity of the procedure by the experiments of Rees (in press) who repeated Benedict's experiments on two captive African elephants which were also fed on a diet consisting largely of hay (82%). His result was an apparent digestibility as low as 22.4%. If this value had been used in the previous calculations, the estimates of the food consumed by the wild elephants would have been reduced by 27.5% and the carrying capacity would consequently have been raised by as much as 35%. These discrepancies should convince us that we have not yet reached the stage when we can plan the management of elephants, or any other species for that matter, on the basis of such calculations.

131

8 *Population dynamics*

A study of the factors which control the number of animals in a particular area constitutes the science of population dynamics. Such studies on elephants have been confined to the African species. While it is important to know how many animals there are in a population, it is often more important to know whether numbers are rising, falling or staying still. In ecology, the term 'population' means a group of animals of the same species which occupies a particular area. A population must be found continuously throughout the region in order to qualify for the title. In effect, any animal in a population has the chance of meeting all others, so that interbreeding is possible, i.e. gene flow can occur across the whole group. This is important, for a population could not otherwise react as a unit to environmental pressures.

It is not always easy to recognize a population. Individuals at each end of the range of a species with a vast distribution are unlikely ever to meet and these animals probably constitute a number of populations. An example of such an uncertainty is found in the elephants of Tsavo National Park. These are, or at least used to be before poaching took its toll, distributed throughout the whole area of the Park but Laws (1969b) believed that there were ten discrete populations (Fig. 8.1). Leuthold and Sale (1973), however, found that some radio-tagged individuals moved over the home ranges of several supposed populations, although such elephants returned to a limited home range in the dry season. It seems likely that the elephants in Tsavo split into separate units at this time of year but the fact that some, at least, intermingle during the wet season suggests that these units are not true populations. On the other hand, their study took place at a time of great upheaval for elephants, following heavy mortality from a severe drought and increased poaching, so that the behaviour might have been abnormal.

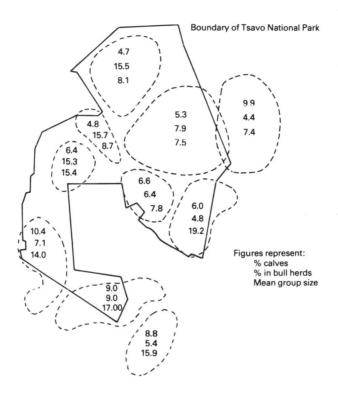

Fig. 8.1 Assumed home ranges of ten elephant populations in and around Tsavo National Park, Kenya. The wide differences in the average values of the population variables suggest that these are distinct groupings. (From Laws, 1969b.)

The question is important in the management of elephants. If there are several populations, the properties of each — such as the birth and death rates — would have to be determined individually, but only one such investigation would be necessary if all the elephants comprised a single population. Management programmes would have to be drawn up for the separate populations instead of just for one. Hence, the first task of the wildlife manager is to find out what he is dealing with and the best way of doing this is to follow a number of elephants that have been marked individually, preferably with radio-transmitters.

Self-regulation of elephant numbers

Regulation of numbers in a population of elephants seems to be effected through a number of factors (see Chapter 4), of which the most effective variable is the inter-calving period. Calf mortality is also important. Less significant are the age of puberty and the reduction of fertility with age, i.e. the age at which the menopause begins. The reality of the dependence of these reproductive variables on the population density of elephants has been demonstrated by Laws (1969b) in the elephants of Kabalega Falls National Park.

Population models

The management use of the information gathered on population dynamics lies in the prediction of future trends in numbers. To do this, it is necessary to make a 'model' of the population. This takes the form of a mathematical equation, which takes into account all the factors controlling population size. Using a computer, it is then possible to calculate the future population, given certain eventualities, such as the doubling of the mortality rate, or females starting to breed a year earlier. The mathematical model is, of course, only as accurate as the information given to it but, nevertheless, it is a very powerful tool for the wildlife manager.

Using a computer model, Hanks and McIntosh (1973) calculated the maximum rate at which an elephant population could increase under ideal ecological conditions. They concluded that, with a low mortality in all age groups, a mean calving interval of 3 years, puberty at 12 years of age and menopause at 55 years, numbers would increase by 4.7% per annum. Real population increases are probably well below this value. Where there have been spectacular rises in numbers, the principal contributory factor has always been immigration and not reproduction. Another model was that of Fowler and Smith (1973), who predicted changes in the population structure of Ugandan elephants that proved to be close to those which actually occurred. The model of Laws et al. (1975) forecasted long-term trends in the elephant population of North Bunyoro, Uganda, and their conclusions will be considered later (p. 139).

Population structure

A good method for investigating the fortunes of an elephant population is to determine its population structure. This is simply the number or proportion of each age and sex class of the animals making up the population, i.e. how many males and females there are in each age group. In the case of elephants, or other large mammals, the age classes chosen are usually annual. The frequency distribution of ages within a population can then be plotted on a graph to give a pictorial representation of the population structure (Fig. 8.2). This can be very informative. Age distributions can be very typical for certain kinds of animals and it is often possible, for example, to identify the population as belonging to a species of fish, bird or mammal from its population structure alone. Species with a high infant mortality show a great reduction in numbers between the first and second age groups. In the elephant, which looks after its young and has a low infant death rate, one would expect the decline to be much less. Large mammals that have survived to maturity normally have a low mortality until old age sets in, when most quickly die. One would expect, therefore, the numbers of animals in the older age groups to fall abruptly. This is normally the case but in elephants, which have no predators, old animals can often survive for years and the drop in numbers with age occurs much more gradually.

Life tables can be constructed from the population structure. Life tables were originally developed by actuaries for use by insurance companies but they have their value in population ecology. Life tables for animals are less reliable than those for people because the precise ages of the animals in the population are rarely known. Nevertheless, they have proved useful as indicators of the general health of a population. Excessive mortality in a particular age group soon shows up in the life table whereas it might not be obvious from casual observation.

Mortality curves, derived from life tables, are as typical of the various animal groups as are population structures. The curve for large mammals usually has a 'fish-hook' shape, which reflects the high mortality early and late in life and the relatively low mortality in youth and middle age. There is often a difference between the

(a)

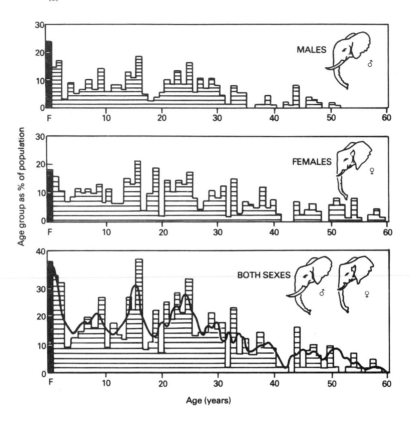

Fig. 8.2 Age structures of elephants shot: (a) in the southern part of Kabalega Falls National Park and (b) in the nearby Budongo Forest, Uganda. The black bands show the numbers of foetuses collected from females in the second half of pregnancy. The continuous lines are 3-year running averages, a technique for smoothing out annual fluctuations. The histograms reveal a better survival in

sexes in mortality rates, with females having better survival. This is true of elephants, although the difference is not apparent after 40 years of age.

The reasons for the sex difference are not always clear. There may be a longer physiological life span in the female, as in the human species, but, in the mammals generally, the more dangerous life led by the male is probably more significant. Males tend to be

(b)

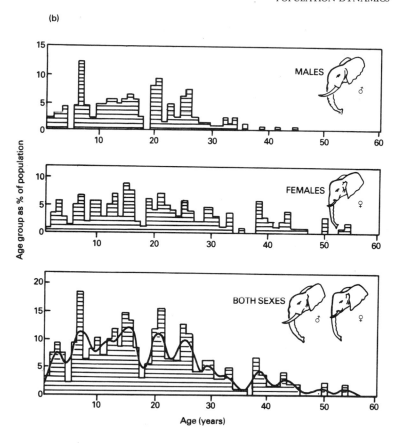

females, as well as indicating that recruitment has declined, especially in Budongo Forest. This analysis illustrates the value of the population structure in giving early warning of a deteriorating situation long before any changes in condition or in the habitat become apparent. (From Laws *et al.*, 1975.)

more aggressive than females and hence are at greater risk from injuries. They are also likely to be more vulnerable to predation. Species which exhibit a rut often suffer high mortality in the males, due to the poor condition of the contestants after the mating season is over. As a result of this bias, it is always best to treat males and females separately in any analysis of the population, unless it can be shown that they do not differ.

137

In the case of African elephants, Laws (1969b) has shown that the death rate varies little over much of the life span. In three populations studied, mortality was more or less constant at about 5 or 6% between the ages of 20 and 50 years for both sexes. Death from disease is mostly confined to old age and, once the hazards of growing up are past, there is little danger of dying. In this, elephants resemble human beings. The principal cause of death in healthy adult elephants is hunting by man and this is likely to be indiscriminate in relation to age. The only exception is that big tuskers are selectively sought out but these are old animals nearing the end of their natural span.

Some information on sex ratios in the African elephant is given by Laws (1969a). The sex ratio at birth is presumably 1:1, judging from a sample of foetuses examined from 171 pregnant females culled in East Africa. Although there was a preponderance of males (93 to 78 females), the difference is not significant. If a further 290 animals up to 2 years old were added to the sample, the number of males (252) then exceeded the number of females (209) by a statistically significant margin, suggesting that survival in the young males was rather better than in females, but the advantage was lost by the time the elephants were mature. Thus, in the five populations considered by Laws, only 44.3% of the adults were males. This swing in the sex ratio away from males to favour females must occur in the sub-adult stage for, as was mentioned earlier, there is little difference between the sexes in the death rate once the elephants are mature.

Smuts (1975) found a somewhat different pattern in the sex ratios of elephants culled in the Kruger National Park (Table 8.1). The only departure from a 1:1 ratio was found in family units but this is hardly surprising, given that these are essentially female groupings. The ratio for the whole population was taken from aerial counts, of elephants both in bull herds and family units, on the assumption that the family units have the same composition as that of the shot sample. Similar results were obtained by Sherry (1975) from a sample of elephants culled in the Gonarezhou Game Reserve in south-eastern Zimbabwe. The foetuses showed an even sex ratio of 92 males to 96 females and there was also no significant difference between the numbers of each sex up to and including 17 years of age

138

Table 8.1 Sex ratios of elephants in Kruger National Park, South Africa*

| Age/Class | Number of | | Ratio | Significance of difference |
	Males	Females	Male/Female	
Embryo/foetus	157	141	1 : 0.90	P > 0.05**
Birth to 14 years	812	827	1 : 1.02	P > 0.05**
Family units	931	1 426	1 : 1.53	P < 0.001
Whole population	15 795	16 518	1 : 1.05	P > 0.05**

*From Smuts, 1975
**Difference not significant

(530 males to 592 females). It was not possible to assess the sex ratio of the adult population because too few adult males were sampled.

It was the population structure in 1966 that first drew the attention of Laws *et al.* (1970) to the deteriorating condition of the elephants in Kabalega Falls National Park in Uganda. The frequency distribution of age classes showed abnormally low numbers of elephants up to 20 years of age, suggesting a reduced birth rate over recent years (Fig. 8.3). This was the first evidence that the elephants were attempting to regulate their own numbers as a result of their density being too high. Laws *et al.* (1975) investigated the matter further by constructing a hypothetical model of the population in 1946, when the decline in the birth rate had apparently started. The model was based on the assumption that the mortality rate, calculated from the observed (1966) population structure, had remained constant and that recruitment had also been constant prior to 1946. The resulting curve shows a steady state system, with births being balanced by deaths.

The model was then adjusted to show the 1966 distribution. This was based on real data from the distribution of elephants over the first 20 years of life. The results showed that losses from death were by then exceeding the gains from birth and growth so that the

139

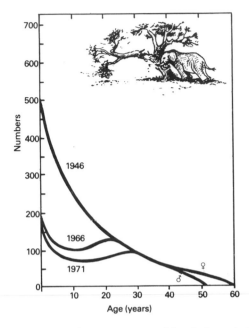

Fig. 8.3 Assumed changes in the age structure of the elephants in Kabalega Falls National Park, south of the Nile, Uganda, based on information from sample culling from 1965 to 1967. The 1971 curve was a forecast at the time the calculations were made. The age corresponding to the point at which a curve diverges from the 1946 curve equals the number of years since the population started to decline as a result of habitat destruction by elephants. A difference between the sexes appears in the survival after 40 years of age. (After Laws *et al.*, 1975.)

population was in decline. Despite the reduction in the net energy passing through the system, the standing crop biomass (i.e. the total weight of all elephants per unit area) had not fallen. This was due to the long life of the elephant. The changes that had taken place were a drop in the birth rate and a reduction in the area over which the elephants roamed.

The model was further developed to enable it to show the population structure at any time in future years and a (then) forecast for 1971 was made. A subsequent study by Malpas (1978) in 1973/74 found a rather different distribution but his sample area was small and changes induced by the culling of a large number of elephants since 1966 may have radically altered the situation. (The forecast was based on the assumption that population variables would remain much the same.)

The technique also enables an estimate of the number of elephants living in the past to be made provided a real count has been made in the present. The total number can easily be added up from the age distribution but. the latter is based on an artificial figure for the initial birth pulse. If the actual number is known, however, a correction factor can be applied to the calculated value and the factor used to adjust the estimates for earlier years. In this fashion, Laws *et al.* (1975) estimated that the population of North Bunyoro was about 16 000 in 1946. This had fallen to about 9400 by 1966. Subsequent counts by Eltringham and Malpas (1980) showed that numbers were still at the 1966 level in 1973 but there was a huge decline over the next 2 years, to about 4000 in 1974 and to a little more than 1000 in 1975. This decline was due to intense poaching for ivory and it illustrates how long-term forecasts may prove futile since such man-made disasters cannot be foreseen. Nevertheless, such forecasts have to be made if management plans are to be drawn up. It would be too defeatist not to bother simply because some future catastrophe might render the whole exercise pointless.

The grim forecast made by Laws *et al.* is included in Fig. 8.3. This suggests that, if matters are allowed to run their course in the Kabalega Falls National Park, the elephant population will not only become very small but will be comprised mainly of middle-aged and old animals so that its future survival will be in doubt. The recent spate of poaching will have certainly deflected the decline of elephants from this course but the ultimate fate of the species may not be so very different.

Information on the Asian elephant is nothing like as detailed. McKay (1973) gives some age distributions, which are based on field estimations of sizes, for elephant populations in Sri Lanka. These show an unbalanced distribution, with far fewer young animals than would be expected in a healthy population, but the sample size is low and the marked variations from year to year suggest that entire populations were not being sampled. On the other hand, it may well be that the elephants in Sri Lanka are suffering a decline through reduced birth rates similar to that recorded in the Ugandan elephants.

The sex ratio of adult elephants observed by McKay was 50 males to 130 females (or 135, there is some doubt) for all four of the populations sampled. The sex ratio at birth and amongst juveniles is thought to be 1:1 so that, as in the African elephant, there is a higher mortality in the sub-adult males than in the females. McKay suggests, alternatively, that the sub-adult males disperse. There is some evidence that they do so but one would expect immigrants to balance those dispersing and the sex ratio ought not to be affected.

Consequences of overpopulation

Overpopulation is a term used to describe a situation in which the number of animals present exceeds the carrying capacity, i.e. the number that the habitat can support without suffering permanent damage. In terms of bio-energetics, overpopulation occurs when the ecosystem loses more energy than it gains through the activities of the species in question. Normally the carrying capacity is never exceeded for long in a natural ecosystem because, once the numbers rise too high, natural checks come into play and the population soon returns to an appropriate level. It is obviously not in the best long-term interests of an animal that the population to which it belongs should exceed the carrying capacity and 'voluntary' reduction in the birth rate has evolutionary survival value under such conditions. It is rare for such a problem to arise with animal species, unless there has been gross human interference, such as the extermination of a predator or the provision of an unlimited supply of food, as in agriculture. Such conditions give rise to pests.

How is it then that elephants have become pests in destroying their habitat in national parks when apparently there has been no human interference? Leaving the latter contention to one side for the moment, we have seen that the elephant is capable of self-regulation of its numbers, but due to its slow reproductive rate and long life, any changes brought about by regulatory mechanisms are not achieved quickly enough to cope with the accelerating decline in the carrying capacity. Even if all births ceased tomorrow, the adults of an elephant population would hardly decrease in numbers for 20, 30 or perhaps even 40 years so that, if the number was excessive to start with, habitat damage would continue throughout that period.

Whereas, in a typical antelope population, a change in recruitment has an effect on the number of breeding females in 1 or at the most 2 years, the period for an elephant population has to be measured in decades.

One can conclude, therefore, that, in the case of elephants, changes in the carrying capacity occur at a rate faster than that at which the population is able to adjust. In theory, this should not happen, for natural selection should have ensured that a population can respond in time to habitat changes; otherwise the species would become extinct. We can only conclude that the rate of change in the carrying capacity is not natural and that we can detect here the hand of man. Thus our assumption in the last paragraph that there has been no human interference is probably naive. The nature of the interference will be covered in Chapter 11. Here only the implications of the inability of elephants to regulate their numbers quickly enough will be considered. These have been discussed in some detail by Laws (1969b), whose diagrams are reproduced in Fig. 8.4.

It should be appreciated that carrying capacity can vary in two distinct ways. In an area with a stable population of elephants, the carrying capacity will fall if large tracts of vegetation are destroyed, e.g. if the elephants themselves rip up the grass by its roots or knock over trees. The carrying capacity can also fall, however, even in the absence of habitat damage, if there is a sudden influx of animals. This appears to have happened with elephants in African national parks, due to the sanctuary offered within against harassment without. This has been called compression. Compression will lead to habitat damage if the number of elephants originally present was already at the carrying capacity.

In the case of elephants, habitat damage quickly follows once the carrying capacity is exceeded because of the destructive feeding habits of the animals. Consequently, the carrying capacity falls. This is an important point: if the number of elephants overshoots the permissible level, it is not simply a matter of waiting until they fall back to that level again, for by then the carrying capacity will have dropped lower still. This problem is not confined to elephants but, in most mammals, the declining population soon overtakes the falling carrying capacity and a new equilibrium is reached. It is possible

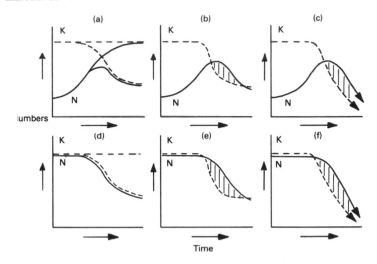

Fig. 8.4 Some possible responses of an elephant population (N) to changes in the carrying capacity (K): (a-c) situations in which the population is initially well below the carrying capacity but subsequently rises as a result of immigration; (d-f) situations in which the carrying capacity falls as a result of environmental changes such as drought. Ideally self-regulation by the elephants should keep the numbers within the carrying capacity (a and d) but, should it fail, the period during which N exceeds K (shaded) is one of habitat damage. The hopeful prognosis is that numbers will quickly adjust (b and e); the gloomy scenario (c and f) assumes that N never falls quickly enough and the elephants become extinct. (After Laws *et al.*, 1969b.)

that this will also happen with elephants but, because of the time scale, observations have not been carried on long enough to be sure. The most pessimistic prognosis is that numbers will never stabilize in time and that the carrying capacity will continue to fall until it reaches zero and the elephants become extinct. If that were to happen, not only the elephants would suffer, but the general biological collapse would bring the whole community of plants and animals crashing down. This is the theoretical basis of the argument that numbers should be artificially and rapidly reduced through culling, so as to bring the population below carrying capacity again. That such a drastic solution should even be contemplated draws attention to the seriousness of the 'elephant problem', a proper consideration of which requires a separate chapter.

9 *The elephant problem*

The elephant has become a problem, mainly because its interests conflict with those of man. Although elephants are very adaptable creatures, able to flourish in a wide variety of habitats, they are in continual retreat before the advance of human settlement. Once the human population reaches a certain level (100 per km^2 according to Watson *et al.*, 1972) the elephants disappear. They are not necessarily killed and most will move on as a consequence of the continual harassment that they receive once an area becomes settled. With the increasing pressure on its living space as human populations expand, the elephant is unlikely to survive for long outside protected areas, such as national parks, or on the remotest mountain tops.

Given the wealth of strategically sited national parks and reserves throughout Africa and Asia, the conservation of the elephants should be assured but, unfortunately, elephants have proved to be so great a nuisance that most parks containing them have what has come to be known as an 'elephant problem'. The elephant, by systematically wrecking its habitat, is putting at risk not only its own survival but also that of most other species in the parks. It does this by ripping up grass tufts by the roots, pulling branches off trees, stripping bark and often knocking over whole trees (Fig. 9.1). Thickets are entered and torn apart until the landscape takes on the appearance of a battleground fought over with tanks.

Why should this happen? We have in the elephant an example of an animal that apparently is not in balance with its resources. This is not a condition that could have evolved naturally so elephants in national parks must be living under conditions to which they are not adapted. This is the real elephant problem which must be solved if the species are to be conserved indefinitely.

It might be argued that the problem is simply one of

Fig. 9.1 Caught in the act of damaging trees. Attacks on trees are often limited to a few individual elephants, usually bulls. Here they are not pushing the tree over but breaking it apart by pulling down the branches.

overcrowding and that elephants damage their surroundings in the same way that cattle can destroy grasslands through overgrazing. It is certainly true that many elephant populations are above the carrying capacity of the region in which they live. This is not due to over-breeding, however, but to the problem of balancing numbers with resources, which is exacerbated by the long life of the elephant. Compression, the immigration of elephants from outside, is the most important factor contributing to overpopulation.

Compression occurs when protection is given to elephants in a particular area, such as a national park. Fig. 9.2 shows this in a diagrammatic way. Suppose Area A is set aside as park, elephants within it are now secure but those outside continue to be shot or harried in other ways. Those in Area C are mostly killed eventually, although some may wander far enough to reach the sanctuary provided by the park. Having arrived there, they have enough sense to stay, for elephants know when they are safe. Most of the

146

elephants in Area B will move into the park because parts of it are probably already within their normal home range and again, they soon learn which parts of that range are safe. This is no conjecture, for anyone at all familiar with elephants cannot help being convinced that they know the position of a park boundary to the metre.

The compression theory, therefore, accounts for the overcrowding, and the long life of the animal explains the inefficiency of the elephants in adjusting their numbers to the new conditions, but how serious is the damage caused? Is the tree destruction merely a minor aberration following a temporary inbalance between the elephants and their resources or is there really a problem wherever the species occurs in a national park?

Fig. 9.2 Compression. This is the probable reason why elephants often suffer from a population problem in national parks. When Area C is settled, most of the elephants are killed. People then begin to infiltrate the band of country (Area B) bordering the national park (Area A), killing some elephants and harrassing others, which flee into the safety of the park, which already has its full complement of elephants.

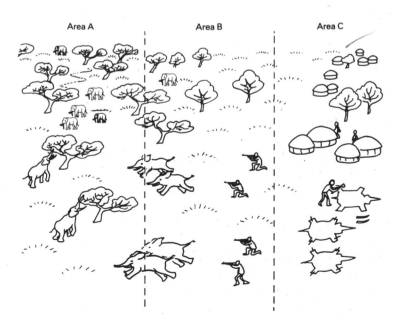

How serious is elephant damage?

There is no doubt that elephants can and do destroy trees but such activities could be no more damaging in the long term than the removal of grass by grazing herbivores. There is an important difference, however, in that grazers do not normally kill the grass plant and the loss of plant tissue is soon made good by rapid growth. A dead tree, on the other hand, will not regenerate and once an elephant has knocked it over, it is usually gone for good. Despite the great numbers of seeds produced by the trees, only a few find the right conditions for germination. Even then, the young shoots may be eaten by herbivores, and the saplings are often snapped off or destroyed by fire. Nevertheless, only one sapling needs to survive to maturity during the lifetime of the parent tree for the woodland to remain. It is when elephants prevent this, that their depredations are serious. Any assessment of elephant damage must, therefore, take regeneration as well as destruction of adult trees into account.

A study by Field (1971) of woodland in the Rwenzori National Park provided clear evidence of loss of trees in the long term. He compared an aerial photograph of the crater region of the Park, taken in 1954, with the distribution of trees in 1968. Of 4671 trees alive in 1954, only 511 remained 14 years later, an annual decline of 14.6%. Over 80% of the living trees were damaged to a greater or lesser extent through being debarked by elephants. In the same Park, I marked all 219 trees on Mweya Peninsula with metal tags (Eltringham, 1980) and within 5 years, 63 of these had disappeared, a loss rate of 6.6% per annum. There is no doubt that if these levels of elephant attack were general, most of the trees would soon be eliminated from the Park.

That stage has already been reached south of the Nile in Kabalega Falls National Park. Now, open grassland, unrelieved by bush or tree, exists where once there was dense jungle. In less than 50 years, the jungle has completely disappeared and there is little doubt that elephants were responsible, for frequent comments were made to that effect in the Annual Reports of the Game Department. Yet, strangely enough, the woodland is still there, at least, in places, for every year hopeful shoots are thrown up by the living rootstocks, only to be cut down by animals or fire. In experimental enclosures, guarded by a deep, wide ditch from all large mammals, shrubs and trees sprout in profusion (Spence and Angus, 1971). It seems that these annual shoots stay above ground long enough to produce sufficient food from photosynthesis to sustain the roots for another attempt in the following year. This is encouraging, for it means that the trend towards grassland is not irreversible and that woodland may be restored by the control of elephants. How far this situation is peculiar to the Kabalega Falls National Park remains to be seen but it is more likely than not to be universal.

Elephant damage has also occurred in Uganda's third national park, Kidepo (Harrington and Ross, 1974). Aerial photographs taken in 1947 were compared with counts made in 1967 on an 11 km^2 study area in the Narus Valley and it was found that about one third of the trees had disappeared, mostly, it was thought, as a result of elephant damage. After 1967, the rate of destruction increased with a reduction in numbers in the study area of 51% over the succeeding 5 years. The only species to escape unscathed was *Balanites aegyptica*. An analysis of the commonest tree, *Acacia gerrardii*, showed that most victims (61%) had died from falling down (mostly pushed over by elephants), 29% from debarking (certainly by elephants) and 10% from natural causes. The regeneration potential was high, about 200 young trees per hectare, but despite this, woodland continued to decline.

A similar picture is seen in Tsavo National Park. When the park was declared, soon after the last war, much of it was covered by Nyika thornbush yet, within 20 years, this has been replaced over wide areas by open savanna. The baobab trees of Tsavo may yet be saved, although they were disappearing through elephant damage at the rate of 2% per annum (Laws, 1969b). This may not seem very high but with no regeneration and a normal life span of several hundred years, the species is very vulnerable.

Leuthold (1977) counted all species of trees along some roads in Tsavo East National Park from 1970 to 1974 and found very extensive reductions, amounting to 95% for one genus. *Melia volkensii*, a tree not eaten by elephants, was the only one to show an increase in numbers. Although mature trees of *Acacia tortilis*, and those of a size to be recruited into the adult population, declined, the number of regenerating trees — those less than a metre in height — increased spectacularly, e.g. from about 74 per km^2 in 1970 to 312 per km^2 in 1974. Few of these young saplings survived, but their high densities emphasize the marked regeneration potential of these tree populations. Again, this is a hopeful sign, suggesting that elephant control would be worthwhile.

Sometimes elephant damage is not an important ecological problem, although it may be serious in management terms. Thus, along the Seronera River, in the Serengeti National Park, bull elephants have been destroying acacia trees, particularly the fever tree, *Acacia xanthophloea*, at a rate of 2.5% per annum (Croze, 1974b). Although Croze maintains that the long-term survival of the trees is not in doubt, the loss of the mature trees has bothered the park authorities, since they have great amenity value and also serve as leopard perches on this very popular tourist route.

Savidge (1968) reports widespread damage to trees on the Ruaha National Park, particularly baobab trees and *Acacia albida*, with losses exceeding regeneration.

The *Acacia tortilis* trees in Lake Manyara National Park, Tanzania, were being rapidly destroyed by elephants in the late 1960s (Douglas-Hamilton, 1973) but elsewhere damage was slight. The elephant population at the time was, at over 5 per km^2, the highest ever recorded in Africa.

Further south, severe damage to *Brachystegia* woodland on Siamagogas Ridge in Chizarira Game Reserve, Zimbabwe, has been documented by Thomson (1975). Extensive damage did not begin until the mid-60s but subsequent loss of trees has been rapid. Of a sample of 500 trees, marked by metal tags in August 1972, 66.8% had been lost by the end of 1973. Of the remainder, 20.4% had been damaged and only 12.8% were alive and undamaged. Another sample of 600 trees suffered a loss of 10% between May and December 1973. During this period, 5.3% received fresh damage. A total of 33 trees died from causes other than elephants but 26 of these had been damaged previously and their final demise can reasonably be scored against the elephants. Most of the damage was removal of bark, which usually leads to the death of the tree. Thomson estimates that all the trees on the ridge, covering some 10% of the game reserve, will have gone in 5½ years.

1 Bull elephant sheltering from the noon sun, Amboseli National Park, Kenya. Elephants in direct sun tend to absorb more heat than they can lose and often have to move into shade. Note the broken right tusk.

2 Elephants drinking from the Chobe River, Botswana. Elephants drink daily when water is freely available and a large bull can take in 100 litres at a time.

3 African elephants feeding in grassland. The large female has pulled up the grass by the roots, a destructive form of grazing, and has paused to wipe her eye with the back of her trunk.

4   Bull in full threat display, Amboseli National Park, Kenya. The flapping ears, the result of vigorous head-shaking, sound like tarpaulins being shaken out. Note the discharge of the temporal gland.

5   Females near Kilaguni Lodge, Tsavo National Park, Kenya, mildly disturbed and holding their trunks like periscopes to test the breeze. They are not excited and, unless alarmed, will resume grazing.

6   Typical family group of elephants consisting of several adult females with their calves of all ages, Tsavo National Park, Kenya. Note the cow on the left which has lost a tusk.

7   Elephant digging for salt in front of Treetops Hotel, Aberdare National Park, Kenya. Elephants use their tusks at salt licks to loosen the salt-impregnated soil, which they then consume.

8   Elephants love to bathe and often immerse themselves completely, using their trunks as snorkels in order to breathe, like this bull in the River Nile, Kabalega Falls National Park, Uganda.

9   Bull elephant in Botswana, fresh from a mud bath, finishing off his toilet with a good scratch on a dead tree.

10   Wild tusker bathing in a river in India. Compare the convex curve of the back
      with the sway-back of the African elephant. The reduced pigmentation of trunk
      and ears is a common feature in the Asian species.

11   Family group of elephants in Sri Lanka taking a dust bath. Asian females are
      always tuskless, as are a high proportion of bulls in Sri Lanka. Note the sparse
      covering of hair on the younger animals.

12   In Kandy, Sri Lanka, the Perahera Day celebration features the tooth relic of the Buddha. This is carried in the shrine borne by the resplendently caparisoned tusker in a procession of up to 100 elephants.

Anderson and Walker (1974) investigated the damage to vegetation in the Sengwa Wildlife Research Area, which forms the south-eastern boundary of the Chizarira Game Reserve. Damage was divided into old and new (before or after the latest rainy season). The proportion of trees showing old damage was 33.9% for all vegetation types and 4.1% had been damaged within the past year. The numbers of dead trees in the various vegetation types were high — 22% in mopane woodland, 27% in miombo woodland and 48% of the riverine canopy trees. Others had been so badly damaged that they had been converted into shrubs, the figures for the above three types being respectively 45%, 33% and 12%. Altogether the loss rate was put at 9%, greatly in excess of replacement, and it is only a matter of time before the woody vegetation goes.

Severe damage has also been caused to woodland at the opposite end of Zimbabwe on the Gonarezhou Game Reserve in the south-east of the country (Sherry, 1975). Damage was first noticed in 1968 and soon reached 'an alarming rate' in all vegetation types, particularly *Colophospermum mopane* woodland, baobab trees and riverine/alluvial communities.

Not only the African species damages vegetation. Mueller-Dombois (1972) reported that the elephants in Ruhuna National Park, Sri Lanka, were causing distortion of the trees by feeding on the branches. Instead of growing into a well rounded crown, the branches turned abruptly downwards, inwards or upwards, often twisting and intertwining with each other. Leader shoots were broken off, resulting in a profusion of stubs sprouting from the branches themselves. Many species of tree were affected in all vegetation types. The percentages of trees with crown distortion were high in some species, with a maximum of 79% in *Feronia limonia*, a very abundant thorny evergreen. Despite the extensive damage, the elephants did not kill the trees by their feeding activity, although Mueller-Dombois mentions that some trees were pushed over by elephants, particularly along actively used pathways. The general lack of destruction was attributed to the low frequency of tusked animals in the population. The females, of course, are tuskless and only 10% of the males are tusked. Some tusk marks were found on trees but there was no extensive bark stripping. Use of the trees as scratching posts resulted in rubbed areas of bark, particularly on *Manilkara* trees, which have deeply fissured, thick bark, but no serious damage ensued.

Mueller-Dombois also thinks that the low density of Sinhalese elephants is a factor in their general non-destructiveness, but the 1.2 elephants per km^2 is higher than that of African elephants in some parks where forests are being wrecked.

Kurt (1974) also reports elephant damage in Sri Lanka — in the Yala National Park. Here the elephants 'scalp' the grass by cutting it off at the roots with their front toenails, so creating ideal conditions for soil erosion. Most of the larger plains in the park now have bare patches, which introduced plants invade, pushing out the food grasses. Elsewhere in Sri Lanka, McKay (1973) records tree destruction by elephants in the course of feeding, although he states that generally elephants do not tear down the entire plant but rather remove twigs or branches.

Some figures are available on the rate at which elephants destroy trees. Croze (1974a) calculated that bull elephants observed by him and Hendricks and Hendricks (1971) in the Serengeti National Park, Tanzania, destroyed trees at the rate of 3 per elephant every 4 days or 0.75 trees per elephant per day. Guy (1976) produced a figure for bull elephants in the Sengwa Research Area, Zimbabwe, that was significantly higher, at 4.5 trees destroyed per bull per day (the figure for cows was 1.5 trees per elephant per day). Taking the group behaviour of bulls into consideration, Guy suggests that the rate might be reduced to 1.6 trees per bull per day. All these levels are much higher than those recorded on Mweya Peninsula, Rwenzori National Park, Uganda, where 39 trees were destroyed between 1971 and 1973 in 9027 'elephant days' (Eltringham, 1980). This low rate, of only 0.004 trees per elephant day, is a reflection of the large number of cows and calves contributing to the elephant days as well as to the less destructive habits of the Mweya elephants.

The verdict

It is clear from this survey that the damage caused by elephants is indeed serious, at least in Africa, and constitutes an important management problem. In many of the parks we have considered, the trees are unlikely to survive for long and it is over-optimistic to assume that matters will sort themselves out. The most pressing problem is to determine the correct balance between elephants and trees but this has yet to be done anywhere, although experimental culling is beginning to throw some light on the problem. One must always remember, of course, that we are trying to conserve elephants and not trees. There are plenty of trees away from elephant haunts, and it is unlikely that any species will become extinct as a result of elephant activity, but we must also remember that trees are essential for the elephants themselves. Apart from providing food, trees are important for shade. In the open grassland of Kabalega Falls National Park, there is no longer any shade and the elephants probably suffer stress as a result. Calves are particularly vulnerable to heat stress, which is believed to be an important cause of the increased mortality of calves in denuded regions.

Trees have other ecological functions. Their deep roots tap water sources far below the ground, so that trees and bushes often remain green and succulent long after the parched grasses have withered away. Nutrients quickly leach from the surface in the ancient African soils and the deep-rooted woody vegetation is important in retrieving these nutrients and recycling them through the ecosystem. There is more to conserving trees, therefore, than preserving a pretty landscape and their destruction by elephants is something that should worry us out of concern for the elephants themselves as well as for the rest of the flora and fauna.

How do elephants damage trees?

Elephants kill or damage trees in a number of ways but the most important are uprooting and debarking. Many savanna trees lack a strong tap root to anchor them in the soil and hence are rather easily pushed over. This is quite deliberate on the part of the elephant which usually lays its trunk vertically up the trunk of the tree so raising its centre of gravity and gaining extra leverage. The elephant then starts to sway backwards and forwards, rocking the tree until its roots are so loosened or broken that it falls over. Sometimes the stem snaps first and the crown of the tree falls off, leaving the broken stump like a post in the ground. Trees snapped in this way invariably die but sometimes a tree that is merely uprooted will survive for years in a recumbent position. Such trees are browsed upon by dikdik, rhinos and other short-legged creatures that would not normally be able to reach its branches. In this way, the elephant is an unwitting benefactor of its neighbours.

Debarking begins by the elephant driving a tusk into the tree trunk and levering up a piece of bark, which is then grabbed by the trunk and peeled upwards, rather like removing the skin of a banana. Very often the bark is not pulled completely away but remains attached at the top of the trunk so that ribbons of drying bark dangle from the branches. Certain *Acacia* species are particularly susceptible to bark stripping but others have thin brittle bark which does not readily strip off. Such trees are more likely to be ring-barked since the elephant will try its luck on another part of the trunk. Trees that are ring-barked will die but, even if only part of the bark is removed, the tree is soon attacked by wood-borers, as well as by fungi. Riddled and rotten, the tree will not survive for long, often toppling under its own weight or falling in a high wind. Even if it is spared these afflictions, with the bark gone the tree has lost its protection from grass fires. The exposed cambium, the growth layer in the trunk, is killed by the flames and, if the loss of bark is at all extensive, the tree will die.

Elephants have further ways of dealing with trees. Sometimes, they simply pull off all the branches until only a stump remains. They may not do this all at once and it may take several years before the last branch is ripped off and the tree eventually dies.

Baobab trees are treated quite differently and are literally hollowed out by the elephants. The wood of a baobab is soft and spongy and easily tusked. Few baobabs in elephant country are free from the scars of past attentions and some contain vast caverns within their stems, for an old tree is huge and may be 30 m in circumference at the base. Sometimes so much of the interior is excavated that there is insufficient wood left to support the trunk, which then falls over. Cases are known of an elephant being crushed as the tree collapses on top of it.

The attack by elephants on regenerating or young trees tends to be concentrated on the leading shoots. In the Budongo Forest, Uganda, up to 47% of the total number of stems showed damage to the leader (Laws *et al.* 1975). The tender shoots are no doubt preferred because of their high protein and low fibre contents. The smaller trees were particularly vulnerable, for 75% of the saplings with damaged leaders were under 2.5 cm in diameter at human breast height and 97.5% less than 10 cm in diameter. Trees larger than this seem to be rarely attacked (Wing and Buss, 1970; Laws *et al.*, 1975). Olivier (1978a) also found that trees more than 10 cm in diameter at breast height were never recorded as being fed upon by Asian elephants.

Thickets, which have less individuality than a tree, are not easily killed but they are broken about by elephants. Branches are snapped off or stripped of leaves and often an elephant disappears completely into a bush, so opening up a passage through which grass fires can enter and further prune back the growth. Sometimes the elephant uproots the thicket by rolling back the base with its tusks, possibly to get at the greener grass growing there. After a while, the thicket is reduced to a few scrawny suckers that do not long survive the attentions of other browsers or the effects of grass fires.

What sort of trees are damaged?

Elephants do not destroy trees indiscriminately. Certain species e.g. *Acacia albida*, *A. tortilis* and baobabs are particularly vulnerable. Guy (1976) found that the trees most often pushed over were not necessarily the most palatable but those that were easiest to push over. A shallow rooting system, as in *Colophospermum mopane*, is important in this respect, as is a thin or brittle stem. The trunk of *Colophospermum* is often hollow and is easily broken by elephants. Not surprisingly this species suffers disproportionately and, of 71 trees which Guy recorded as elephant victims, 35 belonged to this species. The next most frequent victim (6 lost) was *Xeroderris stuhlmannii*, which, although more deeply rooted, has a weak stem liable to be broken off just above ground level.

Tall trees are also more likely to be pushed over than short ones, irrespective of species, presumably because the elephant wishes to get at the green branches, which can be easily reached on a short tree without the need to knock it over. Croze (1974a) uses this as evidence that the function of tree-felling is nutritional and found that 6 m was about the critical height for *Acacia* trees in deciding whether or not they would be pushed over.

Above a certain height, trees are too big even for an elephant to knock down and, although it might be physically possible for an elephant to demolish a tree above a certain size, the rewards might not be worth the effort required. Hence medium-sized trees are the ones most likely to be chosen.

Why do elephants destroy trees?

The need for food would seem to be an obvious reason for elephants to destroy trees but an elephant, because of its size and long trunk, rarely needs to push over a tree in order to obtain browse from the branches. In any case, I have seen elephants in Uganda destroying totally inedible trees and often an elephant will push over a tree and take nothing at all.

Bark has a high calcium content and this has been suggested as a reason for bark-stripping by elephants (Bax and Sheldrick, 1963). However, the normal diet of an elephant contains plenty of calcium without the necessity of eating bark (Weir, 1969; McCullagh, 1969b). Croze (1974a) suggests that bark is a source of roughage but, again, there is sufficient roughage in the normal diet and, in many cases, much of the bark is not eaten but left dangling from the trees.

The attack on baobabs is a special case as elephants chew the moist spongy wood after gouging it from the trunk and it is generally assumed that this is a way of obtaining moisture.

From this evidence, it is difficult to conclude that the pushing over and destruction of trees plays any significant role in nutrition. An alternative hypothesis is that the felling of trees is a display activity of social significance for, although not confined to bulls, it is more common in males. There is little evidence to support this idea, however, as the frequency of tree-felling is too low to function as a display, particularly in the bull herds with their constantly changing membership. Often a subordinate bull will push over a tree, only to be chased off by a more dominant animal (Croze, 1974a).

It seems that no firm conclusion can be drawn over the reasons why elephants destroy trees and, in the process, wreck their own

156

habitat. If the primary objective is to obtain food, the practice would over-exploit this food resource and reduce the capacity of the land to support elephants. There must be an explanation for this seeming paradox but perhaps we should look a little further than present-day elephants in their protected reserves and speculate about the ecology of elephants in the days before modern man appeared on the scene.

A possible explanation of tree felling

One of the constant themes running through the old hunters' tales is that of elephant migratory routes. Modern research has indeed shown that elephants in some areas undertake seasonal movements, e.g. they are known to move from grassland to forest at the onset of the dry season, but the migration is never clear-cut and some elephants are always to be found in each habitat whatever the season. What has never been established, however, is that elephants migrate over long distances. The farthest a recognizable individual elephant has been proved to move is 112 km. Yet, despite the lack of solid evidence that elephants used to move long distances, I believe that they did do so because I cannot see how their ecology makes sense otherwise. What follows is purely speculative, but I put it forward as an hypothesis to explain the elephant problem in Africa.

Years ago, before the advent of modern man, elephants reigned supreme throughout their range. The people lived in villages and, for a number of reasons, did not spread out over the countryside as they do today. Hunting parties no doubt killed many elephants but not enough either to deplete their numbers or to scare them away from any part of their range. With no restrictions the elephants wandered freely over their wide domain, which, I suggest, was probably hundreds of kilometres across.

Within this home range, there would be areas offering better forage and other resources than elsewhere. These may be considered as nutritional 'hot spots', to which the elephants would be attracted. They would certainly be well wooded and contain forests. Within these hot spots, we may assume that elephants behaved much as they do today, i.e. they set about systematically wrecking the habitat. Trees would be debarked or pushed over, bushes broken up and grasses uprooted. But they would go only so far. Before the habitat

157

had been completely laid to waste, the elephants would move on to look for another such hot spot. My reason for assuming this follows from studies that have been made on optimal foraging in birds and other animals. When a bird finds a rich food source it does not remain with it until all the food is consumed but moves away to find another similar food source well before the original food is depleted. This is due mainly to the law of diminishing returns. The less food there is, the more difficult it is to find it and the longer it takes to complete a meal. The time would be better spent in seeking out another food source where the original eating rate can be restored.

So it may have been with elephants. But even if they did wreck the area completely, they would then leave and not return for many years, by which time the vegetation would have recovered and could withstand a further session of abuse from elephants.

Seen in this light, elephant behaviour is not unadaptive and it is only when elephants are prevented from moving to pastures new, that irreversible damage to vegetation occurs. I would go further and say that, not only is elephant behaviour not unadaptive under the assumed circumstances, it is positively adaptive for, in wrecking trees, the elephants convert primary forest to secondary forest, which is a superior habitat for them.

The significance of this hypothesis is that, if it were correct, it would be useless to sit back and wait hopefully for nature to take its course and for the elephants in a national park to come into balance with their resources. The more likely outcome would be for the elephants to continue to wreck the habitat until the whole ecosystem came crashing down, leading to extinction not only of the elephants but of all the other large mammals as well. Admittedly, this is the most pessimistic scenario but dare we take the risk of assuming that it will not take place?

There are alternative and more cheerful hypotheses. One is that of Caughley (1976), who suggests that elephants and trees oscillate in numbers, rather like the lynx and snowshoe hare in the Arctic. His evidence is based on the age distribution of trees in the Luangwa Valley, Zambia, where a large number of baobab trees are around 140 years old, suggesting maximum survival of saplings that long ago. On the assumption that the seedlings survived because there were few elephants around to destroy them, a cycle of 280 years (2 ×

140) is postulated, since elephants are presently at a maximum. On the other hand, it could be argued that, as the baobab is a grassland tree, woodland and forest were at a minimum 140 years ago. This suggests that elephants were then at a maximum, or rather that they had been so some time before, since their numbers trail those of trees by about a quarter of a period. Hence the cycle would occupy 187 years (140 years = ¾ of the cycle). Caughley suggests a round figure of 200 years as a compromise.

Wildlife cycles of 4 or 10 years' duration are well known but they have in common a simple ecosystem with a low input of energy. Such oscillations, or *stable limit cycles*, are unlikely in the tropics, or with species that are as long lived and slow breeding as elephants and trees. The essence of a species that indulges in booms and crashes is rapid reproduction and a short generation time, so that, when conditions permit, recovery of numbers is rapid. The elephant has many admirable qualities but profligate breeding is not one of them and it seems highly unlikely that it could ever become locked into a stable limit cycle. Indeed, there is no example of an ungulate that cycles in this way. A further stumbling block to this theory is that elephants and trees do not show a simple predator/prey relationship with each other. Trees are certainly destroyed by elephants but elephants do not die in the absence of trees. They can and do turn to other foods. Trees are important to elephants, whose health declines when they are gone, but the elephants survive nevertheless.

Another hopeful prognosis is that of Phillipson (1975), who believes that, at least in Tsavo National Park, elephant numbers have often surged and died down again. He suggests that numbers follow the pattern of vegetative production, which in turn fluctuates with rainfall. Droughts are certainly periodic in Kenya and every 50 years or so there is a particularly severe one. Phillipson sees this as a mechanism for regulating elephant numbers and suggests that the cycle should be allowed to run its course and that human interference, in the form of culling to reduce temporary over-abundance, is unnecessary.

I have already discussed these hypotheses in an earlier book (Eltringham, 1979), in which I concluded that neither provided satisfactory solutions to the elephant problem. The evidence for cycling in elephant populations is indirect and tenuous. In particular, I think that Phillipson's estimate of 43–50 years as the interval between severe droughts is far too short a time for an elephant population to complete a cycle. Phillipson supposes that the severe mortality caused by the drought would be followed by a period of 35 years of respite, during which the population would build up to a critical level again, leaving 8–15 years of danger from elephant damage. For a species which at best can produce one calf every 4 years, 35 years is a very short period in which to recover.

It is worth emphasizing that neither Caughley nor Phillipson produce any evidence that elephants undergo a cycle. Caughley has merely produced evidence that elephants were at a maximum (or minimum?) a certain time ago. Phillipson, on the other hand, seems to be supposing that elephants *ought* to cycle because the rainfall, and, therefore, the primary production, does. Neither has shown that elephant numbers ever fluctuated. Even if they had, they still would not have provided evidence of cycling. Let us assume that one of our hypothetical 'hot spots' subsequently became a national park. Biologists examining the trees would find evidence that periodic damage had occurred in the past and would assume that elephant numbers had been high at such times. They would be wrong if they confused periodic visitations with population cycles.

Management implications — the culling dilemma

The issue is an important one because management policy depends on the conclusions drawn. Caughley and Phillipson believe that non-interference is the correct response to the elephant problem. Other biologists, of whom Dick Laws has been the most eloquent, believe that the only solution is to reduce numbers to an acceptable level by culling (shooting) the surplus. These are two very different solutions and it is not surprising that park managers, caught between the cross-fire of conflicting advice, have not known what to do. In such a situation, the best policy is to consider the likely consequences of all alternatives. Deliberate non-interference has several attractions. In the first place, it is cheap in the short term and makes no demands on the usually depressed financial resources of the parks. It is often politically expedient as well as being morally reassuring to the wildlife managers, who feel that their duty is to protect animals, not to shoot them. The emotional repugnance felt by many people towards shooting elephants is an important factor in the culling equation but it should be appreciated that the advocates of culling are also motivated by a compassionate desire to prevent suffering by elephants and yet such persons have to be prepared to be labelled as murderers and butchers, or to be accused of corrupt motives.

If the underlying assumptions are correct, culling restores the balance and allows the elephants to lead a normal, stress-free life. It also prevents other species of plants and animals facing the risk of extinction and halts habitat damage and the possibly irreversible decline to desert. But what if the assumptions are mistaken? This is always a question in the back of the mind of any wildlife manager and it is one that can rarely be answered because controlled experiments cannot easily be carried out. The only solution is to ensure that the culling is not so drastic that the population is unable to recover. It should be possible to tell whether the culling is effective or not by carrying it out in stages and subjecting the culled animals to detailed scientific investigations. Changes in the age distribution or in other population variables should soon reveal whether the culling was serving its purpose.

No one can feel happy about culling and when the species concerned is as valuable as the elephant, one has to be certain that commercial considerations play no part in the decision to cull. A national park could greatly boost its income by slaughtering a proportion of its elephants but no conservationist would support such a proposal. One would also need reassurance over the humane nature of the cull. The animal will inevitably experience a certain degree of suffering but this can be reduced to a minimum by employing skilled marksmen. Professional teams should be used and culling ought not to be regarded as a spare-time occupation for wardens. The culling of elephants in Uganda was carried out by a specialist firm which shot the elephants in family groups, the average size of which was 12 (Laws et al., 1975). The time taken to drop a complete herd from the first shot was 45 to 90 seconds. Of the 800 Ugandan elephants shot in North Bunyoro, only one sub-group escaped (uninjured). By contrast, many of the elephants shot 'on control' by the Uganda Game Department were wounded — perhaps as many as were killed — according to an Annual Report of the Department. Those that escaped unwounded were terrified out of their wits and no doubt spread their alarm to unaffected populations.

If a culling programme is decided upon, large numbers of elephants need not be destroyed once the population has been reduced to manageable levels. Even the initial kill need not be excessively large compared with the numbers being shot anyway. For example, Laws *et al.* (1970) point out that their proposal to cull 4200 elephants over a 4-year period in North Bunyoro is equivalent to only 7 years of the former wasteful (and inhumane) slaughter of some 600 elephants a year under the control programme of the Game Department.

If culling is necessary and is not carried out, elephants may experience much greater suffering. Overcrowding causes stress and leads to the amalgamation of family groups into huge amorphous herds which, by their very size, cause extensive localized damage to the vegetation. In time, much of the rangeland is destroyed, food shortages occur and the elephants lose condition. After years of slow starvation, they begin to die. The old matriarchs are often the first to go and the stable social order begins to crumble.

The elephant problem in the Tsavo National Park is a good example of the dilemma. Numbers had built up to the extent whereby severe losses of trees were occurring. On the one hand were those calling for a reduction of elephants (Laws, 1969b) and on the other were those saying that interference was not required (Harthoorn, 1966; Phillipson, 1975). The initial decision to cull was reversed in the late 1960s and no elephants were shot, apart from a small scientific sample. A particularly severe drought followed in 1970/71 and at least 6000 elephants died from starvation (Corfield, 1973). Both sides felt that this event vindicated their positions. The anti-cullers said that, as predicted, any overpopulation is settled by natural events, which bring numbers down to be in balance with resources. Proponents of culling, on the other hand, claimed that such widespread mortality was not natural but was brought on by the elephants being weakened from the years of sub-standard nutrition that they had experienced as a direct consequence of overpopulation. Far fewer of a healthy population would have died. Long-lived animals, such as elephants, will experience many droughts during their lifetimes but they have evolved to survive them. It was also pointed out that such widespread mortality was wasteful. The meat could not be used, the leather was spoilt and many of the carcases were not found, so that tusks could not be recovered or, if they were, they were often taken by poachers.

So there the matter rests, with both sides claiming victory. It is a pity that elephant management has attracted so much controversy. Any proposal to shoot protected animals needs the most careful consideration and it is right that opponents should insist on the most rigorous evidence for its necessity, but personal considerations should play no part in the deliberations. There can be no victor, whatever decision is made and there can be only one loser, the elephant itself.

Culling programmes in Africa

As far as I know, culling of elephants by shooting has never been practised in Asia, although the capture of animals for working purposes has had a similar effect in reducing the wild populations. Elephant culling in Africa, on the other hand, has frequently been carried out and it is worth examining the few case histories to see why it was thought necessary and whether it was effective.

The cropping in Kabalega Falls National Park involved the shooting of 2000 elephants between 1965 and 1967. This was probably the first cull of elephants to be carried out for ecological reasons. Initially, 17 elephants were shot in April-May 1965. Large-scale culling began in August of that year and continued until May 1967, by which time 2000 elephants had been taken out. Of these, 1200 were shot north of the Nile, and 800 to the south of the river, where the condition of the vegetation had reached a level where only very extensive culling was likely to have much effect. The cull of 800 was more of a preliminary exercise from which the necessary size of the major cull could be determined. In the event, the further cull never took place, for biopolitical and other reasons, and the problem was completely turned around by the catastrophic poaching of the early 1970s. Consequently, the efficacy or otherwise of the cull could not be assessed, although the results of a scientific sampling of elephants in 1973 suggests that the position had improved somewhat (Malpas, 1978). The vegetation was not studied but analysis of the reproductive variables suggested that recruitment through birth was higher than it was at the time of the culling.

Another major cull took place in the Luangwa Valley, Zambia, between 1965 and 1969, when 1464 elephants were killed in the South Game Reserve. This programme was unique in that a permanent abattoir was built on the banks of the Luangwa River to process the carcases. In order to avoid the disturbance caused by rifle shooting, the culling team shot the animals with a dart filled with an overdose of succinylcholine chloride, a drug which breaks down on heating so that the meat from an animal killed in this way can be safely eaten when cooked. An advantage over rifle shooting is that precise aiming is not necessary, for the elephant will go down wherever it is hit, provided it is in a 'meaty' part of the body. Nevertheless, the technique was abandoned in 1968 in favour of shooting. One problem was that complete family units could not be eliminated at once, so that disturbance spread to other elephants. Also the method is inhumane, for, apart from the stress caused to other elephants, the drug kills by paralysing the respiratory muscles so that the elephant suffocates — a particularly distressing form of death. Furthermore, experience with human volunteers suggests that the onset of paralysis is accompanied by severe muscular pains. Despite this, the drug is still used in South Africa, where, admittedly, much of the cruelty is avoided by shooting the animals as soon as they fall over.

Again, it is difficult to assess the effects of the culling because it was halted in 1969, largely as a result of protests from overseas conservationists. Certainly the number killed could have had little effect on the total population in the South Reserve, which was estimated to be about 15 000 in 1964. A later estimate in 1973 produced a figure of 31 600 (Caughley and Goddard, 1975). More recently a survey of the North and South Luangwa National Parks suggested a likely population, including those in the connecting corridor, of 36 510 (Douglas-Hamilton, 1979). Very likely, that is too many and further culling may be necessary.

Zimbabwe has also been the centre of extensive elephant culling but the rationale for it is sometimes obscure. Usually, the aim has been to keep the population at an arbitrarily determined level, even in areas where severe elephant damage has never occurred. No doubt prevention is better than cure and, by preventing elephant numbers from increasing, the authorities are avoiding any risk of a problem. One region where culling is currently taking place is the Wankie National Park, which lies on the fringe of the Kalahari Desert (Cumming, in press). Elephants are seasonal in their distribution and are now dependent during the dry season upon artificial water points. These have led to a deterioration in the vegetation by holding elephants in areas which normally would enjoy a seasonal respite from their maraudings. The resulting (man-made) elephant problem led in 1964 to a decision to cull. The shooting took place between 1971 and 1974 when 3041 elephants were killed. Since then, the policy has been to cull 3 to 4% of the population estimated to be present during the previous dry season, so as to maintain numbers at around the 13 000 level.

The culling is restricted to areas most at risk from elephants and is rarely repeated in the same place in successive years. Sometimes the interval has been up to 5 years or more. Subsequent aerial surveys suggest that elephant densities in regions where culling has taken place remain low for 2 to 3 years afterwards. The aims of the culling programme appear to have been realized for the vegetation in the damaged areas has recovered, although several years of good rainfall have certainly helped.

Culling policies are also being pursued in the Sebungwe region (Cumming, 1981), the Sengwa Wildlife Reserve, the contiguous Chirisa Game Reserve, the Chizarira and Matusadona National Parks and the Gonarezhou Game Reserve. The evidence is too inconclusive as yet to pronounce on the effectiveness of these programmes but preliminary reports are favourable. The culling is experimental in nature and is being carried out in stages, so that it can be immediately stopped if it proves unnecessary or ineffective. There are probably about 30 000 elephants in Zimbabwe (Douglas-Hamilton, 1979), most of whom live in stable or increasing populations and are safe from human exploitation.

Culling in South Africa has taken place in the Kruger National Park, where 95% of South Africa's elephants live. Their density is

165

not high (0.4 per km^2) but the population was rising and the park's authorities wished to stabilize the population at around 7000–8000, which is the estimated carrying capacity of the park during a dry year. Culling started in 1968 and reached its peak in 1971/72, when some 1800 elephants were removed (Smuts, 1975). The population increase was finally curbed in 1974, by which time over 4000 elephants had been shot. Annual aerial counts are made by helicopter and surplus elephants are culled. It is intended to continue this policy indefinitely but it is hoped that, in time, a reliable computerized model of the population can be constructed from which predictions of the population increase can be derived. This would reduce the frequency at which the expensive aerial census would need to be conducted, although regular counts would still be necessary to check on the accuracy of the computer model. The Kruger elephants are isolated from most neighbouring populations and, once the eastern elephant-proof fence is constructed, straying over the border into Mozambique will cease. With such a self-contained population, it should be possible to draw up an effective management programme.

The conclusions to be drawn from this survey of culling are varied. Sometimes, as in Kabalega Falls National Park, the effects of the culling have been swamped by the massive poaching that followed. In other places, such as Tsavo National Park, second thoughts prevailed and the culling was stopped before it could have much effect. We have also seen examples in Zimbabwe of tentative and experimental culling and it is only in the Kruger National Park in South Africa that culling seems to be based on a firm management plan. The Kruger is also one of the few parks in which culling has been undertaken as a precautionary measure before widespread damage has been caused. It is true that elephants had destroyed many trees in the park but not to an extent whereby the future of the habitat was at risk.

Conservation of elephants

Conservation of elephants has been far from satisfactory in the past. The Asian elephant has come perilously close to extinction and the numbers of African elephants are falling in twenty-eight of the thirty-five countries where they still exist (Douglas-Hamilton, 1975), despite model national parks and impeccable conservation laws.

Because of the conflicting interests of man and elephants, the elephant can be conserved only in areas with a sparse human population. The vast food requirements of the elephant mean that the density of its population must be low enough to avoid habitat damage but, on the other hand, it must be high enough to prevent inbreeding. Therefore, only the larger parks or large forest areas are really suitable. Elephants also tend to move into protected areas, so there is a great danger of overcrowding and culling may be necessary.

Translocation of elephants to less crowded areas may be used as an alternative to culling. Young elephants, under sedation, were moved in Rwanda, slung below helicopters, but this was a very costly operation. There are other problems inherent in this procedure. The social coherence of family groups may well be destroyed and the suitability of the release point must be carefully considered.

These remarks apply mainly to the African elephant. The Asian elephants are few in number and exist generally as small scattered units, mainly in the hill forests. This distribution is probably due to the tradition of shifting cultivation in the human population because areas of abandoned agriculture provide an excellent habitat for elephants. The best prospect for the conservation of the Asian elephant would be to continue the traditional land use practice but there is no guarantee that this will happen. Dam-building in Asia is also beneficial to the elephant because the fluctuations in the level of the reservoirs mimic the seasonal flooding of the rivers, resulting in grasslands similar to those found in alluvial flood plains, which are probably the optimal habitat for the Asian elephant (Olivier, 1975).

The high monetary value of elephant carcases provides a great incentive to poachers, despite the protective measures taken by the park authorities. One obvious solution is to ban the trade in ivory and this has been done in Kenya with some success. However, this is only a short-term solution because the question of the disposal of ivory accumulated by natural mortality still remains.

Crop-raiding by elephants is a major problem but it can be reduced by providing barriers around cultivated areas. Sisal, which

167

can be grown as a profitable crop, also acts as a physical deterrent because of its tough leathery leaves with their sharp spikes. Elephant-proof fences can be built, but these are expensive and usually require a ditch to be properly effective and ditches need constant maintenance. Woodley (1965) describes some fenced ditches tried in the Aberdare National Park, the most successful of which was sloped, 2–2.5 m deep, and topped with an angled wire fence on the far side. Electric fences can be effective but they are liable to be pulled down by the non-conducting tusks of the elephants.

Preservation in captivity

It may one day be necessary to rescue elephants by means of a captive breeding programme, but some radical changes in elephant management would be required before such a programme could become standard practice. Most zoos tend to exhibit females only, generally of the Asian species as the African is considered to be untrustworthy. Males of either species tend not to be exhibited for the same reason. The question of untrustworthiness stems largely from the attitudes of the keepers, who look on the elephants as domestic animals and feel that they must be able to enter the enclosures and handle their charges. Ideally, elephants should be kept in large enclosures and in social groups similar to the matriarchal societies found in the wild. They should also be segregated according to sex and species. This would probably be impossible for the average commercial zoo but specialist zoos might find the project worthwhile.

10 *Diseases of elephants*

It is rare to find a diseased wild animal because any creature that falls sick is soon snapped up by predators. The elephant, however, is almost invulnerable to predation. The occasional calf may be taken but man is the only real enemy and, unlike natural predators, he does not seek out the sick and weakly. Consequently, the old and infirm can survive, whereas most other mammals die not long after passing their prime and only a few live long enough to become senile.

Accidents

Accidents are not as uncommon as might be supposed. Despite its bulk, the elephant is quite agile and is adept at clambering up steep slopes. It can make mistakes, however, and cases are known of elephants killing themselves in falls off hillsides. The Douglas-Hamiltons (1975) encountered a dead cow elephant that had slipped and fallen 120 m down the rift valley wall in Lake Manyara National Park and also a bull that had been killed by a falling baobab tree. Presumably, it had been tusking the tree at the time. Sikes (1971) includes a photograph of a remarkable injury to the forelimb of an adult female. The dried ends of the bones of the leg, the radius and ulna, are poking through the foot and are actually taking the weight of the body.

I once saw a severely crippled cow elephant in Lake Manyara National Park. Her right hind leg was twisted into an extraordinary angle with the 'knee' pointing outwards and backwards (Fig. 10.1). In order to walk, she had first to move her injured leg sideways to clear the opposite leg before moving it forwards. She then had to swing the other hind leg out to the side in order to clear the damaged limb when taking her next step — her movements were

Fig. 10.1 Female elephant with deformed hind leg in Lake Manyara National Park, Tanzania. (From a photograph by S.K. Eltringham.)

laborious in the extreme, yet she appeared in good condition and had a healthy calf at heel.

Working elephants in Asia frequently suffer sprains, often as a result of a foot becoming wedged, for example between logs. Evans (1910) found evidence of wild elephants falling down slopes where paths had given way and he once witnessed a fall when a loaded elephant rolled, screaming and trumpeting, some 15 m down a slope after the road collapsed under its weight. Although rescued apparently unharmed, the elephant became so stiff the next day that it could hardly move. One hind leg became very swollen and, although it made a good recovery, the elephant was out of action for a couple of months. Elephants which spend their time shifting huge logs around are vulnerable to strains and pulled muscles. A common injury is that caused when the front legs slip forward as the elephant is coming down a steep slope. To save itself it drops onto its backside and the sudden jar may injure the muscles of the back.

Asian elephants occasionally break a leg when working and may have to be destroyed but, with a simple fracture, the ends of the bone will often knit if the animal is rested for some 3 months. Dislocations are also known but such cases are hopeless, since it is impossible to reset the joint in such a powerful and usually uncooperative animal.

African elephants frequently suffer from accidents with snares set by poachers for antelopes. In the old days, such snares were made of woven grass and elephants had no difficulty in breaking them, should they be caught, but nowadays, wire is used. The elephant is capable of breaking even wire, but, in so doing, the wire cuts deeply into the flesh, causing appalling injuries. In most cases, an elephant caught by the leg develops gangrene and the limb swells up like a balloon, leading to an agonizing death.

Elephants may also be caught by the trunk and, in the resulting struggle to get free, the wire may cut through the trunk and sever it (see p.10). Even if caught lower down and not severed, the trunk may become paralysed and useless for the essential task of feeding. Such animals can now be rescued if noticed in time because they can be immobilized with the help of a dart gun (Eltringham, 1974).

Diseases of the teeth

Elephants sometimes break their tusks but the consequences are rarely serious. A broken tusk will regrow and, because it cannot be used so readily, it is not worn down and so tends to catch up with its partner in length. One-tusked elephants are quite common but one can never be sure whether the missing tusk was absent at birth or was lost by accident. If the latter, the damage was probably done to the developing tusk or to the pulp cavity in the adult stage.

Malformations of tusks occur quite frequently. One such elephant, in the Rwenzori Park, Uganda, had a normal right-hand tusk but the left one emerged from the side of the jaw and curved back towards the 'cheek'. The elephant, therefore, was in danger of piercing its head with the tusk and, left to itself, would probably have died, so it was immobilized by Roger Short in 1965 and the end sawn off. When I saw it again in 1972, the tusk had regrown and was again in danger of penetrating the head. I immobilized it once more and sawed off the offending stump (Fig. 10.2). Fortunately the sawn end of the tusk was flat and had not pierced the flesh but the pressure had set up an inflammation in the socket which was oozing pus. The elephant was probably suffering some pain and was no doubt glad to be rid of the deformity.

Toothache in the tusk must be extremely painful and there are several reported cases of tusk abscesses in African elephants. It is likely that some of the instances of unprovoked aggression by

Fig. 10.2 The author sawing off the end of an abnormal, ingrowing tusk of an immobilized female elephant. Without this treatment, the elephant would probably have died.

elephants against people can be put down to raging toothache. Many of the tusk malformations that have been recorded can probably be attributed to injuries suffered at the hands of man. Bullets or spears passing through the base of the tusk can cause gross deformities, often accompanied by chronic abscesses (Sikes, 1971).

The tusks of Asian elephants sometimes split and, in the case of tame elephants, such tusks can either be capped with brass or iron or bound with an iron band. If the tusk is badly split it may be shortened by sawing off the end, although shortened tusks have a tendency to split. The short tushes of female Asian elephants are liable to be broken off and become diseased. Tuskless males often have such tushes, which are similarly liable to decay.

Dental caries have been reported in Asian elephants (Evans, 1910). This might be expected from the artificial diet given to tame elephants but caries have also been found in wild animals. Another condition frequently found in working elephants is the development of growths on the teeth. These can often reach large sizes and may interfere with mastication of food. Sometimes a tooth may be displaced by a growth on the root and lacerate the inside cheek during mastication. Teeth problems invariably result in a loss of condition in the elephant. The treatment is to cut off the offending growths with a fretsaw or knock them off with a cold chisel.

Before performing dentistry on an elephant it is first necessary to secure the animal and fit a gag. The patience of even the most docile elephant must become strained if the sensations are anything like those we feel in the dentist's chair.

During the culling operations in Kabalega Falls National Park, Uganda, in 1966, Laws and Parker (1968) recorded an appreciable number of elephants (7.5% of 400 examined) with severe abscesses in the teeth and bony swellings on the jaw. Some were very large, as big as a grapefruit, and had prominent drainage passages to the outside of the face. Pus was sometimes exuding from the openings. Subsequent examination of 309 found jaws, i.e. those resulting from natural deaths, in Kabalega Falls Park revealed that 30 (9.7%) showed evidence of abscesses. The level of infected teeth in this park was significantly higher than in elephants elsewhere and it is reasonable to wonder if bad dietary habits were responsible. The elephants were certainly subject to nutritional deficiencies, especially a shortage of protein during the dry season (Malpas, 1977), but Laws and Parker believe that the high incidence of jaw abscesses was due to stress. The increasing tendency for older animals, particularly females, to develop the disease, supports this view.

Abscesses

Abscesses, or healed abscesses, were present on the bodies of several elephants immobilized during studies in the Rwenzori National Park. Most were no more than slight infections following minor injuries, such as a thorn penetrating the skin, and probably caused little pain or inconvenience. Abscesses or septic wounds were a common condition in working Asian elephants often requiring syringing but rarely professional veterinary attention (Williams, 1950).

Diseases of the heart and blood vessels

Cardiovascular disease in elephants has been reported from many regions of Africa. Sikes (1969) made an extensive survey and recorded widespread medial sclerosis, similar to that found in man. In this condition, the main blood vessels to the heart become stiffened by the deposition of calcareous material in the artery wall. Sikes found the condition to be particularly prevalent in elephants from grassland areas and assumed that it reflected a nutritional defect. It is at least as likely that stress due to overpopulation was a contributory factor since most savanna regions can provide the elephant with an adequate diet under normal circumstances. McCullagh (1972) found that the disease was dependent on age, and that older animals, particularly females, were more susceptible than youngsters. Dillman and Carr (1970) came to essentially the same conclusion with elephants from Zambia. Sikes found that some branch arteries become completely blocked by calcareous accretions and, were such occlusions to occur in the coronary arteries, the elephant would suffer a heart attack or, if the carotid arteries were affected, a stroke. It is possible that some elderly elephants die from these familiar human ills but McCullagh (1972) doubts whether such deaths are at all common. He believes that the condition is really a reaction to a weakening of the artery wall.

Calcification of the blood vessels is not always a sign of disease. Because of its huge size and the high blood pressure, the artery wall needs strengthening and this is achieved by reinforcing fibres in the dorsal wall. In elderly elephants, this fibrous arch may become calcified to form a crescent rod.

Fatty deposits are found in the arteries of African elephants at the junction of a small artery and a larger one or where a blood vessel divides (Sikes, 1969). Such deposits are normal in young calves and in pregnant or nursing cows but their presence in other adults is considered pathological. In advanced stages, the fatty deposits lead to

174

the degeneration of the elastic fibres in the arterial wall. The lining of the artery then becomes thickened and calcified, similar to the condition known as atheroma in man. The large volume of an elephant's blood vessels must place a disproportionate strain on the artery wall and aneurysms are not uncommon. Under such circumstances, the artery wall balloons out rather like the weak spot on a bicycle tyre. If one of these were to burst, the elephant would probably drop dead.

Heart disease is known in Asian elephants although the condition has not been investigated so thoroughly as in the African species. Working elephants may suddenly collapse and post-mortem examination often reveals an enlarged and damaged heart. Rupture of the large vessels leaving the heart, usually the left aorta, has been recorded. The result is always rapid death. Asian elephants also suffer strokes following the rupture of blood vessels in the brain. A stroke is not invariably fatal, but elephants which recover frequently suffer some form of paralysis and are useless for work.

Diseases of the blood

There is little information on diseases of the blood itself in African elephants, but such diseases are well known in the Asian species and no doubt similar ones occur in the African elephant. Apart from septicaemia (blood poisoning), a common disease is trypanosomiasis, known in India as *surra* and in Burma as *thut*. It is caused by a protozoan, *Trypanosoma*, which, in Africa, also causes human sleeping sickness and a notorious disease of cattle. The trypanosomes live in the blood serum and are spread by the bite of the tsetse fly (in Africa) and tabanid flies (in Asia). Trypanosomes have been found in the blood of the African elephant but do not cause any apparent disease. In the Asian elephant, however, infection is characterized by fever and general listlessness. There is an overall loss of condition and development of anaemia with dropsical swellings, which may occur between the jaws, in the chest, in the abdomen or in the feet and limbs. Death is by no means inevitable but, when it occurs, it is liable to be sudden, so much so that sometimes snake bite is suspected.

Tick fever, caused by a protozoan parasite, *Piroplasma*, which

Table 10.1   Incidence of microfilariae in African elephants in relation to age*

Age group (years)	Number of elephants examined	% with detectable infection	Number of microfilariae per ml of blood (± standard deviation)
0–5	16	31%	35 ± 78
5–15	47	87%	454 ± 680
15–30	84	83%	351 ± 619
Over 30	48	59%	185 ± 624

*From White, 1980

invades the blood corpuscles, is another well known blood disease in Asian elephants. This parasite is spread by ixodid ticks. The symptoms include high fever, blood-tinged urine, jaundice, anaemia and general weakness. The parasite is likely to be as widespread in the African as it is in the Asian elephant. One species, *Nuttallia loxodontis*, is well known and an undescribed species of *Babesia* (an alternative name for *Piroplasma*) was reported from the blood of a sick African elephant by Brocklesby and Campbell (1963). Although not proven, it is highly likely that this caused the illness.

Microfilariae, the tiny larval stages of nematode worms, have been found in the blood of both Asian and African elephants. Although they can cause serious diseases in many mammals, and are responsible for human elephantiasis, they appear not to cause disease in elephants. The parasites are probably transmitted between elephants by a diurnal biting fly. The incidence of microfilariae in a particularly large sample of 195 African elephants from Uganda was found by White (1980) to be high, with a peak infection in elephants aged from 5 to 30 years (Table 10.1). There was no association between the level of infection and any biochemical property of the blood, nor was there any correlation with other factors such as sex, season or locality. No other blood parasite was found in any of the elephants examined from Uganda.

176

Infectious diseases

Elephants suffer from a great variety of infectious illnesses in captivity but little is known about the incidence of such diseases in the wild. Anthrax certainly occurs in both species but very few instances have been recorded. The disease organism is very resistant and a case is known of anthrax being transmitted to an ivory worker from the dried tusk of an infected elephant. The only elephant we lost during darting operations in Uganda was examined *post mortem* by Mike Woodford, our veterinarian, and was found to have clinical lesions in its lungs similar to those of tuberculosis, but laboratory tests failed to isolate the bacterium. Nevertheless, it is very likely that the elephant was suffering from tuberculosis for the disease is known to occur in 9% of the buffaloes and 10% of the warthogs in the park.

A great many infectious diseases are known in domestic Asian elephants, the most common perhaps being septicaemia, or blood-poisoning, following often minor injuries. Puerperal septicaemia following calving was a further problem in elephant camps and no effective treatment was available until the advent of antibiotics. Haemorrhagic septicaemia, or pasteurellosis, was another scourge. This is a bacterial disease closely resembling anthrax. Progress of the disease is rapid and usually fatal. It is quite common in Asian elephants and may well occur in the African species, although I know of no cases that have been diagnosed with certainty.

Other infectious diseases reported in Asian elephants include foot-and-mouth disease, which is caught from cattle, and elephant pox, which is similar to chicken pox in man. Rabies has also been diagnosed in Asian elephants as well as tetanus, tuberculosis, pneumonia and dysentery. Details of the symptoms of these diseases are given by Evans (1910), who also recommends various treatments. As one might expect from the date, these are more akin to folk medicine than to modern therapy. Evans provides a list of drugs, with their uses and doses, that reads like an inventory of a mediaeval alchemist's treasure house. Many of these drugs were probably effective; others were doubtful or downright dangerous. The general specific for most elephant ills appears to have been an enema.

Parasites

Like most wild animals, the elephant is host to a wide range of parasites but, for the most part, it does not suffer unduly from their presence. A detailed survey of the parasites known to occur in the African elephant (Sikes, 1971), showed that the parasitic flatworms (Platyhelminthes) were represented by two species, one in the gut and the other, a liver fluke, in the bile duct. Cestodes (tapeworms) appear not to have been recorded in the African elephant but they probably do occur, particularly as hydatid cysts are frequently found in the liver of tame Asiatic elephants.

Nematodes (round worms), particularly strongyloids, are well represented. There are at least thirty-one species in the African elephant, not counting the several species of microfilarian worms that occur in the blood.

Ascarids are found in the arteries, limb muscles and bile ducts, an oxyuroid in the gut, strongyloids in the stomach, caecum and intestines, hookworms in the bile duct, gape worms in the respiratory passages and spirurids in the stomach and intestinal walls. Both species of elephants are similarly plagued by these parasites.

Condy (1974) studied the internal parasites of elephants from Zimbabwe and recorded ten genera, mostly nematodes. He considered that cross infection occurred at contaminated water-holes and suggested that, as the water-holes were in any case artificial, it would be better if the water were supplied in tanks with sides 1 m high, to lessen the chance of contamination.

Elephants suffer from a number of ectoparasites and are also bothered by warble or bot flies. These bee-like flies lay their eggs on the surface of the skin and, on hatching, the larvae burrow into the body of the host and undertake a long migration throughout the body, which has not been worked out in the elephant, eventually finishing up in the stomach. Here they feed on the host tissue until well grown, at which point they leave the gut and migrate to the skin of the back, forming swellings, or warbles, on either side of the backbone. When mature, the larvae work their way out to the surface and drop off to pupate on the ground. One African elephant examined by Sikes (1971) was very heavily infested with these maggots, which packed the trunk, mouth, pharynx and gullet as well as the stomach. The elephant had a large open spear wound on its trunk and this may have contributed to the heavy parasite load. Normally, only a few maggots occur. Woodford (1976) found less than ten specimens in each of two elephants that he examined in the Rwenzori National Park, Uganda.

Bot fly larvae are also well known in Asian elephants with patches of up to 100 bots in the gut, usually the stomach, although sometimes in the pharynx, from where they may be expelled through the trunk during a fit of coughing. There are rarely any symptoms, other than apparent irritation when the bots are present in large numbers.

Elephants are not immune from the attentions of other blood-sucking flies, despite the thickness of their skins. Even mosquitoes can cause annoyance and may also transmit diseases. Non-biting flies can be troublesome and elephants expend a lot of energy seeking to avoid their attentions by flapping their ears, swinging their trunks and twitching their tails.

Twenty-one species of ixodid tick have been found in African elephants, of which two species, *Amblyomma thalloni* and *Dermacentor circumguttatus*, are mostly confined to elephants. Ticks are important not so much for the irritation they cause as for their role as vectors of disease.

Only one louse, *Haematomyzus elephantis*, appears to infect elephants and it occurs on both African and Asian elephants. Lice are most likely to be found around the head and neck, under the abdomen and near the root of the tail. They do not appear to transmit any disease to elephants but they cause intense itching and the frequent rubbing to relieve the irritation may open up sores in the skin.

Leeches are the last important group of ectoparasites. They are particularly common in Asia, where land leeches lie in wait amongst the vegetation. They usually attach themselves to their hosts during the wet season and a heavy infestation can lead to a serious loss of blood. They can be removed easily from tame elephants by the time-honoured method of holding a lighted cheroot close to their bodies.

Despite the sometimes heavy parasite loads carried, elephants do not on the whole suffer. Parasitized animals are not usually in bad

179

condition, although they presumably are obliged to feed more in order to support their unwanted guests. Should the habitat deteriorate for any reason, such as drought, and resources become scarce, a heavy load of parasites might tip the balance against survival. Where overcrowding of elephants occurs, as in many national parks, the chances of a parasite finding a new host are increased and parasite burdens are likely to rise. In this case, it certainly makes good sense for the park warden to arrange for the level of infestation to be monitored. This can easily be done by counting the number of eggs in a sample of droppings.

Skin diseases

The skin of an elephant is a sensitive organ liable to the many diseases suffered by the more delicate coverings of smaller animals. The skin is naturally dry but, in the wild, it is kept supple by being liberally plastered with mud or dust and frequently showered with water sucked up in the trunk. In older animals, the skin becomes very wrinkled and inelastic. Evidently, the skin is sometimes itchy, even in healthy animals, but an elephant lacks the dexterity, for example, to scratch its ear with its hind leg. Instead it can use its trunk, but, long and flexible as it is, the trunk cannot reach everywhere and an elephant with an itchy backside has no option but to rub itself against some convenient object. This may be a tree, an ant hill or a large boulder (Fig. 10.3).

Common skin diseases in Asian elephants include scurf, in which small scales are continually shed from the surface, and nettle-rash, which is characterized by eruptions of elastic lumps, usually on the neck, shoulders or abdomen. The causes are probably inadequate or unsuitable diets and the condition usually clears up with no treatment other than good management. Eczema is known in elephants and can occur with various degrees of seriousness. The condition is similar to that in man, with the formation of pustules, which often break, weeping a watery fluid that may turn to pus. The irritation causes the elephant to rub itself on trees etc., so aggravating the condition. The disease may become chronic, with secondary infections causing whole areas of skin to develop into raw patches. Very often, however, the pustules dry up spontaneously

Fig. 10.3 Termite hills or, as here, large boulders are used by elephants to relieve itches in places that cannot be reached by the trunk.

and the affected skin passes through a scaly stage before clearing. Local treatment with powders and ointments can bring a measure of relief.

Ulceration is a common condition in Asian elephants and Evans (1910) shows a photograph of a female which had lost much of its left ear as a result. Such extensive ulceration is unusual and in most cases ulcers soon clear up on treatment with suitable washes. An ulcer is similar to an abscess except that the dead cell tissue is sloughed off and not retained. Most ulcers are stationary but they can affect large areas of skin as in the female elephant mentioned above. Other regions attacked include the tail, which may be completely eaten away.

Not much is known about skin diseases in African elephants. Wild animals have not been examined sufficiently to determine the incidence of the complaint and zoo specimens are usually maintained in conditions too good for infection to occur.

Boils frequently occur in working Asian elephants and are particularly common around the face and shoulders, as well as inside the thighs and belly. Swellings, which are probably boils but may be abscesses, are often seen on wild African elephants. The cause is probably the streptococcal infection of a wound or abrasion on the skin, although some boils arise spontaneously. The swelling, about the size of a tennis ball, is hard and painful to the touch. If left alone, most boils die down without coming to a head and bursting, but they are usually treated with hot water in tame elephants in an attempt to open them.

Diseases of the urino-genital system

Nephritis or inflammation of the kidneys, has been reported in Asian elephants. The symptoms include fever and the frequent passing of small quantities of urine, which is often blood-stained. Cystitis, which is inflammation of the bladder, is indicated by fever and frequent voiding of turbid urine. Diabetes is said to occur in Asian elephants and is also characterized by very frequent urination. Blood in the urine can be caused by factors other than nephritis and may be the result of injury, kidney stones, parasites or, and this is probably most common, the over-zealous use of folk medicines, such as turpentine and cantharidin (Spanish fly). It is, therefore, a symptom rather than a disease in itself.

Ulcers may form inside the urethra of female elephants particularly in old age but venereal disease has never been reported in elephants.

Diseases of the gut

Evans (1910) lists a number of gastro-intestinal diseases in the Asian elephant but one suspects that some, at least, are iatrogenic and require only that the veterinarian should go away for them to be cured. They include acute and chronic indigestion, diarrhoea, excessive purgation (admitted to be due to over-treatment) constipation, colic, enteritis, peritonitis and vomiting. As might be expected, enemas are well to the fore as suggested treatments.

Intestinal obstructions have been reported in Asian elephants and are usually fatal. In most cases, the problem seems to be due to faulty feeding and the condition is unlikely to arise in the wild. Twisting of the gut has also been observed, as has intussusception, a telescoping of a section of the intestine within the following portion. It is usually fatal. Any real disease of the gut in elephants seems to result in death, apart from diarrhoea, which often clears up spontaneously.

Diseases of the eye

Working Asiatic elephants seem to have experienced considerable trouble with their eyes, which Evans (1910) puts down to amateur doctoring by the mahouts. Evans notes that nine of twenty-seven elephants examined by a Major Hawkes had severe impairment of vision, including three that were totally or nearly blind. Wild elephants rarely suffer from eye trouble, unless by accident, until old age, when cataracts may develop. Sikes (1971) records a totally blind old female from northern Nigeria in 1962.

I have noticed that many, if not all, of the elephants I have seen in Ugandan national parks have a frothy white exudate in the corner of the eye, which I suspect is similar to the encrustations which sometimes accumulate in the corners of our own eyes during the

183

night. It does not appear to be pathogenic or disturb the elephant in any way.

Ophthalmia or inflammation of the eyes occurs in working Asian elephants and has a variety of causes, including foreign bodies in the eye and exposure to the glare of the sun. If untreated, the condition may develop into inflammation of the cornea, which becomes infiltrated and cloudy. If this infiltration extends over the pupil, impaired vision will result. The cornea may also become ulcerated, leaving an opaque scar, but ulcers rarely form across the pupil. If the ulcer eats too deeply into the cornea, the pressure of the fluid within the eye may cause the thinned cornea to bulge forwards. This bulge often interferes with the movement of the eyelids and, as a consequence, the blister may burst, releasing fluid from inside the eye. Although this sounds catastrophic, it is in fact remedial and afterwards the eye usually regains its full function.

Treating sick elephants

The introduction of modern immobilizing drugs has made the vet's life much easier, but, in the early days of working elephants, no such aids were available. In a jungle camp, it is not feasible to lift an elephant or throw it onto its side and if it is necessary to operate upon a recumbent animal, the elephant must be persuaded to lie down voluntarily. An elephant can be forcibly restrained, however, and sometimes, as in a painful operation, it is very necessary that it should be. This can be achieved by walking it into a stoutly built timber crush and tying its limbs to the supports. It is also important that the trunk should be secured.

Such draconian measures are best avoided, if at all possible, and most keepers maintain that elephants are intelligent enough to realize that any pain inflicted during their treatment is for their own good. Hence, it is always best to allow the mahout, in whom the elephant has confidence, to carry out any particularly painful treatment. It should rarely be necessary, nowadays, to inflict pain because of the readily available anaesthetics but even so, certain treatments can be frightening and the elephant's confidence should not be lost.

Many operations that need to be done on elephants involve lancing or cleaning out abscesses. Most elephant are cooperative and do not need to be tied up. Working elephants suffer frequently from foot trouble and again, treating cuts on the sole or trimming the nails can be carried out without restraining the animal. The tusks of the male elephants are often sawn off at the tip, a procedure that is usually done with the elephant lying down in a shallow river so that the saw may be cooled frequently in the water. The trunk must be securely lashed to prevent it being accidentally cut. Water should also be available to cool the saw during dentistry on the back teeth. This needs great cooperation on the elephant's part, although gags can be used to prevent the mouth closing on the dentist's arm.

Gags (Fig. 10.4) are sometimes used in giving medicines. The hole in the centre is for the hand to pass through and deposit the pill at the back of the throat. Evans says that the elephant may resist with its tongue and cautions that 'care must be taken that the hand is not pushed to one side between the grinders'. Usually, a pill is enclosed within a ball of pleasant-tasting food and popped into the back of the mouth by the mahout without the need for a gag. Liquid medicines can be pumped into the mouth with an enema syringe or offered in a folded plantain leaf.

Treatment of wild elephants is impracticable if not impossible. In any case, disease is a natural phenomenon and, if it acts as a culling agent in weeding out the old and sickly, it may even be considered desirable. It is a different matter if exotic diseases, to which the elephants have no immunity, enter a population and, in such circumstances, it might be prudent to attempt to get rid of the disease. An extremely virulent disease would be less of a problem than a slowly progressing one, such as tuberculosis, since most affected animals would die before passing on the infection.

Fig. 10.4 Gag used in administering medicine to working Asian elephants.

11 *Elephants and man*

Elephants in art and mythology

The relationship between elephants and man extends back to pre-history. Pictures of the elephant, and of the now extinct mammoths, are found throughout the world in some of the oldest cave paintings known. Paintings and carvings of the African elephant, probably dating from the Palaeolithic, have been found in the Sahara Desert at Tassili Plateau, Wadi Zermei and Sarras. The elephant also features in the art of the ancient Egyptians and there are paintings of elephants on a wall tomb at Thebes dating from 1500 B.C. These look more like Asian than African elephants and are peculiar in being represented as tiny creatures, half the height of a man.

In Asia, artefacts depicting elephants have been recorded from the third millenium B.C. of the pre-Aryan civilization in the Indus Valley, Pakistan. Numerous representations of the elephant occur throughout Asia, dating back to 2 or 3 thousand years ago, on coins, statues, paintings etc. and it is clear that elephants played a large part in religion and legend. Surprisingly, the elephant also figures prominently in European art. The Romans, of course, were familiar with elephants, which they obtained from North Africa, and elephants, easily recognizable as the African species, appear on Roman coins. European artefacts produced some curious representations of elephants and, clearly, most artists had never seen one in the flesh but relied on descriptions brought back by travellers.

Some constant themes appear in the pictures and carvings of elephants. In Europe, the elephant is frequently shown fighting with a serpent or dragon. The latter is usually symbolic of evil, so presumably the elephant must have been considered a symbol of purity. This is generally the case in most traditions and rarely is the elephant regarded as other than on the side of good. The other species which it seems to spend its time fighting in mythology, particularly in the East, is the lion.

Another recurrent theme is the castle on the elephant's back. Elephants certainly are burdened with howdahs but no howdah has ever reached the size of the castles shown in mediaeval representations. 'Elephant and Castle' is a common name for public houses in England and may well be derived from such illustrations rather than from the more commonly suggested 'Infanta de Castile'.

Elephants in war

Despite the firm conviction of many authorities that the African elephant is untameable, it was probably the African species that was first domesticated. It is likely that the elephants were originally tamed for military reasons. In the days when the cavalry was the most mobile and effective instrument of war, the use of elephants as a counter weapon had obvious advantages. A naive enemy who had never seen an elephant would be terrified at the approach of such monstrous creatures. In fact, their value was more psychological than practical. Elephants are more difficult to control than horses and they tended to run amok in battle, causing as much damage to their own side as to the enemy. Further, they are not aggressive animals and are easily frightened. Ranks of infantry men who stood firm and slashed at the elephants with swords and spears soon put them to flight.

One of the earliest occasions in which elephants were used in warfare was the Battle of Ipsus in 301 B.C., when King Antigonus, erstwhile general of Alexander the Great, was decisively beaten by his rival Lysimachus. As the battle site was in Phrygia in Asia Minor, the elephants were presumably Asian.

The most famous military elephants are undoubtedly those used by Hannibal in his crossing of the Alps in 218 B.C. Hannibal's problems were not confined to scaling the mountains, for he had first to negotiate the Rhone above Arles, at a point where the river is some 300 m wide. This he did, according to Polybius, using a series of rafts.

Evidence from coins minted at the time suggests that Hannibal's elephants included both African and Asian species. Polybius

187

mentions that the Asian elephants were bigger and stronger than the African ones, so presumably the African elephants were of the forest race (*cyclotis*). It is possible that the elephants were young ones, but their ears, as shown on Carthaginian coins, are distinctly rounded, like those of *cyclotis*.

Elephants were sometimes armoured for battle, often with a coat of chain mail, although it is doubtful that the protection was effective. Perhaps the most famous battle in history in which elephants featured was that between Alexander the Great and the Indian King Porus in 326 B.C. Alexander had reached the River Hydaspes, now called the Jhelum, which is a tributary of the Indus in present day Pakistan. Facing him was the Indian Rajah Paurava (Porus) with an army of cavalry, chariots, infantry and elephants. Leaving some of his army and elephants in camp, Porus marched forward with a force which included 200 elephants. Upon reaching the selected battle ground, he lined up his elephants at the front, about 100 m apart, as an impregnable line from which his infantry could in due course advance. On either end of the line he placed elephants carrying huge wooden 'towers' (presumably howdahs), containing armed men.

Battles never go according to plan and, in the event, the elephants wreaked as much havoc amongst the Indians as amongst the Macedonians. Eventually most of the elephants were killed or so severely wounded that they took no further part in the action.

Elephants as beasts of burden

African elephants
The most useful role which elephants have played in human affairs is as a beast of burden. A tame elephant is a tractable beast and can be trained to carry out numerous tasks. It forms an ideal means of transport in country that no car could penetrate and it is capable of carrying loads of up to 550 kg on its back. Dr Andrew Laurie, who studied the Indian rhino in Nepal, found that the only possible way of observing rhinos in the 3-m high grass was from elephant back. Elephants are used to take visitors around the Indian and Nepalese national parks but this means of transport has not been

tried in African parks. The incentive is less since the latter are more open and easily accessible by car but to approach wildlife silently on elephant back must be a sublime experience. Moreover, in India, wild elephants do not seem to notice people riding on tame animals.

The usual argument, that the African elephant is untameable, can easily be countered. Elephants from North Africa were domesticated in antiquity and, in this century, elephant training stations were set up at a number of places in the then Belgian Congo. The scheme was started in 1899 by order of King Leopold and organized by a Commandant Laplume, who sited his first station at Kiravunga in the rain forest of the Bas Uele province. The initial attempts at taming elephants were none too successful but eventually some thirty-five were trained. Only immature animals were captured and, because of their small size, it was some 10 years before they were trained and big enough to work.

In 1925, the station was transferred to Api and, in 1930, a second station was opened at Gangala na Bodio, near the Garamba National Park. This is the only station still existing. Only nine elephants remained in 1976, of which the oldest, Doruma, was captured in 1926. The youngest was born in 1954 but the latest wild-caught elephant was acquired in 1957. Only one was a male and it had been castrated. The elephants are trained with the help of older, reliable animals known as *moniteurs*. Of the nine, only four are *moniteurs*, although two others were considered to be potentially suitable for the role. The eighteen attendants are growing old too so unless some more elephants and men are trained soon, the project will die a natural death. The elephants are no longer worked but they are kept in training by collecting loads of fodder from the forest and bringing it back to the station.

Asian elephants
The use of the Asian elephant as a beast of burden is well documented and a good account of everyday life in an elephant station is given by Williams (1950). The principal function of elephants is to remove logs cut from deep inside the forest. Today their task is more often carried out by tractor and elephants have a use only on the most precipitous slopes but, even here, mechanical winches have largely taken over. The change is not for the better, not only

because yet another traditional skill is dying out but because the more powerful winches often scour deep trenches with the logs as they are dragged uphill, destroying vegetation and forming foci of erosion.

The days of the working elephant in Asia are numbered, if not already over. One reason is that the elephant is really an inefficient machine; because of its bulk it has to feed for much of the time and its working day is short. It works only 3 days in succession before being given 2 days rest and, in Burma at least, the working year is only 9 months long. Hence there are only 162 working days in the year. Elephants are expensive to maintain and it is obviously uneconomic to use them now that their job can be done by machine. Nevertheless, it is interesting to recall the training and working life of an elephant.

CAPTURING ELEPHANTS

Many working elephants are born in captivity or at least to tame animals, although very often the calf is sired by a wild bull. Other elephants are captured from the wild. Methods of capture have not changed much since the time of Pliny, who describes how wild herds were driven into enclosures and tamed down through hunger. More recent techniques involve going into the enclosure on tame elephants to take out the wild animals. The tame elephants move alongside a wild one while one of the men jumps off and daringly slips a noose around the hind foot of the captive. The free end of the rope is then attached to the collar of the tame elephant, which leads its charge over to a tree to which it is tethered. Other tame elephants may crowd round the wild one to ensure that it does not break away or to control it if it should become obstreperous.

Such catching operations are rare for they take considerable organization and are expensive. The corral, or *keddah*, has to be constructed of stout timbers and needs to be large, often enclosing several hectares of jungle. Many hundreds of beaters are required to drive the elephants towards the *keddah*. This must be done slowly to prevent the elephants breaking back and the process may take several weeks. Obviously, it is not worth going to all this trouble unless fair numbers of elephants are involved.

Williams considers that 15–20 years is the ideal age for a

captured wild elephant because it soon becomes large enough to carry out heavy work. Breaking-in is a lengthy process and it is much simpler to train a calf born in captivity, although it is many years before it is big enough to work.

Calves are trained together from the age of about 5 years, when they are fully weaned. Each is pushed into a cage and its rider lowered onto its neck. (The usual practice was to assign a young boy to each calf as its future mahout so that they could grow up together.) The calf objects strongly at first but, in time, accepts the rider, whereupon a heavy block of padded wood is lowered onto its back. Again the calf vigorously objects but the block is lifted off after a few moments. It is then raised and lowered a number of times until the calf eventually sits down when it feels the block on its back. This is considered an advance, for the animal sits or stands depending on whether or not the load is placed on its back. These movements are accompanied by shouts of command until the calf will respond to the voice only. It is then considered broken and is released from the cage.

Further training takes place with the help of an adult elephant, which takes its charge for walks into the jungle at the end of a rope. The calves are not fully trained and put to work until they are about 19 years old. They are first taught words of command and the meaning of pressure applied to the back of their ears (turn right or left), to the top of the head (kneel), or to the back (stop). By the age of 8 years, they are big enough to carry a light pack and to begin to earn their keep.

WORKING THE ELEPHANTS

The elephants' harness for dragging logs is simple (Fig. 11.1). There is no collar and the animal's pull is transmitted through a breast band. A light wooden saddle is placed over a cushioning pad and secured with a belly band. A double sling is hung from the saddle to just above the level of the chest and the ends of the breast band are passed through the two loops. The breast strap, about 12-cm wide, is fitted with eyelets at each end, through which hooks with swivel links are passed. Trace chains are clipped onto these hooks and the

Fig. 11.1 A Burmese elephant harnessed for dragging logs.

free end attached to the load. The pulling gear is thus only loosely attached and the elephant can easily throw it off by turning round and stepping inside the chains. This it will do if it miscalculates and finds the log slipping and threatening to pull it over a precipice. Some ill-behaved elephants cast off their harness for devilment and, with these, it is necessary to secure the gear with a crupper and a sling around the tail, through which the dragging chains are passed (Fig. 11.2).

The usual task for an elephant during logging operations is to drag a log, from the place where the tree has been felled, along a ridge to a point where it can be unshackled and pushed down the slope towards the river. Great delicacy is required during the process and the elephant has to position the log carefully with its fore feet before giving the final heave. It then has to move down the slope and 'manhandle' the log into the river. The logs often weigh up to 4 tonnes each and even an elephant cannot move these more than a few yards at a time before pausing for breath. The dragging chains are usually threaded through a hole cut into the end of the log but sometimes a small wheeled cart is used to support the log.

The harness for an elephant used as a pack animal is rather different. Unlike that of a horse, the elephant's backbone forms a prominent ridge and can be easily damaged if any weight is put directly upon it. Consequently, the gear is designed to avoid

192

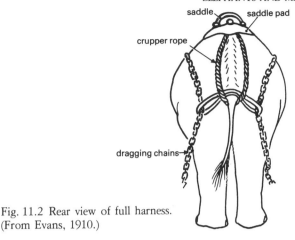

saddle   saddle pad

crupper rope

dragging chains→

Fig. 11.2 Rear view of full harness.
(From Evans, 1910.)

pressure on the spine. First a pad (*guddela*) of cloth is put over the back and a cushioned pad (*guddee*) placed on top. This pad (Fig. 11.3a) has a central opening to accommodate the spinal ridge. Next, an iron saddle with rings on each corner (Fig. 11.3b) is placed on top of the pad and secured with a tight girth. The lower bars of the saddle should be wrapped with soft ropes to prevent chafing and a network of rope should be woven between the bars to stop small articles falling onto the elephant's back (Fig. 11.3c). A neck rope is

Fig. 11.3 (a) Saddle pad or *guddee*. (b) Iron saddle. (c) Iron saddle wrapped and ready for use. (From Evans, 1910.)

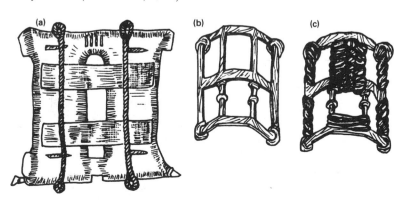

(a)   (b)   (c)

Fig. 11.4 (a) Iron crupper pipe. (b) Crupper rope threaded through crupper pipe. (From Evans, 1910.)

looped around one of the front rings of the saddle, passed under the elephant's head and knotted onto the other corner. This prevents the saddle from slipping backwards and a crupper rope prevents it moving forwards. The rope is passed through a hollow crupper pipe (Fig. 11.4) under the tail and secured to the rear corners of the saddle in the same way as the neck rope is attached to the front.

The load is then tied onto this contraption with a long rope to ensure that each side is properly balanced. Simple panniers or howdahs may be used to carry the loads (Fig. 11.5) and more elaborate ones for riding purposes. In such cases, the howdah normally replaces the saddle. Some of the howdahs used in ceremonial processions are very elaborate affairs, with canopies and silken seats, but the usual type is more like a simple box, useful for hunting as the marksman can move about to take aim. For simple transport purposes, outward-facing bench seats, like the saddle of a zoo elephant, are often used.

Fig. 11.5 Burmese howdah. (From Evans, 1910.)

194

Fig. 11.6 (a) Driving hook with bamboo handle. (b) Iron driving hook. (From Evans, 1910.)

CONTROLLING ELEPHANTS

The driver of the elephants, *mahout* in India or *oozie* in Burma, sits on the animal's neck with his feet behind its ears. Most of the commands are given verbally but they can be reinforced by kicks and pressure behind the ears from the mahout's bare feet or knees. Sometimes a driving hook (Fig. 11.6) is used to goad the elephant but this is frowned upon by good drivers. The goad is regularly used, however, for leading the elephant, when it is hooked over the top of the ear close to the head. The elephant is usually mounted after commanding it to sit down on its brisket with the front legs extended forwards.

After a day's work, the elephant is turned out into the jungle to feed but, in order to prevent it from wandering too far, the front feet are often fettered with chains, which are rather like a pair of handcuffs. Some wily elephants are adept at undoing these hobbles and for them, a special spring lock is necessary. If the elephant is inclined to wander, a 14-m length of chain may be attached to the fetter between the fore legs and allowed to trail.

Next day the mahout tracks the elephant, calling out to it when close in order not to surprise it and cause it to bolt or charge. The elephant is then unhobbled and ridden back to camp. It is important to ensure that all the males are properly fettered in case they start fighting at night. An unfettered tusker can inflict serious damage on a fettered opponent, even if the latter is a bigger animal.

While tethered in camp, an elephant is usually secured by one fore leg only to a chain wound round a tree or post but, if a male is coming into musth, all four legs are tied separately to posts.

Fig. 11.7 Hind foot fetter or *soolay*. (From Evans, 1910.)

BOLTING

Some elephants are given to frequent bolting and mahouts have devised various ways of halting runaway beasts. Blindfolding the animal with a cloth has been known to work but, normally, sterner measures are necessary. A length of chain is often looped around the hind leg and stowed on the saddle. At the opportune moment, this can be thrown overboard in the hope that it will become entangled in some obstacle. Sometimes a small log is attached to the end to increase its effectiveness or an anchor may be formed from the head of a pick axe. Alternatively a fetter with inwardly pointing barbs (*soolay* in Burmese), suspended by a cord, may be placed loosely around the limb so as not to hurt the elephant under normal circumstances (Fig. 11.7). A length of chain and an anchor is attached to the ring and released when required. The barbs dig into the flesh and soon cause the elephant to pull up.

Other techniques include threading a string through a hole in the ear. If the elephant give signs of trouble, the mahout pulls on the string and this apparently brings the animal back under control. A more drastic treatment is to place a large hook over the top of the ear close to the head. When the elephant starts to bolt, the attendant pulls on a string attached to the hook, driving the point into the ear.

CATCHING ESCAPED ELEPHANTS

Occasionally elephants refuse to return to captivity when turned out into the jungle. Bulls on musth often do so if they are not tied up. If possible, they are left until they become tractable again but should they start attacking people, they have either to be recaptured quickly or shot. The methods used in recapture are generally barbaric to a greater or lesser degree. One is simply to shoot the animal in the foot in order to incapacitate it sufficiently for it to be roped. Another technique is to load the gun with pieces of pointed bamboo, which

196

Fig. 11.8 *Kya-pazat*.
(From Evans, 1910.)

lodge in the foot and lame the animal.

A slightly more humane method with an elephant which will allow a man to approach but not handle it, is to place a *kya-pazat* around the hind leg. This instrument is shaped rather like a pitchfork, with backward pointing barbs on the prongs (Fig. 11.8). These slip round the leg easily enough but the hooks dig into the flesh if an attempt is made to pull it off. The wooden handle soon becomes detached but the head is tied to a rope which becomes entangled in bushes as the elephant moves away.

If the escaped elephant is not too big, it can often be recaptured with the help of other elephants, which close in on each side and march the miscreant back to camp.

Elephants in zoos

Most elephants kept in zoos have been of the Asian species, although perhaps the most famous of all, London's Jumbo, was an African elephant. The first elephant to walk on English soil since Pleistocene days was probably the one given to King Henry III by King Louis IX of France in 1254. Judging from a drawing, this was of the African species. It was accommodated in a specially constructed elephant house in the Tower of London by order of the King. A further donation of an elephant from the Crown of France to that of England is recorded during the reign of Elizabeth I. When the menagerie in the Tower was closed down in the reign of William IV, the stock included an elephant, which was passed on with the other animals to the newly formed collection in Regent's Park.

A bull Asian elephant named Chunee was used on the stage in Covent Garden in 1810 but it soon became an embarrassment to the management, who were glad to send it to Exeter Exchange, an

197

indoor menagerie which used to stand just off the Strand in London. It was most unsuitable accommodation for an elephant and, eventually, probably during a period of musth, Chunee ran amok. Fearing that it would break out of its enclosure, Mr Cross, the manager, decided to put it down and called in a detachment of Foot Guards, but they proved to be less than efficient, for they took 152 shots to kill the maddened beast.

Jumbo, the most well known of all zoo elephants, probably came from what is now Zimbabwe. He was taken to the Cape and sold to the Jardin des Plantes in Paris. From there, in 1865, he went to London Zoo in exchange for a rhinoceros. At this time he was thought to be about 4 years old, being some 1.5 m high at the shoulder.

Jumbo's story has been told many times and a full biography has been written by Jolly (1976). He was placed in the charge of Matthew Scott, under whose care, Jumbo grew apace until he was about 3.5 m high. He was used as a riding animal, being usually quiet and reliable, but after 15 years, when he was about 20 years old and full grown, he began to show signs of truculence and, during these periods, he damaged his quarters considerably. He was probably on musth but, as Sikes (1971) points out, his fifth set of molars would have been erupting and it is possible that he was suffering from teething troubles. He may have suffered permanently from his teeth for, after his death, his right upper molar was found to be misshapen and most likely could not function properly.

The attacks on his quarters were so violent that he broke off both tusks close to the skull and, on growing out again, the broken ends penetrated the flesh, setting up abscesses. With great courage, Bartlett, the Zoo's Superintendent, and Scott stood under the elephant and cut through the skin around the tusk roots with a razor-sharp hook, allowing the pus to escape. The operation was completely successful and the tusks grew out through the cuts without further trouble.

Despite his improved health, Jumbo continued to be unpredictable and only Scott could handle him when he started to play up. It is interesting that Jumbo became much calmer if he was taken out of his quarters and walked around the gardens. Fearing that Jumbo might one day run amok when surrounded by visitors, the Council of the Zoological Society were relieved when, in January 1882, the American showman, Phineas T. Barnum offered to take him off their hands for £2000 and the sale was announced.

There followed one of the most remarkable outbursts of chauvinistic hysteria ever seen in England. One might have thought that the Americans had kidnapped the lions in Trafalgar Square. Letters to the press and public indignation meetings failed to sway the stony heart of Barnum who, recognizing a publicity stunt when he saw one, did his best to encourage the controversy. New heights of pathos were reached when Jumbo refused to leave the Zoo! Nothing would persuade him to enter the specially prepared crate and, when it was decided to walk him to the docks instead, he lay down in the road and refused to budge. The ship he was to travel on had to leave without him and there is more than a suspicion that Matthew Scott, his keeper, was partly responsible for Jumbo's reluctance to depart. Suspecting that Scott was secretly signalling to Jumbo, Bartlett told Scott that he was thinking of replacing him by an American elephant trainer, but at the same time said that Barnum had made him a generous offer if he would go to the USA with the elephant while his job at the Zoo was held open. The next day Jumbo became much more cooperative and immediately entered the crate! Another passage was booked but had to be cancelled because of legal action by dissident Fellows, who attempted to restrain the Zoo Council from selling Jumbo. They were unsuccessful and a few weeks later Jumbo left for the docks in a procession that must have rivalled that for the Queen's Golden Jubilee 5 years later.

Jumbo's subsequent life in the USA was as a circus elephant, although he was not called upon to perform tricks. His role was to lead a procession of some twenty or thirty Asian elephants, over whom he towered by a metre or so, into the ring. He was also used as a riding elephant. With one exception, when he knocked a hole in the wall of his enclosure, he showed no sign of the truculence that led to his sale by London Zoo. His end was sad for he was knocked down on 15th September 1885 by a railway engine when returning to his quarters with the circus train during a visit to St Thomas, a little town in Ontario. Mortally injured, Jumbo died shortly afterwards with Scott, who had remained with him, by his side.

Jumbo's skin was stuffed and used with his mounted skeleton as a central attraction at Barnum's shows but the remains eventually found their way into museums. The stuffed Jumbo was destroyed by fire in 1975 at Tuft's University in Medford, Massachusetts, but his skeleton is on display at the Museum of Natural History in New York.

London Zoo has kept many elephants in its time. One of the first, Jack, an Asian tusker acquired in 1831, was as famous in his day as Jumbo was to be later on. He was mentioned in the writings of Thackeray and Dickens and was immortalized as a corpse in a drawing by Landseer. His other claim to fame is that he killed an Indian rhinoceros in a neighbouring pen by repeatedly tusking it when it came too close to the dividing railings.

Other African elephants were kept at the Zoo during the last century. One, Alice, arrived a few months after Jumbo and was alleged to be his sorrowing wife by those trying to stop Jumbo's sale. There is in fact no evidence that the two were ever kept together. Alice followed Jumbo to the USA in 1886 as another of Barnum's elephants but she was killed in the same year in a fire.

Jumbo's successor was a young African male called Jingo, who arrived in 1882, the year Jumbo was sold. He eventually became troublesome and in 1903 he too was sold to the USA, but for only a tenth of Jumbo's price. Unfortunately he died on the voyage, from sea sickness it is said, and was pitched overboard much to the surprise of the crew of another ship who came across the improbable corpse floating in mid-Atlantic.

Plenty of other zoos in Britain have kept elephants. Bristol received its first specimen in 1869 from the Rajah of Mysore and it lived until 1911. Like many other zoos, Bristol used to keep only one elephant at a time, due to the expense of upkeep and general shortage of space. Belle Vue Zoo, Manchester, was an exception and always kept a group. The main function of the zoo elephant was to give rides and it was one of the few inmates to earn its keep. When London Zoo first started to charge tuppence each for elephant rides, soon after Jumbo's departure, they were startled to find that the proceeds came to between £600 and £1200 a year, a lot of money in those days — or these for that matter. Tips for elephant rides had previously been taken by the keeper so it is no wonder that elephant attendant was a much sought-after job or that Matthew Scott had discouraged attempts to provide him with an assistant and been so reluctant over Jumbo's departure.

Few zoos have managed to breed elephants and most do not even keep a bull. Several Asian but very few African calves have been born in captivity. There have been successful births at the Hellabrun Zoo in Munich, where a bull calf was born in 1943, and in the private zoo at Kronberg, near Frankfurt, where two calves were born to the same mother in 1966 and 1968 respectively. Another birth occurred at Basle Zoo in 1966. The most remarkable birth, however, took place at Chester Zoo, England, in 1977, when a female Asiatic elephant gave birth to a hybrid calf. Such inter-generic crosses are very rare and, indeed, I cannot recall any other case with large mammals. The calf, unfortunately, did not survive.

Elephants in circuses

Elephants move smoothly from zoo to circus and back again. Indeed the distinction is difficult to draw because some zoos, such as that in West Berlin, train their elephants to perform tricks. Jumbo, of course, became a circus elephant, although it was considered undignified for him to perform tricks, and so did Alice, his erstwhile 'wife'. Rosie, the Ceylon elephant that lived for years in Bristol Zoo, was an ex-circus performer and continued to display the exaggerated swaying motion which she had been taught to do to dance music in her circus days.

Elephants make suitable circus animals as they readily learn tricks without coercion. There are, no doubt, cases of cruelty in the training of elephants but, in most cases, the trainer simply encourages them to intensify natural movements, such as the swaying which many chained animals carry out as a substitute for walking. Wild elephants have been seen to stand on their hind legs to reach titbits in trees and can easily be persuaded to rear up in captivity. The familiar procession of elephants walking on their hind legs with the fore feet resting on the elephant in front is not difficult to arrange, for the elephants' position is not far removed from the mating stance.

During the days of the Romans, circuses were certainly not at all innocent. At first, elephants were encouraged to fight each other in the amphitheatre, but later they were pitted against other animals, including fighting bulls. The first record of the use of elephants in circus fights comes from Livy, who mentions combats between men and elephants around 131 B.C. The elephants were attacked by gladiators and archers and often ran amok, as much to the danger of the spectators as to that of the contestants. Pliny also gives bloodthirsty accounts of elephants being matched against men during the Consulship of Pompeius. The 'fights' were not all one-sided and men were killed or injured as well as the elephants. Many species of wild animals featured in the Roman circuses and it is quite likely that the extensive slaughter in the circuses hastened the extinction of big game in North Africa.

Not all the Roman circuses were brutal and elephants were also used in processions around the amphitheatre. Seutonius and other Latin writers tell of elephants that had obviously been trained to a high level to perform tricks in public. Circuses with animal performers fell into abeyance after the Roman period and were not revived until the eighteenth century, first in England and then on the Continent and in America. It was not until the second half of the nineteenth century that circuses became a popular entertainment for the masses, with Barnum in the USA, Lord George Sanger in Britain and Hagenbeck in Germany. Numerous circuses emerged in the early years of this century and spread to all parts of the world. Recent trends have been towards displays by acrobats, clowns and conjurers rather than by animals. Animal acts are, in fact, dying out, partly because of expense but also because of pressure from animal welfare bodies opposed to the exploition of animals. Misgivings have been expressed, not only about possible cruelty in training but also about the conditions under which the animals are kept between performances.

Those concerned with the conservation of elephants should welcome the decline of animal acts in circuses. Elephants are rarely bred in captivity and most circus elephants are caught from the wild.

Elephant fights were not confined to Roman times, for, until quite recently, Indian princes showed a pronounced taste for them. The elephants, however, were pitted against one another, not against men, and it was rare for any to be killed. The fight usually consisted of a trunk-wrestling match across a low wall, between contestants which were often tethered by a hind foot. Elephants on musth were preferred because they needed little incentive to fight but sometimes mahouts would ride on the elephants and goad them into combat. Occasionally the wall would be knocked down and untethered combatants would grapple with one another and could be separated only with great difficulty. Deaths were not unknown after such encounters. Reports of large-scale combats between rival herds of wild elephants driven into an arena seem rather far-fetched in view of their peaceful behaviour in the wild.

Ceremonial elephants

Ceremonial elephants were once used widely in religious processions or in ostentatious display by potentates. Elephants are still used for this purpose in Asia, e.g. the annual procession of the Buddha's Tooth on Kandy Perahera Day in Sri Lanka (Plate 12). The ceremonial elephant is richly caparisoned with a gorgeous *guddela* across its back and an intricately decorated shield over its forehead. The skin is usually painted with naturalistic or abstract designs, particularly on the front of the trunk and down the fore legs. The tusks are often bangled with precious metals. The howdah is the centre piece. Intricately carved, furnished with silk and capped with a canopy of elaborate design, it is a conveyance fit for a prince, who indeed was the usual occupant in the days when even a minor ruler would have several hundred elephants in his stables. Nowadays, the princely stables are no more and only a few ceremonial elephants remain to continue the tradition.

White elephants were particularly desirable for ceremonial purposes. These are elephants with reduced pigmentation but they are not usually albinos. Their colour is dirty grey rather than white and they often disappoint visitors at side shows where they are exhibited. Barnum tried to cash in further on the elephant mania generated by Jumbo by showing a white elephant, Toung Taloung, which he had acquired in 1883 from Siam. Londoners were most unimpressed when the grey creature with pink blobs on its ears and trunk was put on display at the Zoo. In the USA, a fake, painted white, proved to be far more popular with the public.

The status of white elephants was very different in the East where they have always been accorded near-divine rank. This is no doubt due more to their rarity value than to any attraction in their appearance. Some may have been true albinos but evidence for their existence stems mainly from travellers' tales, which are notoriously unreliable. Such elephants were never worked, nor even expected to carry the king, because they were considered to be of equal rank with the monarch. On capture, the white elephant was treated with the greatest respect and anointed as a Buddhist lord with conse-crated water. It was housed in a sumptuous palace, fed with the choicest foods and accorded a splendid funeral at its death. Its behaviour was closely watched by the priests, who interpreted its every action to the king. It seems that the policies of the state were sometimes altered to accommodate the supposed 'opinions' of the white elephant.

12 *The ivory trade*

Characteristics of ivory

Ivory, with its grain and lustrous whiteness, has always had a curious fascination for man. It was well known in classical times and its use in India and China dates back to prehistory. The ease with which it can be shaped has long attracted carvers and some of the most exquisite artefacts ever produced are made of ivory. It has also been widely used as an inlay in wooden tables or other furniture. Billiard balls, knife handles and piano keys were amongst items made of ivory but, nowadays, other substances are more commonly used and ivory has little utilitarian function. Its principal value, at least in the West, is as currency, rather like gold. It is still widely used in the East for making items of jewellery and has also been used medicinally, in powdered form, as an emetic and as a cure for worms.

Ivory is graded by merchants according to its weight and shape as follows:

a) Vilaiti — tusks weighing over 40 lb (18 kg). Tusks of this size are almost all from adult males.

b) Cutchi — tusks weighing from 20–40 lb (9–18 kg). This again is predominantly a male class for few female tusks weigh over 20 lb (9 kg).

c) Calasia — tusks from females weighing more than 10 lb (4.5 kg) and between 2 and 3 in (5 and 7.6 cm) in diameter.

d) Fankda — tusks from males weighing between 10 and 20 lb (4.5 and 9 kg).

e) Maksub — tusks from either sex weighing between 5 and 10 lb (2.3 and 4.5 kg).

f) Dandia — tusks from either sex weighing less than 5 lb (2.3 kg).

g) Chinai — defective tusks of any weight.

The price of ivory roughly follows this sequence. Vilaiti is the most valuable if the tusk is particularly large. Otherwise Calasia, which exceeds Cutchi in value, is worth more weight for weight. A tusk is defective if broken, split, slightly weathered or if it shows abnormal growth pearls. The latter tend to cause splintering of the ivory during carving.

Badly weathered ivory is classed as rotten and is worthless commercially. The straighter tusks are better for carving than markedly curved ones because there is less wastage, so Calasia is generally preferred, especially that from the forest elephant, which has almost straight tusks.

Ivory is further classified as soft or hard. The really hard ivory comes only from *L. a. cyclotis* of the equatorial rain forests. Hard ivory falls into the same categories but each is qualified by the word 'Gandai', e.g. Vilaiti Gandai.

Ivory was not always highly valued in Africa and was often put to mundane uses by local tribesmen, e.g. as fences for penning cattle. Nevertheless, the Ugandan kings in the last century tended to collect ivory; Kamrasi, the Omukama of Bunyoro, had accumulated a vast quantity and the Kabaka of Buganda had an ivory courtroom.

The extent of the ivory trade

With the coming of the Arab slavers, the African kings found that ivory could be exchanged for goods. This trade continued long after the suppression of slavery with new markets opening up in the West in addition to the traditional markets in Asia.

Spinage (1973), in his review of the ivory trade in Africa, points out that over-exploitation of elephants started with the Romans who, by A.D. 50 had exhausted supplies of all but small tusks from African sources and had to turn to India. Their excessive demands probably led to the disappearance of elephants from North Africa. The Romans, in A.D. 100, were also said to be importing large quantities from the East African coast but the trade was probably not very great. Ivory was well known, but scarce, throughout the Dark Ages and mediaeval period and it was not until the seventeenth century that African ivory began to reach Europe in quantity.

Much of it came from West Africa. The Dutch are said to have exported 23 000 kg a year from Laongo, north of the mouth of the Congo River, between 1608 and 1612. With the introduction of firearms around 1635, elephant hunting was intensified and extended inland as far as present-day Kinshasha. The trade eased off in the eighteenth century but, by the beginning of the nineteenth, the Portuguese began exporting ivory on a large scale until, by the 1860s, there were no elephants left along the Angolan coast and ivory had to be brought in from the Congo. Between 1888 and 1902, an average of 214 180 kg of Congolese ivory was being exported to Antwerp each year. Most came from the forest elephant, *Loxodonta africana cyclotis*.

South Africa was never an important source of ivory because its elephant population was all but wiped out very early on. Even towards the end of the nineteenth century, only 4000 kg a year was exported.

The ivory trade on the east coast of Africa was long-established but did not amount to much until around 1840 when Arabs from Zanzibar began to organize ivory-collecting expeditions to the interior. By the end of the century, Zanzibar was exporting an average of about 180 000 kg of ivory annually, equivalent to well over 10 000 elephants.

Another ivory-producing region was northern Uganda and the Sudan, whose outlet was Khartoum. The peak period was from 1853 to 1879, during which time an average of 137 000 kg of ivory was exported each year to just one firm in Antwerp. The trade died out after 1879, due to the Madhist rebellion, but, in any case, the supply of ivory was beginning to run out.

It is difficult to calculate the total amount of ivory leaving the African continent but, in the early 1880s, it was estimated that Zanzibar supplied 20% of the total crop (Spinage, 1973). If this figure is accurate, some 900 000 kg a year were being taken out by the end of the century. With an average tusk weight of 8.5 kg, this represents an annual crop of about 53 000 elephants. As a percentage of the probable total of elephants then in Africa, this would not have been excessive if evenly spread throughout all populations but, most probably, there was local over-exploitation. One obvious effect was a reduction in the proportion of large 'tuskers', due to preferential hunting, with a resulting fall in the average age of the

207

exploited populations. Brooks and Buss (1962) showed that the average age of a population hunted in Uganda declined by 6 years over a 32-year period.

The East African ivory trade continued to expand throughout the early years of the twentieth century (with the occasional marked declines, as during World War 2), reaching a peak in the 1950s of about 660 000 kg in one year. There was an abrupt drop in the 1960s, following the unrest in the Congo (Zaire), suggesting that the equatorial rain forests remained the principal source of the ivory.

The export of ivory from French-speaking West Africa, on the other hand, fell away after 1909 to negligible quantities between the Wars. There was a slight, short-lived, revival immediately after World War 2. This pattern probably reflects the near exhaustion of ivory stocks.

During the inter-War period, and for some years afterwards, the price of ivory fluctuated very little and there was small incentive for illegal killing of elephants. Most poaching was carried out as much for meat as for ivory. In the 1970s, however, the price of ivory began to climb steeply. Ivory then took on an intrinsic value, similar to that of gold, and investors began to purchase it as a hedge against inflation. It soared in price, from less than £1 a pound in the 1960s to around £15 a pound in the late 1970s.

Given this huge leap in value, ivory not surprisingly became big business. Whereas, in the old days, most of it was legally acquired, large quantities of poached ivory began to reach the market, often with the connivance of politicians and high officials. Soon the elephants had all but been shot out in the traditional hunting areas and the poachers turned to the national parks. Kenya lost about two thirds of her elephants and Uganda suffered a near extinction of her populations. Of a healthy 60 000 or so at the beginning of the 1970s, less than one tenth remained at the end of the decade. The drop was well documented, e.g. from 14 337 in 1973 in Kabalega Falls National Park to 2246 in 1975 (Eltringham and Malpas, 1980). In the same period, numbers in the Rwenzori National Park dropped from 2714 to 931. A further holocaust followed the overthrow of Amin's regime in 1979 and now the elephants number about 1300 in Kabalega Falls National Park and less than 150 in Rwenzori National Park (Malpas, 1980).

The quantities of ivory presently leaving Africa are as great, if not greater, than they were at the height of the trade in the last century and there is little doubt that the elephants are now being over-exploited. A continuation of the trade at its present level can lead only to the extinction of the African elephant. Estimates of the annual official export of African ivory in recent years range from 991 000 kg in 1976 to 827 000 kg in 1977 and 766 000 kg in 1978. These are minimal figures, derived from the returns of countries importing large quantities of ivory and they take no account of the exports to small markets or of smuggled ivory, which probably accounts for a high percentage of the total crop. Douglas-Hamilton (1979) estimated that the number of elephants providing the ivory exported in 1976 could have been anything from 100 000 to 400 000.

Control of the ivory trade

One solution to the problem is simply to ban the ivory trade as Kenya has done (see p.167). If the trade is to continue, and there is certainly an economic case for it to do so, some way must be found of regulating it. This ought not to be difficult; ivory, unlike drugs or diamonds, is bulky and not easily smuggled except with official connivance. An incorruptible ministry and customs service, therefore, is an essential prerequisite. Dealers in ivory are few and well known and their activities could easily be monitored, given the will. It would be helpful if the dealers disciplined themselves and refused to trade in illegal ivory but the financial incentive to accept a forged document at its face value must be immense. Also, an ivory trade based on a sustainable crop might not be large enough to support all the present dealers and few men are likely to agree to organize their own bankruptcy.

There seems no easy way out of the dilemma. Ratification by all countries of the Washington Convention on the Ivory Trade, which promotes the conservation of elephants, would be a helpful step. Some of the ivory-producing countries have yet to do this. A further suggestion is the formation, by the producer countries, of an ivory exporters' cartel to control the world price and to export the ivory on a sustained yield basis. If such a scheme could be properly organized, it might well be a solution. Proposals that artificial ivory should be manufactured and sold to reduce demand for the genuine article are unlikely to be realistic.

Passing laws is rarely a contribution to conservation, unless the laws can be enforced and, if there is to be a legal trade in ivory, tusks must be clearly marked and accompanied by unforgeable documents of legal ownership. Tusks could be identified by metal tags riveted onto the inside pulp cavity and sealed, if necessary, to prevent them being tampered with. The trade has been brought within the ambit of the Convention of Trade in Endangered Species (CITES), to which all countries involved, both exporters and importers, should subscribe but not all do.

The income engendered by the ivory trade is not large, even by Third World standards, and although it is highly profitable for individuals, its loss would cause hardly a ripple in foreign exchange earnings.

13 *The ancestry of elephants*

The fossil record of the Proboscidea is good and the group has frequently been used in school and university textbooks to illustrate the workings of evolution. The doyen amongst palaeontologists in this field was Professor Fairfield Osborn, whose monograph on the group was published in two massive tomes in 1936 and 1942 respectively. At that time, some 330 species of proboscids were known to science. A mass of new, or previously unstudied, museum material has been examined since Osborn's day and new species described. At the same time, some of Osborn's species have been shown to be only variants so that the total number of full species has not greatly increased. As usual, palaeontologists are constantly changing their ideas as new evidence is dug out of the ground. Most popular accounts of elephant evolution, and even those in university textbooks, are out-of-date and the following version leans heavily on the monograph published by Maglio in 1973, which is based on a wealth of new fossils found in Kenya in 1965 and 1967.

These Kenyan sites were the first good fossil beds of Pliocene* age to be found in Africa and the study of the remains led to a re-evaluation of the ancestry of elephants. The following account is no doubt simplified and it may not meet with the approval of all specialists but there does now seem to be a clearer picture emerging. Many individual fossils, often known only from teeth or fragments of bones, have been given separate specific, or even generic, status but Maglio tends to group many such fossils into single species unless it can be shown that they are really distinct.

The first forms of ancestral elephants are found in Eocene deposits but elephants themselves date only from the Pliocene, no more than

---

*A geological time scale is given in Table 13.1.

Table 13.1 A geological time scale (There is no general agreement over the timing and the figures given are only approximate. Periods are given only for the Cenozoic Era)

Era	Period	Millions of years since beginning	Duration in millions of years	Animal features
CENOZOIC	RECENT	(10 000 yrs)	(10 000 yrs)	Human civilizations
	PLEISTOCENE	1	1	Giganticism common
	PLIOCENE	13	12	First elephants
	MIOCENE	27	14	'Golden Age' of mammals
	OLIGOCENE	37	10	First true proboscids
	EOCENE	52	15	First horses, whales and carnivores
	PALAEOCENE	63	11	First primates
MESOZOIC		230	167	Age of reptiles
PALAEOZOIC		600	370	All invertebrate types present, fish abundant
PROTEROZOIC		1700	1100	First worms and sponges and other primitive invertebrates
ARCHAEOZOIC		3000	1300	Protozoans
AZOIC		?	?	No life

6 or 7 million years ago, yet, in that short time, they have spread over most of the world and split into some thirty species.

True elephants belong to a distinct family, Elephantidae, within the order Proboscidea but their family tree can best be understood if it is set in the broader context of proboscid evolution.

There has been much parallel evolution in the proboscids and some lineages once thought to be closely related have since been shown to be far apart. Consequently, the classification of the order

212

has changed radically over the years. Simpson (1945) modified Osborn's scheme considerably but, more recently, workers have tended to revert to an arrangement not so very different from that proposed by Osborn (Maglio, 1973). A working classification embodying modern ideas is given in Table 13.2.

Watson (1946) summarizes the parallel evolutionary trends which have occurred within the proboscids. These include: an increase in size and weight, a delayed eruption of the molars, a great increase in the area of the grinding surface of the molars compared with the milk teeth, an increase of the number of lamellae or ridges on the molars, an increase in complexity of the pattern on the worn surface of the molars, an increase in the height of the molars (i.e. a tendency towards hypsodont teeth), a gradual backward movement of the palate and increased height of the posterior (occipital) region of the skull. There is thus both a shortening and a heightening of the skull, trends which are very obvious in the true elephants. There was also a general tendency for the symphysis (the region of union between the two halves of the lower jaw) first to elongate and then to shorten. Mandibular (i.e. lower jaw) tusks were present in earlier types but these were soon lost in most evolutionary lines, although they persisted in a few. Maxillary (upper) tusks are universal, though with a tendency to become reduced or vestigial in living forms. One extinct group, the deinotheres, possessed only mandibular tusks but these creatures are of doubtful affinity with the proboscids.

Most of the convergent evolution in the proboscids can be related to an increase in bulk. The evolution of the teeth is very closely linked with that of body size. A mere scale increase in the size of the teeth as the body becomes larger would not have sufficed because the grinding area of a tooth increases only by the 0.66 power of the weight while the food requirements rise by a power probably close to 0.75. Hence the larger the animal, the more food, in absolute terms, that it must eat and, consequently, the faster the teeth will wear down. If the duration of life is not to be curtailed, the evolution of hypsodont (high crowned) teeth is inevitable.

The extreme convolutions in the enamel of the molars and the increase in the number of ridges can be related to a change to a grass diet. Such developments in structure effectively increase the grinding efficiency of the tooth without increasing its size.

213

Table 13.2   A classification of the Proboscidea*

ORDER PROBOSCIDEA

Suborder   Deinotherioidea
Family   Deinotheriidae
Genus   *Deinotherium*

Suborder   Moeritherioidea
Family   Moeritheriidae
Genus   *Moeritherium*

Suborder   Barytherioidea
Family   Barytheriidae
Genus   *Barytherium*

Suborder   Mammutoidea
Family   Mammutidae
Genera   *Mammut* (or *Mastodon*), *Zyglolophodon*
Family   Stegodontidae
Genera   *Stegodon, Stegolophodon*

Suborder   Gomphotherioidea
Family   Gomphotheriidae
Subfamily   Phiomanae
Genera   *Phiomia, Palaeomastodon*
Subfamily   Trilophodontinae
Genus   *Trilophodon*
Subfamily   Tetralophodontinae
Genera   *Tetralophodon, Morrillia*
Subfamily   Anancinae
Genera   *Anancus, Pentalophodon*

Subfamily   Eubelodontinae

   Genera   *Eubelodon, Cuvieronius*

Subfamily   Serridentinae

   Genera   *Serridentinus, Trobelodon, Platybelodon*

Subfamily   Rhynchorostrinae

   Genera   *Rhynchotherium, Aybelodon*

Subfamily   Amebelodontinae

   Genus   *Amebelodon*

Family   Elephantidae

Subfamily   Stegotetrabelodontinae

   Genus   *Stegotetrabelodon*

Subfamily   Elephantinae

   Genera   *Primelephas, Loxodonta, Elephas, Mammuthus*

---

*Partly after Maglio, 1973

Survey of proboscid groups

Suborder Deinotherioidea

The deinotheres should probably be put into a separate order, as their relationship with other proboscids is obscure. Nevertheless, they must have looked like elephants, being large and possessing a trunk. They lacked tusks in the upper jaw, however, although the premaxillae were very long as in normally tusked proboscids. *Deinotherium* did possess a pair of tusks but these were found in the lower jaw and their shape was unique. Instead of pointing forwards as in all other proboscids, the tusks pointed downwards and curved backwards.

Deinotherium first appeared in the late Miocene and persisted into the Pliocene in Europe and the Pleistocene in Africa, i.e. for some 15 million years, during which time they changed very little, other than to increase in size. (The first to appear were the size of a modern elephant, standing some 250 cm at the shoulder, but later types were bigger.) The presence of a long proboscis is suggested by the posterior nares being high up on the face, as in elephants.

215

Deinotheres departed from the true proboscids in the nature of their molar teeth, which remained low crowned and primitive, even in the later types. There were two premolars and three molars in each half-jaw, with three ridges on the first molar and two on each of the others.

Suborder Moeritherioidea

To return to the mainstream of proboscid evolution, the earliest fossil that can be assigned to the order comes from the upper Eocene of Egypt. This is *Moeritherium*, a bulky animal about the size of a pig, standing about 60 cm at the shoulder. Apart from its stocky build, there is little that is elephantine about it but certain features foreshadow those of later forms.

The skull was long with the eyes well forward — features which are not typical of modern elephants — and it is in the dentition that the first signs of proboscid relationships appear. At first glance, the teeth seem unremarkable but the second incisors of both jaws were tusk-like and enlarged, although they probably did not protrude beyond the mouth. The upper tusks projected downwards and the lower ones pointed forwards but, because of the foreshortened jaw, their tips met. There was a marked diastema (i.e. a gap between incisors and molars) with the lateral lower incisors and the lower canines missing. The molars were primitive, with low crowns and simple cusps, an arrangement technically known as *bunodont*. The nostrils were well forward on the skull so there was probably no trace of a trunk or even a tapir-like proboscis. The lower jaw was very deep posteriorly, a common feature in the proboscids and one that is shared with the hyrax. The skull of *Moeritherium* shows certain resemblances to those of hyraxes and sirenians, underlining the common ancestry of these three orders.

Moeritherium survived into the lower Oligocene but remained within Africa. It probably did not become extinct but rather evolved into later types.

Suborder Barytherioidea

This is an obscure group, known only from a few fragmentary remains from the Eocene of Africa, which have been assigned to the genus *Barytherium*. The dentition shows proboscid affinities and recent work suggests a distant relationship with the deinotheres (Maglio, 1973).

None of these three groups is recognized as a proboscid by Maglio (1973), although most authors include them in this order. *Deinotherium* and *Barytherium* should probably be excluded but *Moerotherium* has some claim to consideration as an ancestral type, if not the ancestor, of the proboscids.

Suborder Mammutoidea

FAMILY MAMMUTIDAE

Members of the family Mammutidae are called mastodons because the grinding surface of the tooth is in the form of conical tubercles which were thought by Cuvier, who coined the name in 1806, to have a fanciful resemblance to the human breast. The term has no phyletic significance.

The mammutids were mastodons which arose in the Miocene and died out in the Pleistocene probably no more than 10 000 years ago. Their fossils are found in both Eurasia and North America but they were derived from ancestors which originated in Africa. These mastodons showed considerable convergent evolution with elephants in such features as their large size, short, high skull, huge tusks in the upper jaw and a reduced lower jaw from which the tusks had completely disappeared in later forms. The USA is particularly rich in the remains of these creatures. Some still have skin and hair attached, from which we know that the American mastodon (*Mastodon americanus*) was covered in long, reddish brown hair. Although the skeleton is similar to that of present-day elephants, the head was held more horizontally and, in life, the creature probably had a typical 'mastodon' stance which would clearly distinguish it from an elephant. The teeth were quite unlike those of an elephant and remained low crowned, with simple ridges lacking cement. The inference is that mammutids fed on soft vegetation, not on grass. The teeth were elephant-like at least in that only two at the most were in wear at any one time in each half-jaw.

FAMILY STEGODONTIDAE

Fossil stegodonts are found from the Pliocene and Pleistocene of

217

Africa. The group has been shuffled around by taxonomists over the years. Osborn (1936) originally included them with the true elephants but later he removed them to form a new suborder, Stegodontoidea, maintaining that the elephant-like features were the result of convergent evolution. Simpson (1945) returned the stegodonts to the Elephantidae, considering them to have been primitive elephants, representing a transitional stage between mammutids and elephants proper. Recent ideas, however, have reverted to Osborn's conception of *Stegodon* as belonging to an independent line quite distinct from the elephant lineage. A similar but little known form, *Stegolophodon*, sometimes considered to be ancestral to *Stegodon*, also shows convergence with elephants and was once classified with them. It occurred in the Pliocene of Europe and from the Pliocene to the Pleistocene in Asia.

The skulls of the *Stegodon* fossils were rather longer than those of elephants but were otherwise very similar. Later forms of the genus showed further shortening of the skull, which also became very deep, as did the lower jaw, until the head was almost indistinguishable from that of an elephant. Only the teeth provide evidence that these were not true elephants at all but a distinct evolutionary line whose origins probably lie in some as yet unknown early mastodon group. The teeth of stegodonts are ridged like those of elephants but the number of ridges is less. Each ridge of the stegodont molar is continuous but the crest is divided into from six to ten conelets, a condition never found in elephants.

The tusks were well developed and curved, much like those of the modern African elephant, and later stegodonts grew immensely long tusks. Tiny vestiges of a second pair of tusks were present in the symphysis of the lower jaw.

Suborder Gomphotherioidea

This suborder gathers together a large miscellany of early and advanced proboscids. It contains 'mastodons', mammoths and modern elephants, as well as primitive forms which had yet to

Fig. 13.1 Reconstructions of some extinct proboscids. The trunks shown on the more primitive forms are conjectural as are the shapes of the ears.

Gomphotherium (Trilophodon)

Palaeomastodon

Moeritherium

Mammut

Platybelodon

Gnathobelodon

Dinotherium

Mastodon

Woolly mammoth (Mammuthus primigenius)

Imperial mammoth (Mammuthus imperator)

develop a trunk. One of the two families, the Gomphotheriidae, underwent an explosive adaptive radiation in the Miocene but the many evolutionary lines that sprang up had all died out by the Pleistocene. The classification given in Table 13.2 is no more than a tentative grouping of the main evolutionary lines.

FAMILY GOMPHOTHERIIDAE

One of the earliest gomphotherids was *Phiomia*, with four species, from the lower Oligocene. It can readily be derived from a *Moeritherium*-like ancestor. A similar form was *Palaeomastodon*, also from the lower Oligocene of Egypt. All these early proboscid families are found in Africa, which is clearly where the group originated. *Phiomia* was about 120 cm high at the shoulder and of a bulky build. Elephant-like developments include the deepening of the skull and the flattening of its posterior surface for the attachment of the neck muscles necessary to hold up the heavy head. Much of the flattening was achieved by the development of pneumatic spaces in the skull.

A peculiarity of *Phiomia* is the elongation of the lower jaw, a feature which was to become greatly exaggerated in many of its descendants. Both upper and lower jaws possessed short tusks but no other front teeth. Because of the elongation of the lower jaw, the tusks did not meet and could not have been used for biting food. Possibly, the upper pair served as weapons while the lower tusks were used for grubbing food, a function which those of the later forms almost certainly possessed. The space in front of the relatively short upper jaw was probably filled by a long tapir-like snout but this would in no sense have been a trunk. The molar teeth remained primitive but showed an advance over those of *Moeritherium* in possessing three ridges instead of two and in the appearance of accessory cusps, resulting in a rather pig-like tooth.

These bunodont gomphotheres soon increased in size and even some of the earlier Oligocene types reached the proportions of a modern elephant. They also spread from Africa and occupied all parts of the globe, except Australia, Antarctica and desert regions. They had their heyday in the Miocene and most had died out before the Pleistocene.

Gomphotherium (or *Trilophodon*) was a typical Miocene genus whose members were about twice the size of *Phiomia*. The lower jaw was extremely elongated and contained a pair of well developed but short tusks. The tusks in the upper jaw, however, had elongated and, unlike the condition in *Phiomia*, they extended as far as the lower tusks. It is likely that these early forms did not possess the rudimentary trunks that are often shown in pictorial reconstructions. At most, there may have been a flexible snout rather like that of a pig.

The cheek teeth remained unspecialized with all the molars in place at once and with permanent teeth replacing the milk dentition as in most mammals.

Further development of these long-jawed gomphotheres resulted in the 'shovel-tuskers', which were probably polyphyletic, i.e. included several evolutionary lines. The lower incisors widened still further to form a flat ivory surface. This was short and wide in *Platybelodon* but long and narrow in *Amebelodon*. In one genus, *Gnathobelodon*, the mandibular tusks were lost and the lower jaw had the form of a bony spoon covered in life, presumably, by tough skin. These animals were quite large, some reached the proportions of an elephant, and the elongated jaws enabled them to reach the ground to feed. The alternative, of developing a long neck, as in antelopes, was not open to them because of the massive head. (The hippopotamus has solved the problem by developing short legs.)

It is usually assumed that these creatures dabbled in muddy swamps and fed on aquatic vegetation, which they shovelled into their mouths with the aid of short trunks but, as Spinage (1972) has pointed out, it is at least as likely that they used their flattened incisors to crop grass or other vegetation in the same way as the hippopotamus uses its broad muscular lips to pluck grass. There is therefore, no reason to assume that they possessed trunks although, as with *Trilophodon*, reconstructions always show them with such appendages. One feels that trunks would not be drawn in on reconstructions of these fossils had the group not developed forms with a long proboscis.

There is no direct evidence, of course, since the soft parts did not fossilize, but the positioning of the bony nostrils high on the skull is assumed to indicate the presence of a trunk since these two features occur together on modern elephants. This may well be so but the

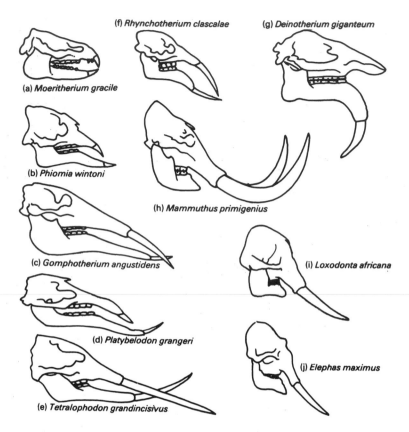

Fig. 13.2 Evolution of the proboscid head and lower jaw from the ancestral condition found in *Moeritherium*. Note that the lower jaw tends to lengthen and to curve upwards or downwards before experiencing an abrupt shortening. These anatomical changes are probably due to selection for the most mechanically efficient jaw mechanism, which results in a change in importance from the lower to the upper tusks. Consequently, the lower tusks tend to be lost and the upper to become bigger. (After Spinage, 1972.)

trunk need not necessarily be free at the tip. In order to be functional, such a trunk would need to be fairly long. Although it is possible that such a novel structure could have evolved, it seems more plausible to assume that the nostrils developed into a trunk when they became 'left behind' by the shrinking of the lower jaw and the flattening of the face (Fig. 13.2).

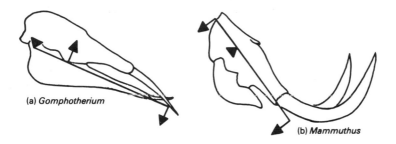

Fig. 13.3 Change in the jaw mechanism from a third order lever to the more efficient first order lever during the evolution of the skull and lower jaw in the proboscids. The lever was: (a) the lower jaw in *Gomphotherium* and (b) the skull in *Mammuthus*. Note that the shortening of the weight arm in *Mammuthus* is facilitated by the upward curve of the tusks. (From Spinage, 1972.)

Why did the lower jaw recede? This would not have been possible were it not for the development of the trunk, which offered an alternative method of reaching the ground. I think it would be wrong to assume that the lower jaw shortened because the trunk developed and made a long jaw superfluous because this is to confuse cause and effect. The development of a trunk certainly permitted the jaw to shorten, and there are very good biomechanical reasons why it should have done so. Spinage (1972) has pointed out that the gomphothere mandible comprised a third order lever, with the fulcrum at the posteriorly situated coronoid process of the jaw and the whole supported by the masseter muscle (Fig. 13.3). The advantage of this arrangement was that only a small muscular movement was required but there was a disadvantage in that the effort necessary to move the lever was greater than the load lifted, i.e. the mechanical advantage was less than 1.

As greater size evolved in the group, the stress upon the masseter muscle must have increased out of proportion to the work achieved. Movement of the jaw therefore, would have been very expensive in energy terms. Some forms, such as *Platybelodon*, tried to overcome this defect by carrying the mandible forwards. Presumably it then fed by pushing with the whole weight of the body behind its lower jaws. This would have been equally effective whether the animal was

223

indeed a swamp feeder or a grazer. Further development resulted in a downward curve in the mandible, bringing the lower tusks nearer to the ground as in *Rhynchotherium*. The mandible was effectively as long as ever but the bony jaw had receded and was replaced by the lower incisors. Meanwhile the upper tusks bent downwards to keep in contact with the descending jaw.

The evolution of the elephant-type skull and lower jaw took place when the upper incisors took over from the lower as the principal feeding organs. Now, the skull, and not the lower jaw, becomes the lever; this time of the more efficient first order, with the fulcrum at the junction of head and neck and with the power provided by the splenius muscles linking the back of the skull with the neck. Anchorage of the lever is provided by the *ligamentum nuchae*, a strong ligament in the neck. Operation of the 'lever' results in an upward movement of the premaxillae and, consequently, there is a tendency for the tusks to curve upwards.

The disadvantage of this arrangement is that the muscular movement is greater than in the third order lever but the over-whelming bonus is that the mechanical advantage is greater than 1, i.e. the muscular power required is less than the load moved. The increased efficiency of the first order lever was of great selective advantage in evolution and rapidly spread throughout the proboscids. Hence, we see, in many evolutionary lines, the same shortening of the lower jaw, the disappearance of the lower incisors, which had lost their function, the development of the upper incisors as upward curving tusks and the flattening of the back of the skull to provide attachment for the powerful splenius muscles. None of these modifications would have been possible without the development of the long prehensile trunk as a feeding organ. So efficient is the trunk that it has taken over from the tusks, which have, therefore, become superfluous in food gathering. This may well be the reason for the reduction in the size of tusks in modern elephants, and even their complete regression in females of the Asiatic species. The tusks still retain a function as weapons in inter-male rivalry and presumably have been retained for this reason.

Whereas *Trilophodon* and its relatives formed the principal gomphothere group in the Miocene, the Pliocene saw the rise of a line which closely paralleled the evolution of elephants. The representative genus is *Tetralophodon*, of Europe, Asia and America. The lower jaw had become relatively shortened but the mandibular tusks remained moderately long. The premaxillae had also shortened but carried long straight tusks. The cheek teeth became high crowned (hypsodont) and showed an elephant-like sequence of eruption with only a few molars in wear at any one time.

Similar convergent evolution occurred in the Anancinae, whose type genus, *Anancus*, was characterized by exceptionally long straight tusks which were not much shorter than the length of the body. Like many other gomphotheres, it flourished in the Pliocene and persisted well into the Pleistocene with a worldwide distribution. Another branch, represented by *Cuvieronius*, did not become extinct until the Christian era, for its remains have been found in Ecuador with artefacts dating from A.D. 200 to 400 (Watson, 1946). This animal was elephant-like in appearance with spirally twisted tusks. The lower tusks had disappeared, but its molar dentition was primitive, showing that it was well off the main line leading to the evolution of the elephants.

The serridentines parallel the evolution of the trilophodonts but were generally smaller and, hence, the structural changes were less extreme. They were distinguished by the structure of the molars, which lacked central conules but possessed extra ridges to increase the grinding area. When worn, these ridges formed trefoil loops, which resemble those formed from the wear of central conules of other groups. There was a tendency for the eruption of molar teeth to be spread out in time but to a lesser extent than in the case of contemporary groups. The presence of two premolars was another primitive feature. Widely distributed throughout the world, serridentines evolved into a diversity of forms, with a tendency for the lower tusks to widen, culminating in the 32-cm wide shovel of *Torynobelodon*.

The rhynchorostrines were characterized by a downwardly curved symphysis bearing forwardly directed tusks. The lower jaw was still very long, with no trace of the typical shortening seen in so many groups. The curious curvature of the lower jaw and tusks was probably related to the biomechanical principles discussed earlier.

All these many gomphothere lines diversified in the Miocene, flourished in the Pliocene and died out in the Pleistocene, some very

225

recently. A number of trends can be discerned in their evolution. Some, such as *Platybelodon*, retained the primitive long lower jaw, which became extremely specialized as a feeding organ. Others showed a reduction in the lower jaw and the loss of the lower tusks. This trend was followed independently in several evolutionary lines, including that leading to the elephants. Other evolutionary changes common to these groups were a flattening of the face, through an increase in height of the skull and a decrease in its length, and changes in the lower jaw. In addition to becoming shorter, the latter became very deep while the shrinking symphysis remained as a 'chin'. The only other vertebrate with a chin is the human species, although it is formed in quite a different fashion and for very different reasons.

FAMILY ELEPHANTIDAE

The elephant 'facies', as we might call it, has therefore evolved several times and one might ask what in fact defines a 'true elephant'. The answer, of course, lies in the teeth. A proboscid develops into an elephant when its molars become high crowned (i.e. hypsodont) and bear a large number of transverse ridges (i.e. lophodont), usually invested with cement. The change is significant and is not due to a chance variation for it marks a radical change of diet from soft, leafy vegetation to tough grass. The low crowned, cusped (i.e. bunodont) teeth of the 'mastodon' type were inefficient at dealing with grass and it may well be that the ability to exploit the readily available food, provided by the expanding grasslands of the Pleistocene, helped the elephants to survive while many of the other proboscids became extinct. Side by side with the development of lophodont dentition came a change in the manner of chewing. Mastodons and gomphotheres chewed their food in a manner similar to that found in most herbivores, i.e. with a side-to-side rotation of the jaws. Such a technique was adequate for proboscids feeding on rich herbage, or for the smaller antelopes, but the elephant, turning to grass, which although plentiful is poor in quality, needed to eat so much that side-to-side chewing was not sufficient to grind up the food properly. Consequently there was a change to a fore-and-aft masticatory movement (Fig. 13.4).

The function of the elephant's molar can best be understood by

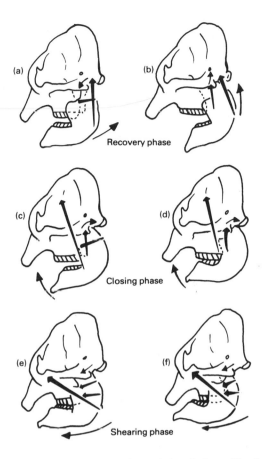

Fig. 13.4 Chewing motions of the jaws in an Asian elephant. The fine lines show the direction of movement of the lower jaw and the heavy lines represent the average direction of pull of the main muscle masses. The sequence shows: (a and b) the elephant opening its mouth to receive food; (c and d) the jaws closing on the food; (e and f) the lower jaw sliding forward to slice the food between the ridges of the upper and lower molars. (From Maglio, 1973.)

considering it in relation to the opposing molar against which it is grinding. The ridges of one tooth cross those of the other at a narrow angle as the two teeth slide over one another and so the edges of the enamel ridges form an efficient shearing system, similar to the blades of a pair of scissors (Fig. 13.5). It is obvious that the

227

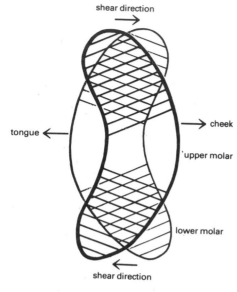

shear direction

tongue ←

→ cheek

·upper molar

lower molar

shear direction

Fig. 13.5 The shearing action of an elephant's teeth, which move fore and aft, not side to side, during chewing. The upper molars are represented by the heavy lines and the lower molars by the fine lines; their curvature is much exaggerated. As the lower jaw slides forward, the cutting angle between the ridges moves towards the cheek at the front end of the tooth and in the reverse direction at the back. This arrangement results in the effective shear width being greater than the width of the ridges since some of the food will be moved from one side of the tooth to the other during a single stroke of the lower jaw.

efficiency of this type of chewing depends on the length of the enamel edge of the ridges. This may be increased firstly by broadening the tooth, secondly by folding the enamel and thirdly by increasing the number of ridges in a given length of tooth. A fourth possibility, that of increasing the length of the tooth, is precluded because of the finite length of the jaw and, although during evolution there was an increase in the width of the tooth, this was possible only to a limited degree. Consequently the second and third methods are those that are particularly exploited in elephant evolution.

Because of the curvature of the teeth as a whole, the shearing angles vary. At the anterior end of the grinding surface, the shear angle moves outwards, towards the cheek, as the two teeth pass over each other. At the posterior end of the tooth, however, the shear angle moves across the tooth in the reverse direction, i.e. towards the tongue. Food tends to be trapped in the shear angle and moves across the tooth towards the cheek at the anterior end. Some of this food then comes into contact with the posterior part of the tooth as the jaw moves forward and is subjected to a shearing movement in the opposite direction. Thus the effective length of the shearing surface is increased as the food moves from one side of the tooth to the other during the same stroke.

The efficiency of an elephant's tooth, therefore, depends on the length of the enamel ridge. Its thickness is not important and thinning of the enamel is a general trend in elephant evolution. Thinning is advantageous because it makes room for an increased number of ridges. The only problem is that thin enamel wears down more quickly but this is compensated for by the development of extremely hypsodont teeth. In some lineages there was a sixfold increase in the height of the crown of the molar teeth during evolution.

There is no difficulty in accommodating a high crowned upper molar in the skull of an elephant but the lower jaw cannot increase in depth beyond a certain point, for mechanical reasons, and it is not possible for the lower molars to be as high as the upper. (Elephants' teeth do not grow continuously from an open root like those of rodents and the height of a plate is determined before it erupts.) The expected result of two teeth of different heights rubbing against one another is that the lower molar will wear out before the upper. This is avoided by a change in the angle at which the plates carrying the enamel ridges meet the surface of the tooth. In the gomphotheres and early elephants, the ridges were vertical, or inclined slightly forwards in the lower teeth and slightly backward in the upper teeth. Hence the upper and lower ridges cut against each other, leading to excessive wear but this was of little consequence because of the thickness of the enamel. In the more advanced elephants, the angle which the lamellae make with the surface is greatly increased and the ridges point backwards in the lower teeth, not forwards. The lower ridges, therefore, face away from the direction of shearing; so much reducing the degree of wear that the lower teeth last for as long as the upper.

Studies on the shearing efficiency of teeth in primitive elephants, using a formula derived by Maglio (1973), show that many of the fossil elephants, far from being primitive, were much more highly evolved than the living forms.

Before discussing further the technical definition of an elephant, we need briefly to summarize the various types that existed. The recent revision of the group by Maglio (1973) recognizes only five genera: the four-tusked *Stegotetrabelodon*, which is put into a separate subfamily; the primitive *Primelephas*, with low crowned molars; the living elephants, *Loxodonta* and *Elephas*; and the mammoths, assigned to the genus *Mammuthus*.

The evolution of the Elephantinae

The elephantines arose towards the end of the Pliocene and have persisted up to the present day. Maglio (1973) recognises twenty-three species, two belonging to the primitive *Primelephas*, three to *Loxodonta*, eleven to *Elephas* and seven to *Mammuthus*. In addition, some fragmentary remains have been found which cannot safely be placed in any genus but they have been given names which often appear in the literature. Three of them have been assigned to the genus *Archidiskodon* and a fourth to *Metarchidiskodon*.

The probable course of the evolution of the elephants is shown in

Fig. 13.6 Probable evolution of elephants. (From Maglio, 1973.)
Key: *(E.c.) Elephas celebensis; (E.e.) E. ekorensis; (E.f.) E. falconeri; (E.i.) E. iolensis; (E.n.) E. namadicus; (E. plf.) E. planifrons; (E. plc.) E. platycephalus; (E.r.) E. recki* (evolutionary stages 1-4); *(L.ad.) Loxodonta adaurora; (L.at.) L. atlantica; (M. af.) Mammuthus africanavus; (M.ar.) M.armeniacus; (M.c.) M. columbi; (M.i.) M. imperator; (M.m.B) M. meridionalis* (Bacton Stage); *(M.m.L) M. meridionalis* (Laiatico Stage); *(M.m.M) M. meridionalis* (Montavarchi Stage), *(M.p.) M. primigenius; (M.s.) M. subplanifrons; (P.g.) Primelephas gomphotheroides; (P.k.) P. korotorensis; (S.o.) Stegotetrabelodon orbus; (S.s.) S. syrticus.*

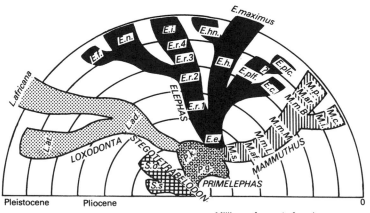

Millions of years before the present

Fig. 13.6. This scheme is due to Maglio (1973), although it closely resembles that proposed by Aguirre (1969), and it is only the latest of many such family trees. It may yet be discarded as unsatisfactory but it has the advantage of being based on an analysis of the new fossils found in the Kenya Rift Valley.

There is no doubt that elephants originated in Africa, but not from the stegodonts as has almost universally been assumed in the past. The genuine ancestor was probably one of the gomphothere lines but, whereas Aguirre (1969) believes that the ancestral gomphothere arose from *Stegolophodon*, Maglio (1973) disagrees because that genus was well on the road to *Stegodon* and it is difficult to derive elephant dentition from that of *Stegolophodon*. On the other hand, a gomphothere molar can readily be converted into an elephant's tooth (Fig. 13.7).

Maglio takes the early stegotetrabelodonts as the ancestral group from which both the later stegotetrabelodonts and short-jawed elephants arose. He believes that, in the very late Miocene, the primitive elephantine, *Primelephas*, evolved from the basic stegotetrabelodont stock. The one group did not evolve directly into the other, however, for species of both genera are found in the same geological deposits. The molars of *Primelephas* are low crowned and

Fig. 13.7 Evolution of the elephant molar from the primitive condition in the Miocene proboscid *Gomphotherium* to the advanced state found in the woolly mammoth: (a) *Gomphotherium angustidens*, (b) *Stegotetrabelodon syrticus*, (c) *Primelephas gomphotheroides*, (d) *Mammuthus subplanifrons*, (e) *Mammuthus africanavus*, (f) *Mammuthus primigenius*. Note the progressive consolidation of the cone pairs, loss of the median cleft, fusion of accessory columns, increase in plate number and thinning of the enamel. (From Maglio, 1973.)

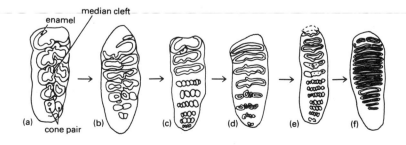

show many common features with stegotetrabelodont dentition. The only species with numerous fossil remains is *P. gompho-theroides*, which could well be ancestral to all other elephants. The lower jaw was short, as in all elephants, but still retained a pair of small but prominent incisors.

Three new lines arose from *Primelephas*. The first and least changed is the genus *Loxodonta*, to which the living African elephant belongs. The first recognizable loxodont species was *L. adaurora*, which lived from the early to late Pliocene in Africa. Very probably it gave rise to two later species in the Pleistocene, *L. atlantica* and the living *L. africana*. The genus is unknown outside Africa and *L. atlantica* is so called because its remains were first found near the Atlantic coast of North Africa. Subsequently a separate race was described from South Africa while some specimens have turned up in Ethiopia. It was a large animal, exceeding the living African elephant in size and in many ways was more advanced in its anatomy. Its disappearance in the face of the survival of *L. africana* is a mystery but it may have had rather special ecological requirements. This is suggested by its replacement in fossil beds by *Elephas recki*, the dominant elephant in Africa at the time.

The second evolutionary line led to *Elephas*, represented today by the living *E. maximus*. The *Loxodonta* line is simple and confined to Africa but the ancestry of *Elephas* is much more complex. Apart from containing more species, the genus had a much wider geographical distribution, extending to Europe and Asia, as well as Africa where it originated (Fig. 13.8). There are, in fact, two branches of *Elephas*, the Afro-European-Asiatic, derived from *E. recki*, and the purely Asiatic, which split off from the African species *E. ekorensis* in the late Pliocene.

The African elephants were dominated by *E. recki*, which spread all over the continent and is known in four progressively more advanced morphological types representing, presumably, a direct evolutionary descent. *E. iolensis* appears to be the culmination of this particular branch. The species which spread into Europe was *E. namadicus*, whose remains have been found throughout the continent and also at many sites in Asia from the Middle East to Japan. The European fossils were once separated under the name *E. antiquus* but, according to Maglio (1973), new fossil evidence no

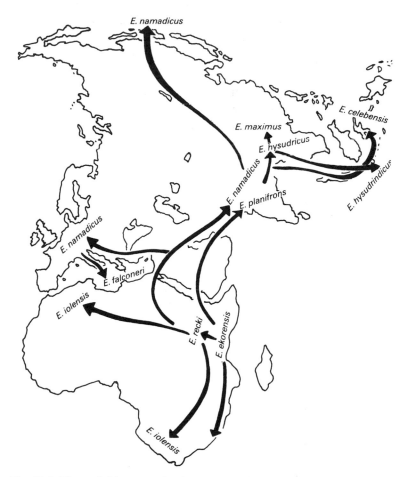

Fig. 13.8 The probable geographical expansion of the various species of *Elephas* that evolved from the ancestral *Elephas ekorensis*. The lines do not represent exact migratory routes. (After Maglio, 1973.)

longer supports such a distinction. The existence of these Asiatic fossils of *E. namadicus* destroys the neat division of *Elephas* into Asiatic and European branches but it seems that the Asiatic *E. namadicus* was distinct from the other *Elephas* species in Asia. There must, therefore, have been two independent invasions of Asia by *Elephas* from Africa.

Fossils of dwarf elephants have been recovered from several

233

islands in the Mediterranean and all have been referred to a single species, *E. falconeri*. There were true pygmy elephants standing only about a metre at the shoulder. The phenomenon of island dwarfing is widespread in many groups of animals but such dwarves are not always specifically distinct. It is likely, therefore, that *E. falconeri* was no more than a pygmy race of *E. namadicus*. Similar dwarfing occurred in the other *Elephas* line as we shall see.

The elephant which gave rise to the Asiatic species of *Elephas* other than *namadicus* was *E. planifrons*. This elephant lived during the late Pliocene to early Pleistocene in the Middle East and Asia, with fossils coming from as far apart as Bethlehem and Shansi Province in China. It can be derived from the African *E. ekorensis* and it, or an unknown intermediate form, probably emigrated from Africa in the late Pliocene. It was a smallish elephant and a branch which spread through Java into the island of Sulawesi (Celebes), underwent rapid dwarfing into *E. celebensis*.

Soon after the arrival of *E. planifrons* in Asia, a separate type split off, known as *E. hysudricus*, which showed the greatly expanded parietal and occipital regions of the skull that are so characteristic of its living descendant, *E. maximus*. It did not itself become extinct but rather evolved into further species. One was the living Asiatic elephant and the other was *E. hysudrindicus*. The latter was once thought to be ancestral to *E. maximus* but there are clear morphological distinctions between the two that make such a relationship unlikely.

One species of *Elephas* does not fit into this grand pattern. This is the little known *E. platycephalus* from the early Pleistocene of India. As the name suggests, this elephant had a flattened and very primitive skull with small tusks. Its relationship remains obscure and perhaps it is best regarded as an aberrant offshoot from *E. planifrons*.

The mammoths of the genus *Mammuthus* form the third evolutionary line within the Elephantinae. As with the other elephants, this group originated in Africa but later spread even further than *Elephas* and passed into North America along the land bridge, which then existed across the Bering Straits. Their evolution followed a linear progression until the middle Pleistocene. Mammoths then split into two branches, one mainly European and the

234

other American.

Mammoths were not particularly large animals relative to other elephants and their distinction was mainly in the dentition. Later species had a very large number of lamellae in the molars. The tusks were rather larger than those of living elephants and tended to grow in a spiral. Another mammoth feature was the shape of the skull, which was even shorter and higher than in the living elephants. Not all mammoths were hairy but the thick fur of the woolly mammoth shows how elephants can adapt to cold climates.

Mammoths originated in the late Pliocene of Africa and can be derived from *Primelephas gomphotheroides*. The relationship between mammoths and the living elephants, therefore, is very close, and *Mammuthus* is probably nearer to *Elephas* than either is to *Loxodonta*. The first recognizable mammoth is *Mammuthus subplanifrons*, whose remains are found in East and southern Africa. Once thought to be ancestral to all the elephants, it is now considered to have given rise only to the mammoths. Some of the teeth referred to this species may in fact belong to early species of *Elephas*, or even to *Loxodonta*. At the very base of elephant evolution, the teeth of all types were similar and hard to separate, especially as many of the remains are fragmentary. The teeth of *M. subplanifrons* were very primitive and it would not be recognizable as a mammoth but for a typically curved tusk found with one specimen. The subsequent evolution of the mammoths follows a gradual change from one form to another. *M. africanavus* is more recognizably a mammoth from the remains of its skull and tusks. Its molars were at about the same evolutionary stage as those of *Loxodonta adaurora*. There is little doubt that *M. africanavus* arose from *M. subplanifrons*, or a species very similar to it, but, because of the paucity of fossil evidence, one cannot be sure.

The evolution of the important *M. meridionalis* from *M. africanavus* is more certain. This species has such a good fossil record that we can trace the detailed evolutionary changes that took place. It is the first mammoth to be found outside Africa and the earliest remains came from Europe. Maglio (1973) recognizes three groups of mammoths within this species, which he believes represent successive evolutionary steps and, for this reason, considers that all of them should be included under the same name. These early

Fig. 13.9 The probable geographical expansion of mammoths that evolved from the ancestral mammoth, *Mammuthus subplanifrons*. The lines do not represent exact migratory routes. (After Maglio, 1973.)

mammoths spread right across northern Europe during the middle Pliocene to early Pleistocene. By the middle Pleistocene they had reached North America (Fig. 13.9). Further speciation took place there to produce the magnificent 'imperial mammoth', *M. imperator*, a massive animal measuring perhaps 4 to 4.5 m at the shoulder. The later forms of *M. meridionalis* were also very large and it is these fossils which have caused 'mammoth' to be a synonym for 'huge' in everyday speech. A closely related species was *M. columbi*, which, if not identical to *M. imperator*, certainly branched off from it. It is found in the late Pleistocene of North America and differs from *imperator* only in its more progressive dentition.

We have to retrace our steps to *M. meridionalis* of the middle Pleistocene in Europe to pick up the second branch of mammoth evolution. While one branch of this species migrated into North

America, another evolved in Europe into *M. armeniacus*, whose main claim to fame is that it, in turn, gave rise to the woolly mammoth, *M. primigenius*. The fossil record for these species is extremely good and in the case of the woolly mammoth, even the soft anatomy is known from frozen carcases in the permafrost of Siberia.

M. primigenius is inaptly named, for it was not the first born of its line but rather the culmination of elephant evolution. It was the most highly evolved mammoth and was more advanced than either of the living elephants. It arose in the late Pleistocene of Europe and persisted well into the human era, often being represented in cave drawings. It was not particularly large — no bigger than an Asiatic elephant — but its tusks were huge. Whereas very few tusks of the African elephant exceed 3 m in length, those of the woolly mammoth often reached 5 m. The shape was also different, for the tusks grew in a tighter spiral and often crossed in front of the trunk.

M. primigenius migrated right across northern Europe, following in the footsteps of *M. meridionalis* and crossing the Bering Straits to enter North America. It was, therefore, the fourth mammoth to occur on that continent but it followed a separate evolutionary path from the other three, which differed by having broader molars, a more massive jaw and minor variations in the skull. The woolly mammoth of North America, therefore, is the same species as that found in Europe. From the carcases recovered from the tundra, we know exactly what the woolly mammoth looked like. Even its food is known from fragments of grass in the mouth and from the stomach contents. The woolly mammoth showed many morphological adaptations for its frozen world. It had small ears, covered with fur, and a thick undercoat of fine hair about 3 cm in length, over which there was a further coat of coarser hair some 50 cm long. The skin was thicker than that of a living elephant and underneath there was a layer of fat, 9-cm deep, which presumably acted as an insulating layer. In colour, the woolly mammoth was a rusty reddish brown. The mammoth was not much like living elephants in appearance, having a high domed forehead and sloping back as well as curling tusks.

The woolly mammoth is thought to have become extinct some 10 000 to 20 000 years ago but its remains are so plentiful that it is tempting to wonder if its demise was not more recent. There was a brisk trade in mammoth ivory within historic times, with an annual sale of nearly 23 000 kg at Yakutsk in eastern Siberia, representing the remains of between 180 and 200 mammoths (Carrington, 1957). Altogether, it is estimated that the tusks of at least 45 000 mammoths from Siberia have been sold in the last 300 years. The possibility has even been raised that this species still exists. It is unlikely to be living on the tundra, for a population of any size would surely have been noticed but, if it were now preferentially a forest animal, like its living relatives, it could well be overlooked in the vast areas of unexplored coniferous forest in the northern USSR.

Evolutionary rates in the Elephantinae

The rate of evolution in terms of a particular character can be measured directly but it is more difficult to compare the rates at which the character developed in different groups, or to say whether one evolutionary line has evolved faster than another. A method of

Fig. 13.10 Evolutionary rates of some molar features in three evolutionary lines of elephants: *Loxodonta* (African elephants), *Elephas* (African, European and Asian elephants) and *Mammuthus* (mammoths). Note that the most rapid evolution occurred in the mammoths while the purely African elephants changed very little. (After Maglio, 1973.)

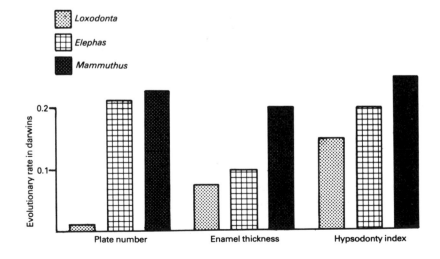

overcoming this problem was suggested by Haldane (1949). He proposed that the unit of evolutionary change should be the darwin, which he defined as an increase or decrease in a character by a factor of 10^3 per 1000 years. Thus a rate of evolution of 1 darwin would result in a character doubling or halving its size (or any other measurable feature) every 1 million years. Another approach is to measure the time taken for taxonomic groups to evolve, e.g. the time required for the evolution of one species from another or, conversely, the number of species evolving in a particular lineage over a given period — say a million years. This is a more subjective measurement, but, in practice, the method can be useful and informative.

Both techniques have been used by Maglio (1973) and some comparisons between *Loxodonta*, *Elephas* and *Mammuthus* for a number of characters are shown in Fig. 13.10. These reveal that the most rapid evolution took place in *Mammuthus* and that evolution in *Loxodonta* was a relatively slow affair. Evolutionary change is not necessarily constant with time and, in the case of molar characters in mammoths, the rates were very irregular (Fig. 13.11). Over the first 3 million years the molars changed slowly (although much faster than in *Loxodonta*) but, during the middle Pleistocene, there was a marked increase in the rates, coinciding with rapid changes in the mandible and tusks, as well as in the carriage of the head. These changes can be correlated with a number of external factors, including the appearance on the European scene of a possible competitor, namely *Elephas namadicus*, and an advance in the glaciation of northern Europe. Selection pressure was obviously intense, leading to ecological separation between the two species as *Mammuthus* became adapted to the sub-Arctic conditions and evolved into the woolly mammoth.

A similar variation in the evolutionary rate is seen in the molars of the African representatives of the *Elephas* group, although the timing is quite different (Fig. 13.12). Change was rapid early in the evolution of the line, reflecting the major changes, including the loss of the lower tusks, which took place during the evolution of *E. ekorensis* from *Primelephas gomphotheroides*. After this initial change, evolution proceeded at a slower rate throughout the early and middle Pleistocene but, in the late Pleistocene, another burst of

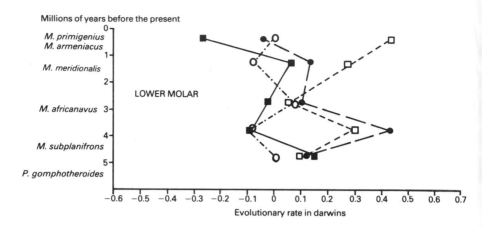

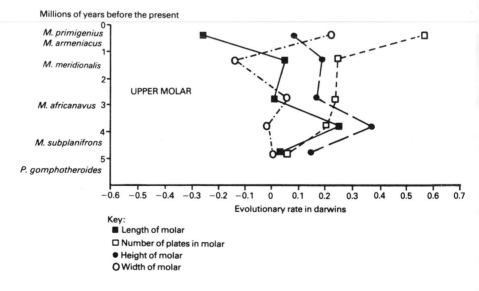

Fig. 13.11 Changes in the rates at which some molar characteristics evolved during the evolution of the woolly mammoth (*Mammuthus primigenius*) from the ancestral *Primelephas gomphotheroides*. The rapid change in the width of the molar in the Pleistocene was probably due to the emergence of a potential competitor in *Elephas namadicus*. (From Maglio, 1973.)

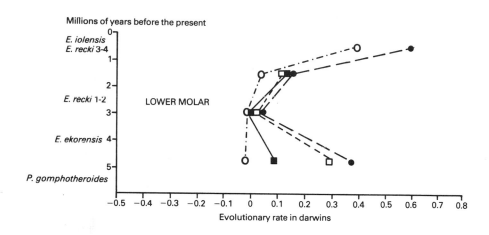

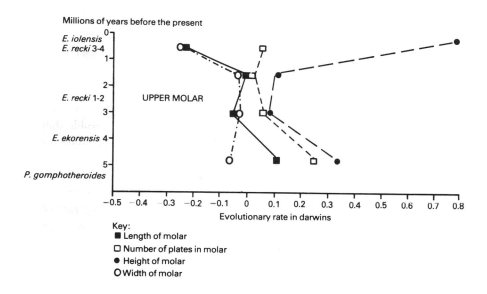

Fig. 13.12 Changes in the rates at which some molar characteristics evolved during the evolution of the African species of *Elephas* from the ancestral *Primelephas gomphotheroides*. The rapid change in molar width seen in *Elephas recki* was probably due, as in the mammoth line, to the emergence of a potential competitor, in this case *Loxodonta atlantica*. (From Maglio, 1973.)

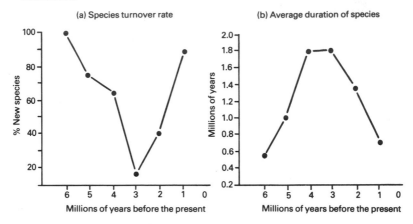

Fig. 13.13 Evolutionary rates in the elephants. (a) The percentage of new species of elephants appearing in the fossil record relative to the total number then in existence for each period of one million years. Note that the group was still actively evolving in the Pleistocene with over 90% of the species then alive arising during that period. (b) The average duration of elephant species. Those that appeared three or four million years ago lasted the longest. (From Maglio, 1973.)

evolutionary activity took place in the molars (Fig. 13.12), culminating in the evolution of *E. iolensis*. Again, it is possible that the risk of competition with another species, in this case *Loxodonta atlantica*, resulted in the evolutionary spurt.

In the Asiatic branch of the *Elephas* group, there was a high but steady rate of evolutionary change without the fluctuations seen in the African branch and in *Mammuthus*. The evolutionary rate of *Loxodonta* was also steady, but much lower than in the other groups of elephants.

Perhaps the most rapid rates of evolution in elephants occurred in the dwarfing which took place several times with island forms. The dwarf Mediterranean elephant, *Elephas falconeri*, shrank to one quarter or one fifth of its original size within a few thousand years. Such a rate is in the order of 10 darwins, which is extremely rapid in comparison with other evolutionary changes in elephants, as reference to Fig. 13.10 to 13.12 will show.

The appearance of new species was not constant, nor was the period over which each species survived. The most enduring species,

242

with an average life span of 1.8 million years, existed between 2 and 4 million years ago. Earlier and later species persisted for around half a million years (Fig. 13.13).

One of the most interesting facts about the evolution of elephants is that, even as late as the end of the Pleistocene, the group was still expanding and new species were being formed. The number of species had never been higher and very little extinction had occurred (Fig. 13.13). Of the twenty-seven known species in the Elephantinae, fourteen were still extant during the last 1 million years and eleven made their first appearance in this period. Yet this thriving group was suddenly extinguished, leaving only two representatives. Why this should have happened is not clear but it is only part of the greater puzzle of the wholesale Pleistocene extinctions which occurred in all groups of mammals. No satisfactory explanation has yet been given for these extinctions although there are many theories (Martin and Wright, 1967). An external factor may be suspected in the case of elephants since there was no sign of racial senescence; on the contrary, the group was showing an active adaptative radiation immediately before its decline.

Appendix: Numbers and distribution

Fig. 1 Distribution of the African elephant in 1976. Although numbers may have changed subsequently, this is essentially the distribution of the elephant today. In historic times, the elephant was found throughout Africa apart from in the Sahara Desert and similarly desert regions. (After Douglas-Hamilton, 1979.)

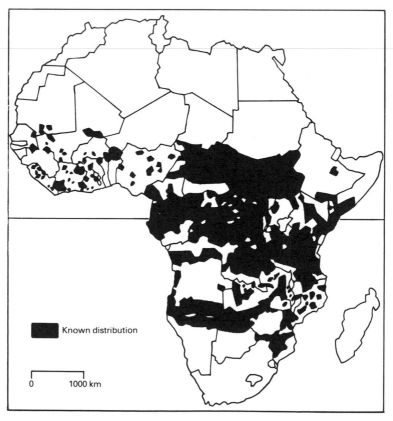

Known distribution

0   1000 km

Table 1   Total numbers in 1979 of wild African elephants in all countries where the species is known to occur*

Country	Number of elephants	Country	Number of elephants
Angola	12 400**	Mozambique	54 800**
Benin	900**	Namibia	2 700**
Botswana	20 000	Niger	1 500**
Cameroon	16 200**	Nigeria	2 300**
Central African Republic	63 000**	Rwanda	150**
Chad	15 000**	Senegal	450**
Congo	10 800**	Sierra Leone	300**
Equatorial Guinea	1 300	Somalia	24 300**
Ethiopia	900**	South Africa	7 800
Gabon	13 400	Sudan	134 000**
Ghana	3 500**	Tanzania	316 300
Guinea	300**	Togo	80**
Ivory Coast	4 000**	Uganda	6 000**
Kenya	65 000**	Upper Volta	1 700**
Liberia	900**	Zaire	377 700**
Malawi	4 500	Zambia	150 000**
Mali	1 000**	Zimbabwe	30 000
Mauritania	160**		

Grand total for Africa 1 343 340

*From Douglas-Hamilton, 1979

**Elephant numbers probably declining

245

Fig. 2 Past and present distribution of the Asian elephant. (After Olivier, 1978b.)

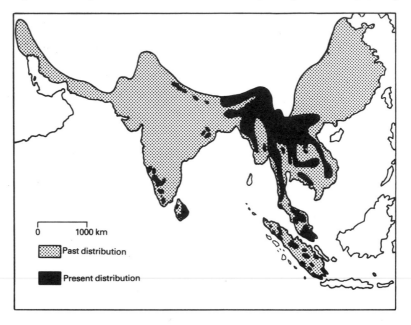

Table 2 The numbers of wild Asian elephants throughout the geographical range of the species*

Division	Region	Number of elephants		
		Regional totals	Divisional totals	Grand total
Indian sub-continent	West sub-Himalayan foothills	500		
	Peninsular India (Western Ghats)	4 500		
	Central Peninsular India	900–2 000		
	North-eastern India	4 000–8 000		
			9 950–15 050	
Continental South-East Asia	Burma	5 000		
	China	100		
	Thailand	2 500–4 500		
	Kampuchea, Laos and Vietnam	3 500–5 000		
			11 100–14 600	
Islands and Peninsular South-East Asia	Andaman Islands	30		
	Borneo	2 000		
	Malaya	3 000–6 000		
	Sri Lanka	2 000–4 000		
	Sumatra	300		
			7 330–12 330	
				28 380–41 930

*According to Olivier, 1978b

Bibliography

Afolayan, T.A. (1975) 'Effects of elephant activities on forest plantations in the Kilimanjaro forest-game reserve in northern Tanzania' *Oikos* **26**, pp. 405-10.

Agnew, A.D.G. (1966) 'The use of game trails as a possible measure of habitat utilization by larger mammals' *E. Afr. Wildl. J.* **4**, pp. 38-46.

Aguirre, E. (1969) 'Evolutionary history of the elephant' *Science* **164**, pp. 1366-76.

Albl, P. (1971) 'Studies on assessment of physical condition in African elephants' *Biol. Conserv.* **3**, pp. 134-40.

Alexandre, D.-Y., (1978) 'Le rôle disséminateur des éléphants en Forêt de Tai, Côte-d'Ivoire' *Terre Vie* **32**, pp. 47-72.

Altmann, J. (1974) 'Observational study of behavior: sampling methods' *Behaviour* **49**, pp. 227-67.

Amoroso, E.C. and Perry, J.S. (1964) 'The foetal membrane and placenta of the African elephant (*Loxodonta africana*)' *Phil. Trans. R. Soc. Ser. B* **248**, pp. 1-34.

Anderson, G.D. and Walker, B.H. (1974) 'Vegetation composition and elephant damage in the Sengwa Wildlife Research Area, Rhodesia' *J. S. Afr. Wildl. Mgmt Ass.* **4**, pp. 1-14.

Barnes, R. (1979) *Elephant Ecology in Ruaha National Park, Tanzania* Ph. D. Thesis, University of Cambridge.

Bax, P.N. and Sheldrick, D.L.W. (1963) 'Some preliminary observations on the food of elephants in the Tsavo Royal National Park (East) of Kenya' *E. Afr. Wildl. J.* **1**, pp. 40-53.

Benedict, F.G. (1936) *The Physiology of the Elephant* Carnegie Institute, Washington.

Brocklesby, D.W. and Campbell, H. (1963) 'A *Babesia* of the African elephant' *E. Afr. Wildl. J.* **1**, p. 119.

Brooks, A.C. and Buss, I.O. (1962) 'Trend in tusk size of the Uganda elephant' *Mammalia* **26**, pp. 10-34.

Brown, I.R.F. and White, P.T. (1980) 'Elephant blood haematology and chemistry' *Comp. Biochem. Physiol.* **65B**, pp. 1-12.

Brown, I.R.F., White, P.T. and Malpas, R.C. (1978) 'Proteins and other nitrogenous constituents in the blood serum of the African elephant' *Comp. Biochem. Physiol.* **59A**, pp. 267-70.

Brownlee, J.W. and Hanks, J. (1977) 'Notes on the growth of young male African elephants' *Lammergeyer* **23**, pp. 7-12.

Buss, I.O. (1961) 'Some observations on food habits and behavior of the African elephant' *J. Wildl. Mgmt* **25**, pp. 131-48.

Buss, I.O. and Estes, R. (1971) 'The functional significance of movements and positions of the pinnae of the African elephant *Loxodonta africana*' *J. Mammal.* **52**, pp. 21-7.

Buss, I.O. and Johnson, O.W. (1967) 'Relationships of Leydig cell characteristics and intratesticular testosterone levels to sexual activity in the African elephant' *Anat. Rec.* **157**, pp. 191-6.

Buss, I.O. and Smith, N.S. (1966) 'Observations on reproduction and breeding behaviour of the African elephant' *J. Wildl. Mgmt* **30**, pp. 375-88.

Buss, I.O. and Wallner, A. (1965) 'Body temperature of the African elephant' *J. Mammal.* **46**, pp. 104-7.

Carrington, R. (1957) *Mermaids and Mastodons* Chatto & Windus, London.

Carrington, R. (1958) *Elephants* Chatto & Windus, London.

Caughley, G. (1976) 'The elephant problem — an alternative hypothesis' *E. Afr. Wildl. J.* **14**, pp. 265-83.

Caughley, G. and Goddard, J. (1975) 'Abundance and distribution of elephants in the Luangwa Valley, Zambia' *E. Afr. Wildl. J.* **13**, pp. 39-48.

Coe, M. (1972) 'Defaecation by African elephants (*Loxodonta africana africana* (Blumenbach))' *E. Afr. Wildl. J.* **10**, pp. 165-74.

Coe, M., Cumming, D.H. and Phillipson, J. (1976) 'Biomass and production of large African herbivores in relation to rainfall and primary production' *Oecologia* **22**, pp. 341-54.

Condy, J.B. (1974) 'Observations on internal parasites in Rhodesian elephant, *Loxodonta africana* Blumenbach 1797' *Proc. Trans. Rhod. Scient. Ass.* **55**, pp. 67-99.

Corfield, T.F. (1973) 'Elephant mortality in Tsavo National Park, Kenya' *E. Afr. Wildl. J.* **11**, pp. 339-68.

Croze, H. (1972) 'A modified photogrammetric technique for assessing age-structures of elephant populations and its use in Kidepo National Park' *E. Afr. Wildl. J.* **10**, 91-115.

Croze, H. (1974a) 'The Seronera bull problem. I. The elephants' *E. Afr. Wildl. J.* **12**, pp. 1-27.

Croze, H. (1974b) 'The Seronera bull problem. II. The trees' *E. Afr. Wildl. J.* **12**, pp. 29-47.

Cumming, D.H.M. (in press) 'On the management of elephant and other large mammals in Zimbabwe'.

Debbie, J.G. and Clausen, B. (1975) 'Some haemotological values of free-ranging African elephants' *J. Wildl. Dis.* **11**, pp. 79-82.

Dillman, J.S. and Carr, W.R. (1970) 'Observations on arteriosclerosis, serum cholesterol and serum electrolytes in the wild African elephant (*Loxodonta africana*)' *J. Comp. Path.* **80**, pp. 81-7.

Dougall, H.W. and Sheldrick, D.L.W. (1964) 'The chemical composition of a day's diet of an elephant' *E. Afr. Wildl. J.* **2**, pp. 51-9.

Douglas-Hamilton, I. (1973) 'On the ecology and behaviour of the Lake Manyara elephants' *E. Afr. Wildl. J.* **11**, pp. 401-3.

Douglas-Hamilton, I. (1979) *The African Elephant Action Plan* IUCN/WWF/NYZS Elephant Survey and Conservation Programme.

Douglas-Hamilton, I. and O. (1975) *Among the Elephants* Collins, London.

Dunham, K.M. (1980) 'The feeding behaviour of a tame impala *Aepyceros melampus*' *E. Afr. Wildl. J.* **18**, pp. 253-7.

Eisenberg, J.F. and Lockhart, M. (1972) 'An ecological reconnaissance of Wilpatta National Park, Ceylon' *Smithson. Contr. Zool.* **101**.

Eisenberg, J.F., McKay, G.M. and Jainudeen, M.R. (1971) 'Reproductive behavior of the Asiatic elephant (*Elephas maximus* L.)' *Behaviour* **38**, pp. 193-225.

Elder, W.H. (1970) 'Morphometry of elephant tusks' *Zool. Afr.* **5**, pp. 143-59.

Eloff, A.K. and van Hoven, N. (1980) 'Intestinal Protozoa of the African elephant *Loxodonta africana* (Blumenbach)' *S. Afr. J. Zool.* **15**, pp. 83-90.

Eltringham, S.K. (1974) 'The rescue of distressed large mammals in national parks using drug immobilization' *E. Afr. Wildl. J.* **12**, pp. 233-8.

Eltringham, S.K. (1977) 'The numbers and distribution of elephant *Loxodonta africana* in the Rwenzori National Park and Chambura Game Reserve, Uganda' *E. Afr. Wildl. J.* **15**, pp. 19-39.

Eltringham, S.K. (1979) *The Ecology and Conservation of Large African Mammals* Macmillan Press, London and Basingstoke.

Eltringham, S.K. (1980) 'A quantitative assessment of range usage by large African mammals with particular reference to the effects of elephants on trees' *Afr. J. Ecol.* **18**, pp. 53-71.

Eltringham, S.K. and Malpas, R.C. (1980) 'The decline in elephant numbers in Rwenzori and Kabalega Falls National Parks, Uganda' *Afr. J. Ecol.* **18**, pp. 73-86.

Evans, G.H. (1910) *Elephants and Diseases. A Treatise on Elephants* Government Printing, Rangoon.

Fairall, N. (1979) 'A radio tracking study of young translocated elephants'. In *A Handbook on Biotelemetry and Radio Tracking* Amlaner, C.J. and MacDonald, D.W. (eds), Pergamon Press, Oxford.

Ferrier, A.J. (1948) *The Care and Management of Elephants in Burma* Steel, London.

Field, C.R. (1971) 'Elephant ecology in the Queen Elizabeth National Park, Uganda' *E. Afr. Wildl. J.* **9**, pp. 99-123.

Field, C.R. and Ross, I.C. (1976) 'The savanna ecology of Kidepo Valley National Park. II. Feeding ecology of elephant and giraffe' *E. Afr. Wildl. J.* **14**, pp. 1-15.

Fowler, C.W. and Smith, T. (1973) 'Characterizing stable populations: an application to the African elephant population' *J. Wildl. Mgmt* **37**, pp. 513-23.

Frade, F. (1955) 'Ordre des Proboscidiens (Proboscidea — Illiger 1811)' In *Traité de Zoologie* Grassé, P.P. (ed.), **17** Paris.

Franzmann, A.W. (1972) 'Environmental sources of variation of bighorn sheep physiologic values' *J. Wildl. Mgmt* **36**, pp. 924-32.

Gee, E.P. (1964) *The Wild Life of India* Collins, London.

Gilchrist, W. (1851) *A Practical Treatise on the Treatment of the Diseases of the Elephant, Camel, and Horned Cattle, with Instructions for Preserving their Efficiency* Calcutta.

Goddard, J. (1967) 'Home range, behaviour and recruitment rates of two black rhinoceros populations' *E. Afr. Wildl. J.* **5**, pp. 133-50.

Guy, P.R. (1975) 'The daily food intake of the African elephant, *Loxodonta africana* Blumenbach, in Rhodesia' *Arnoldia, Rhodesia* **7**, 1-8.

Guy, P.R. (1976) 'The feeding behaviour of elephant (*Loxodonta africana*) in the Sengwa area, Rhodesia' *S. Afr. J. Wildl. Res.* **6**, pp. 55-63.

Guy, P.R. (1977) 'Coprophagy in the African elephant (*Loxodonta africana* Blumenbach)' *E. Afr. Wildl. J.* **15**, p. 174.

Haldane, J.B.S. (1949) 'Suggestions as to quantitative measurement of rates of evolution' *Evolution* **3**, pp. 51-6.

Hanks, J. (1969) 'Seasonal breeding of the African elephant in Zambia' *E. Afr. Wildl. J.* **7**, p. 167.

Hanks, J. (1972a) 'Aspects of dentition of the African elephant, *Loxodonta africana*' *Arnoldia, Rhodesia* **5**, pp. 1-8.

Hanks, J. (1972b) 'Reproduction of elephant (*Loxodonta africana*) in the Luangwa Valley, Zambia' *J. Reprod. Fert.* **30**, pp. 13-26.

Hanks, J. (1972c) 'Growth of the African elephant (*Loxodonta africana*)' *E. Afr. Wildl. J.* **10**, pp. 251-72.

Hanks, J. (1973) 'Reproduction in the male African elephant in the Luangwa Valley, Zambia' *J. S. Afr. Wildl. Mgmt. Ass.* **3**, pp. 31-9.

Hanks, J. (1977) 'Comparative aspects of reproduction in the male hyrax and elephant'. In *Reproduction and Evolution* Calaby, J.H. and Tyndale-Biscoe, C.H. (eds), pp. 155-64. Australian Academy of Science, Canberra.

Hanks, J. (1979) *A Struggle for Survival. The Elephant Problem* Country Life Books.

Hanks, J. and McIntosh, J.E.A. (1973) 'Population dynamics of the African elephant' *J. Zool., Lond.* **169**, pp. 29-38.

Harrington, G.N. and Ross, I.C. (1974) 'The savanna ecology of Kidepo Valley National Park. I. The effects of burning and browsing on the vegetation' *E. Afr. Wildl. J.* **12**, pp. 93-105.

Harthoorn, A.M. (1966) 'The Tsavo elephants' *Oryx*, **8**, pp. 233-6.

Heath, B.R. and Field, C.R. (1974) 'Elephant endurance on Galana Ranch, Kenya' *E. Afr. Wildl. J.* **12**, pp. 239-42.

Hendricks, H. and Hendricks, U. (1971) *Dikdik und Elephanten* Piper, Munich.

Huggett, A. St. J. and Widdass, W.R. (1951) 'The relationship between mammalian foetal weight and conception age' *J. Physiol., Lond.* **114**, pp. 306-17.

Janis, C. (1976) 'The evolutionary strategy of the Equidae and the origins of rumen and caecal digestion' *Evolution* **30**, pp. 757-74.

Jainudeen, M.R., Katongole, C.B. and Short, R.V. (1972) 'Plasma testosterone levels in relation to musth and sexual activity in the male Asiatic elephant, *Elephas maximus*' *J. Reprod. Fert.* **29**, pp. 99-103.

Janzen, D.H. (1975) *Ecology of Plants in the Tropics* Arnold, London.

Jewell, P.A. (1966) 'The concept of home range in mammals' *Symp. zool. Soc. Lond.* **18**, pp. 85-109.

Johnson, O.W. and Buss, I.O. (1965) 'Molariform teeth of male African elephants in relation to age, body dimensions, and growth' *J. Mammal.* **46**, pp. 373-84.

Johnson, O.W. and Buss, I.O. (1967a) 'The testis of the African elephant (*Loxodonta africana*). I. Histological features' *J. Reprod. Fert.* **13**, pp. 11-21.

Johnson, O.W. and Buss, I.O. (1967b) 'The testis of the African elephant (*Loxodonta africana*). II. Development, puberty and weight' *J. Reprod. Fert.* **13**, pp. 23-30.

Jolly, W.P. (1976) *Jumbo* Constable, London.

Krumrey, W.A. and Buss, I.O. (1968) 'Age estimation, growth and relationships between body dimensions of the female African elephant' *J. Mammal.* **49**, pp. 22-31.

251

Kühme, W. von (1963) 'Ethology of the African elephant (*Loxodonta africana* Blumenbach 1797) in captivity' *Int. zoo. Yb.* **4**, pp. 113-21.

Kurt, F. (1974) 'Remarks on the social structure and ecology of the Ceylon elephant in the Yala National Park' *IUCN Publ. N.S.* **24**, pp. 618-34.

Lang, E.M. (1980) 'Observations on growth and molar change in the African elephant' *Afr. J. Ecol.* **18**, pp. 217-34.

Laurie, W.A. (1978) *The Ecology and Behaviour of the Greater One-horned Rhinoceros* Ph.D. Thesis, University of Cambridge.

Laws, R.M. (1966) 'Age criteria for the African elephant, *Loxodonta africana*' *E. Afr. Wildl. J.* **4**, pp. 1-37.

Laws, R.M. (1967a) 'Eye lens weight and age in African elephants' *E. Afr. Wildl. J.* **5**, pp. 46-52.

Laws, R.M. (1967b) 'Occurrence of placental scars in the uterus of the African elephant (*Loxodonta africana*)' *J. Reprod. Fert.* **14**, pp. 445-9.

Laws, R.M. (1969a) 'Aspects of reproduction in the African elephant, *Loxodonta africana*' *J. Reprod. Fert.* Supplement 6, pp. 193-217.

Laws, R.M. (1969b) 'The Tsavo Research Project' *J. Reprod. Fert.* Supplement 6, pp. 495-531.

Laws, R.M. (1970) 'Biology of African elephants' *Sci. Progr. Oxf.* **58**, pp. 251-62.

Laws, R.M. and Parker, I.S.C. (1968) 'Recent studies on elephant populations in East Africa' *Symp. zool. Soc. Lond.* **21**, pp. 319-59.

Laws, R.M., Parker, I.S.C. and Archer, A.L. (1967) 'Estimating live weights of elephants from hind leg weights' *E. Afr. Wildl. J.* **5**, pp. 106-11.

Laws, R.M., Parker, I.S.C. and Johnstone, R.C.B. (1970) 'Elephants and habitats in north Bunyoro, Uganda' *E. Afr. Wildl. J.* **8**, pp. 163-80.

Laws, R.M., Parker, I.S.C. and Johnstone, R.C.B. (1975) *Elephants and their Habitats. The Ecology of Elephants in North Bunyoro, Uganda* Clarendon Press, Oxford.

Leuthold, W. (1977) 'Changes in tree populations of Tsavo East National Park, Kenya' *E. Afr. Wildl. J.* **15**, pp. 61-9.

Leuthold, W. and Leuthold, B.M. (1975) 'Parturition and related behaviour in the African elephant' *Z. Tierpsychol.* **49**, pp. 75-84.

Leuthold, W. and Sale, J.B. (1973) 'Movements and patterns of habitat utilization of elephants in Tsavo National Park, Kenya' *E. Afr. Wildl. J.* **11**, pp. 369-84.

Lord, R.D. (1959) 'The lens as an indicator of age in cottontail rabbits' *J. Wildl. Mgmt.* **23**, pp. 358-60.

McCullagh, K. (1969a) 'The growth and nutrition of the African elephant. I. Seasonal variations in the rate of growth and the urinary excretion of hydroxyproline' *E. Afr. Wildl. J.* **7**, pp. 85-90.

McCullagh, K. (1969b) 'The growth and nutrition of the African elephant. II. The chemical nature of the diet' *E. Afr. Wildl. J.* **7**, pp. 91-7.

McCullagh, K.G. (1970) *Arteriosclerosis in the African Elephant* Ph.D. Thesis, University of Cambridge.

McCullagh, K.G. (1972) 'Arteriosclerosis in the African elephant. I. Intimal atherosclerosis and its possible causes' *Atherosclerosis* **16**, pp. 307-35.

McCullagh, K.M. and Lewis, M.G. (1967) 'Spontaneous arteriosclerosis in the African elephant. Its relation to disease in man' *Lancet* ii, pp. 492-5.

252

McKay, G.M. (1973) 'Behavior and ecology of the Asiatic elephant in south-eastern Ceylon' *Smithson. Contr. Zool.* 125.

Maglio, V.J. (1973) 'Origin and evolution of the Elephantidae' *Trans. Am. Phil. Soc.* 63, pp. 1-149.

Malpas, R.C. (1977) 'Diet and the condition and growth of elephants in Uganda' *J. appl. Ecol.* 14, pp. 489-504.

Malpas, R.C. (1978) *The Ecology of the African Elephant in Rwenzori and Kabalega Falls National Parks* Ph.D. Thesis, University of Cambridge.

Malpas, R.C. (1980) *Wildlife in Uganda 1980. A Survey.* A report to the Minister of Tourism and Wildlife, Uganda, New York Zoological Society & WWF/IUCN.

Martin, P.S. and Wright, H.E. (1967) *Pleistocene Extinctions* Yale University Press, New Haven.

Martin, R.B. (1978) 'Aspects of elephant social organisation' *Rhod. Sci. News* 12, pp. 184-7.

Merz, G. (1977) *Untersuchungen über Ernährungsbiologie und Habitatprä-ferenzen des Afrikanischen Waldelefanten*, Loxodonta africana cyclotis, *Matschie, 1900* Unpubl. Ms., University of Heidelberg.

Mgaah, E.E. (1979) 'Observations in Tsavo National Park, Kenya' *Elephant* 1, p.22.

Morrison-Scott, T.C.S. (1947) 'A revision of our knowledge of African elephants' teeth with notes on forest and "pygmy" elephants' *Proc. zool. Soc. Lond.* 117, pp. 505-27.

Moss, C. (1977) 'The Amboseli elephants' *Wildl. News* 12, pp. 9-12.

Mueller-Dombois, D. (1972) 'Crown distortion and elephant distribution in the woody vegetations of Ruhuna National Park, Ceylon' *Ecology* 53, pp. 208-26.

Nirmalan, G., Nair, S.G. and Simon, K. (1967) 'Haematology of the Indian elephant (*Elephas maximus*)' *Can. J. Physiol. Pharmacol.* 45, pp. 985-9.

Olivier, R.C.D. (1978a) *On the Ecology of the Asian Elephant* Elephas maximus *Linn. with particular reference to Malaya and Sri Lanka* Ph.D. Thesis, University of Cambridge.

Olivier, R. (1978b) 'Distribution and status of the Asian elephant' *Oryx* 14, pp. 379-424.

Osborn, H.F. (1936) *Proboscidea.* Vol. I. American Museum Press, New York.

Osborn, H.F. (1942) *Proboscidea.* Vol. II. American Museum Press, New York.

Perry, J.S. (1953) 'The reproduction of the African elephant, *Loxodonta africana*' *Phil. Trans. R. Soc. Ser. B* 237, pp. 93-149.

Perry, J.S. (1954) 'Some observations on growth and tusk weight in male and female African elephants' *Proc. zool. Soc. Lond.* 124, pp. 97-105.

Petrides, G.A. and Swank, W.G. (1965) 'Estimating the productivity and energy relations of an African elephant population' In *Proc. 9th. Int. Grassland Conf., San Paulo, Brazil* pp. 831-42.

Phillipson, J. (1975) 'Rainfall, primary productivity and "carrying capacity" of Tsavo National Park (East), Kenya' *E. Afr. Wildl. J.* 13, pp. 171-201.

Poole, J. and Moss, C. (1981) 'Musth in the African elephant *Loxodonta africana*' *Nature, Lond.* 292, pp. 830-31.

Rees, P.A. (in press) 'Gross assimilation efficiency and food passage time in the African elephant' *Afr. J. Ecol.*

Rodgers, D.H. and Elder, W.H. (1971) 'Movements of elephants in Luangwa Valley, Zambia' *J. Wildl. Mgmt* **41**, pp. 56-62.

Savidge, J.M. (1968) 'Elephant in Ruaha National Park: a management problem' *E. Afr. agric. for. J.* **33** (Special issue), pp. 191-6.

Savidge, J.M., Woodford, M.H. and Croze, H. (1976) 'Report on a mission to Zaire' *Mimeo. Rep., UNDP/FAO Kenya Wildlife Management Project (KEN/71/526).*

Seidensticker, J. (1976) 'Ungulate populations in Chitawan Valley, Nepal' *Biol. Conserv.* **10**, pp. 183-210.

Sherry, B.Y. (1975) 'Reproduction of elephant in Gonarezhou, southeastern Rhodesia' *Arnoldia' Rhodesia* **7**, 1-13.

Short, R.V. (1966) 'Oestrous behaviour, ovulation and the formation of the corpus luteum in the African elephant, *Loxodonta africana' E. Afr. Wildl. J.* **4**, pp. 56-68.

Short, R.V., Mann, T. and Hay, M.F. (1967) 'Male reproductive organs of the African elephant, *Loxodonta africana' J. Reprod. Fert.* **13**, pp. 517-38.

Sikes, S.K. (1966) 'The African elephant, *Loxodonta africana*: a field method for the estimation of age' *J. Zool. Lond* **150**, pp. 279-95.

Sikes, S.K. (1968) 'The African elephant, *Loxodonta africana*: a field method for the estimation of age' *J. Zool. Lond.* **154**, pp. 235-48.

Sikes, S.K. (1969) 'Habitat and cardiovascular disease: observations made in East Africa on free-living wild animals, with particular reference to the African elephant' *Trans. zool. Soc. Lond.* **32**, pp. 1-104.

Sikes, S.K. (1971) *The Natural History of the African Elephant* Weidenfeld & Nicolson, London.

Simpson, G.G. (1945) 'The principles of classification and a classification of the mammals' *Bull. Am. Mus. Nat. Hist.* **85**, pp. 1-350.

Slade, H. (1903) 'On the mode of copulation of the Indian elephant' *Proc. zool. Soc. Lond.* **1**, pp. 111-13.

Smith, F. (1890) 'The histology of the skin of the elephant' *J. Anat. Physiol.* **24** (N.S.4), pp. 493-503.

Smith, N.S. and Buss, I.O. (1973) 'Reproduction of the female African elephant' *J. Wildl. Mgmt* **37**, pp. 524-33.

Smith, N.S. and Ledger, H.P. (1965) 'A method of predicting live weight from dissected leg weight' *J. Wildl. Mgmt* **29**, pp. 504-11.

Smuts, G.L. (1975) 'Reproduction and population characteristics of elephants in the Kruger National Park' *J. S. Afr. Wildl. Mgmt Ass.* **5**, pp. 1-10.

Spearman, R.I.C. (1970) 'The epidermis and its keratinisation in the African elephant (*Loxodonta africana*)' *Zool. Afr.* **5**, pp. 327-38.

Spence, D.H.M. and Angus, A. (1971) 'African grassland management — burning and grazing in Murchison Falls National Park.' In *The Scientific Management of Plant and Animal Communities for Conservation* Duffey, E. and Watt, A.S. (eds), Blackwell, Oxford.

Spinage, C.A. (1972) 'Evolution of the Proboscidae' *Saugetierkundliche Mitt.* **20**, pp. 152-6.

Spinage, C.A. (1973) 'A review of ivory exploitation and elephant population trends in Africa' *E. Afr. Wildl. J.* **11**, pp. 281-9.

Sykes, A.R. and Field, A.C. (1973) 'Effects of dietary deficiencies of energy, protein and calcium on the pregnant ewe' *J. agric. Sci. Camb.* **80**, pp. 29-36. 29-36.

Thomson, P.J. (1975) 'The role of elephants, fire and other agents in the decline of a *Brachystegia boehmii* woodland' *J. S. Afr. Wildl. Mgmt Ass.* **5**, pp. 11-18.

Vancuylenberg, B.W.B. (1977) 'Feeding behaviour of the Asiatic elephant in south-east Sri Lanka in relation to conservation' *Biol. Conserv.* **12**, pp. 33-54.

Watson, D.M.S. (1946) 'The evolution of the Proboscidae' *Biol. Rev.* **21**, pp. 15-29.

Watson, R.M., Bell, R.H.V. and Parker, I.S.C. (1972) 'Men and elephants' *Africana* **4**, pp. 20-21.

Weir, J.S. (1969) 'Chemical properties and occurrence on the Kalahari sand of salt licks created by elephants' *J. Zool. Lond.* **158**, pp. 293-310.

Weir, J.S. (1972) 'Spatial distribution of elephants in an African National Park in relation to environmental sodium *Oikos* **23**, pp. 1-13.

White, P.T. (1980) 'Blood parasites in free-living African elephants' *Zool. Gart. N.F.* **1**, pp. 45-8.

White, P.T. and Brown, I.R.F. (1978) 'Haematological studies on wild African elephants (*Loxodonta africana*)' *J. Zool. Lond.* **185**, pp. 491-503.

Whitehead, R.G. (1965) 'Hydroxyproline-creatinine ratio as an index of nutritional status and rate of growth' *Lancet* **ii**, pp. 567-70.

Williams, J.H. (1950) *Elephant Bill* Hart-Davis, London.

Williamson, B.R. (1975) 'The condition and nutrition of elephant in Wankie National Park' *Arnoldia, Rhodesia* **7**, 1-20.

Williamson, B.R. (1976) 'Reproduction in female African elephant in the Wankie National Park, Rhodesia.' *S. Afr. J. Wildl. Res.* **6**, pp. 89-93.

Wing, L.D. and Buss, I.O. (1970) 'Elephants and forests' *Wildl. Monogr.* **19**.

Woodford, M.H. (1976) *A Survey of Parasitic Infestation of Wild Herbivores and their Predators in the Ruwenzori National Park, Uganda.* FRCVS Dissertation, Royal College of Veterinary Surgeons, London.

Woodford, M.H. and Trevor, S. (1970) 'Fostering a baby elephant' *E. Afr. Wildl. J.* **8**, pp. 204-5.

Woodford, M.H., Eltringham, S.K. and Wyatt, J.R. (1972) 'An analysis of mechanical failure of darts and costs involved in drug immobilization of elephants and buffalo' *E. Afr. Wildl. J.* **10**, pp. 279-85.

Woodley, F.W. (1965) 'Game defence barriers' *E. Afr. Wildl. J.* **3**, pp. 89-94.

Wyatt, J.R. and Eltringham, S.K. (1974) 'The daily activity of the elephant in the Rwenzori National Park, Uganda' *E. Afr. Wildl. J.* **12**, pp. 273-89.

Index

Numbers in *italics* refer to black and white illustrations. Numbers in bold refer to colour plates.

Aberdare National Park, 168
Abscesses, 171–2, 173–4, 185
Acacia, 154, 156
    albida, 150, 155
    gerrardii, 149
    tortilis, 149, 155
    xanthophloea, 150
Accidents, 169–71, *170*
Addo National Park, 24
Aerial
    photography, 36–7, *37*
    survey, 49
Age determination, 8–9, 28–30, *28, 29*
Age of bulls, 57
Aggression
    circus fights, 201–3
    between elephants, 71–2, *72*
    towards man, 10, 65
    towards other species, 72–3
Amboseli National Park, 24, 56, 77, 81, **1, 4**
Amebelodon, 215, 221
Anaemia, 175
Anal flap, 18, 27, 36
Anancus, 225
Anatomy, 4–21
    female, *20*, 21
    male, 19–21, *20*
Aneurysm, 175
Anthrax, 177
Archidiskodon, 230
Assimilation efficiency, 131
Atheroma, 175
Aunties, 82
Aybelodon, 215

Babesia, 176
Balanites, 149
Baobab trees, 149, 151, 154, 155, 156, 158–9, 169
Barking of trees, 102, 148, 152, 153–5, 156
Barnum, Phineas T., 199, 200, 203
Barytherioidea, 214, 216–7
Barytherium, 214, 216, 217
Bathing, 112–13, **8, 10**
Behaviour
    reproductive, 74–8
    social, 52–73
    study techniques, 43–5
Birth, 82, 201
Blood
    chemistry, 121–3
    diseases, 175–6
    serum, 32
    system, 18
Bohr effect, 122
Boils, 182
Bolting, 196
Bone marrow, *31*, 31–2
Bot flies, 178–9
Brain, 16–17
Breeding seasons, 39–40, 78–81, *79*
Budongo Forest 84, 85, 87, 154–5
Bull herds, *54*, 57, 60–62
Bunodonty, 216

Caecum, 17, 89
Calf, 12, **11**
    hybrid, 201
    mortality, 153
Calving interval, 39, 74, 86–8, 134

256

Captive breeding, 168
Capture, 190–91
Carrying capacity, 130–31, 142, 143–4, *144*, 146
Cave paintings, 186
Ceremonial elephants, 203–4
Chewing action, 7, 226–9, *227*, *228*
Circuses, 199, 201–3
Clan, 64
Classification, 2–3, 214–15
Clitoris, 21
Colon, 89
Colophospermum mopane, 151, 155
Communication, 64–7
Compression, 143, 146–7, *147*
Conception, 40, 78–80, *79*
Condition, 30–32, 123–6
Conservation, 167–8
Control shooting, 161–2
Copulation, 21, 75
Coprophagy, 91
Corpus luteum, 21, 38
Corral, 190
Counting elephants, 48–51
Courtship, 74–6
Crop raiding, 167–8
Crupper, 192, *193*, 194, *194*
Culling, 144, 160–66
Cuvieronius, 215, 225
Cystitis, 182

Daily activity, 107–17, *108*
Darwin unit, 239, 240, 241, 242
Defaecation, 116–17
Deinotherioidea, 213, 214, 215–16
Deinotherium, 214, 215, 217, *219*, *222*
Deme, 64
Density
    and culling, 165–6
    and fecundity, 87, 88
    in African reserves, 87
    in forests, 106
Dental caries, 173
Dental formula, 7
Diabetes, 182
Diarrhoea, 183
Diastema, 216
Diet
    of Asian elephant, 98–9
    of bush elephant, 92–7
    of forest elephant, 97–8
    quality, 123–6
    seasonal changes, 93–6
Digestion, 89–92
Digestive system, 17–18
Disease, 169–85
    and age, 174
    treatment, 184–5
Display
    social, 156
    threat, 11, 65, **4**
Distribution, 244–7
Domestication, 187–97
Drinking, 10, 112–13, **2**
Driving hook, 195, *195*
Droppings
    analysis, 33, 97
    counts, 49–50, 106, 116
    measure of food intake, 34, 99, 131
    parasites in, 43, 182
Drought, mortality from, 162–3
Drug immobilization, *44, 45, 47*, 45–8, 173
Dusting, 113, 180
Dysentery, 177

Ears
    anatomy, 11
    use in display, 64–5, **4**
    measurements, 11
    shape, 3–4
    temperature regulation, 114, 119–21, *120*
Eczema, 180, 182
'Elephant and Castle', 187
Elephant as a beast of burden, 188–94
Elephant
    beds, 110, 117
    facies, 226
    pox, 177
    problem, 145–68
    training stations in Africa, 189
Elephant in
    art, 186–7
    mythology, 186–7
    war, 187–8
    zoos, 197–201

257

Elephant-proof fences, 168
Elephantidae, 212, 215, 218, 226–43
Elephantinae, 215, 230–43
Elephas, 232–4, 235, *238*, 239, *241*,
    242
   antiquus, 232
   celebensis, *233*, 234
   ekorensis, 232, *233*, 234, 239,
     241
   falconeri, *233*, 234
   iolensis, 232, *233*, *241*, 242
   maximus, 3, 222, 230, 232,
     246, 247
     indicus, 3
     maximus, 3
     summatranus, 3
   namadicus, 232, *233*, 239
   planifrons, 233, 234
   platycephalon, 234
   recki, 232, *233*, *241*
Eubelodon, 215
Enamel thickness, *238*
Energy budget, 129–30
Evolution
   Elephantinae, 230–38
   molars, 213, 231, *231*, *238*,
     239, *240*, *241*, *242*
   skull, 213
   trunk, 221–2
Evolutionary rates, *238*, 238–43,
    240, *241*, *242*
Excretion, 130
Eye, 22
   disease, 183–4
   lens weight, 30

Faeces, 17–18, 33, 34, 97, 118
Family units, 52–7, *53*, *54*, 115, 6,
   11
Fat
   measurement, *31*, 31–2
   metabolism, 32, 123–6, *126*
Femur, 16, 31
Feeding behaviour,
   bark stripping, 102
   daily pattern, *108*, 108–10
   feeding methods, 6, *93*, *94*,
     109, 3, 5
   feeding rates, 99–102
   food preparation, 101–2

   food quantities, *96*, 99
   seed dispersal, 97
   study techniques, 32–5
Feronia limonia, 151
Fetters, 195, *196*
Flehmen, 76
Food, 91, 92–103
   availability, 34, 130–31
   digestibility, 129
   diversity, 102–3
   intake index, 34
   passage time, 91
   quantity, 99, 129
   rainfall, effect of, 93
   seasonal variation, 93
   stomach contents analysis, 32–
     4, 103, 123–4
   trees, 156
   trunkful, 34
Foot, 12–13, *13*
Foot and mouth disease, 177
Foramen mentale, 29
Forests, *105*, 106, 158
Fostering, 83–4

Gag, 185, *185*
Gal Oya National Park, 60, 103,
   117
Gastroenteritis, 183
Geological time scale, 212
Gestation period, 86
Gnathobelodon, *219*, 221
Gomphotherioidea, 214, 218–30
Gomphotherium, 214, 218, *219*,
   222, *223*, *231*
Gonarezhou Game Reserve, 85, 87,
   138, 151, 165
Graviportal features, 16
Group size, 54, 58–60, 62
Growl, 66–7
Growth, 125–9
   brain, 17
   measurement, 35–8
   rate, 37, 124, *126*, 126–9
Guddee, 191, *193*
Guddela, 193, *193*, 203

Habitat damage, 143–4, 145, *146*,
   148–56
Haemoglobin, 121–3

Haematomyzus elephantis, 179
Hair, 12
Hannibal, 187–8
Herderian gland, 22
Harness, 191–4, *192, 193, 194*
Hearing, 22
Heart, 18
    disease, 174–5
    rate, 118
Heat production, 130
Height to weight ratio, 30
Hind leg weight, 25, *26*
Home range, 64, 67–70, 106, 157
Howdah, 194, *194*, 203
Humerus, 16
Hydroxyproline-creatinine ratio, 38,
    124–5
Hypsodonty index, *238*
Hyrax, 1, 2, 216

Incisors, 4
Inclusive fitness, 61
Indigestion, 183
Informed estimation, 51
Injuries, 169–71, *170*
Inter-calving period, 39, 74
Inter-specific reactions, 72–3
Intestines, 17
Itching, 180, *181*
Ivory, 5, 167, 205–10, 237–8

Jacobson's organ, 75
'Jap', 23, 34, 41–2, 114, 116, 117,
    128
Jaw, 14, 223–6
'Jumbo', 197, 198–200, 201, 207

Kabalega Falls National Park, 23, 24,
    27, 54, 56, 57, 58, 62, 78,
    79, *79*, 80, 84, 85, 87, 88,
    123, 124, 125, 126, 127,
    134, 139, *140*, 141, 148,
    153, 163, 166, 173, 208, **8**
Kalahari, 69, 165
Kandy Perahera Day, 203, **12**
Kasunga National Park, 24
Keddah, 190
Kidepo Valley National Park, 94, 95,
    149
Kidney fat index, 31, *124*, 123–6

Kikumbi, 25
Kin selection, 61, 82
Kinship group, 56, 62–4, *63*
Kruger National Park, 24, 68, 80,
    85, 87, 89, 138, 139, 165
Kya-pazat, 197, *197*

Lactation, 39
Lactational anoestrus, 86
Lahugala Tank, 60, 117
Lake Manyara National Park, 24, 56,
    62, *63*, 64, 67, 71, 85, 87,
    88, 150, 169, 170
Lamella *see* Lamina
Lamina, 7–9, *8*, 29, 238
Laminary index, 29
Lanugo, 12
Leeches, 179
Life tables, 135
Ligamentum nuchae, 227
Liver fluke, 178
Locomotion, 14
Logging operations, 192
Lop ear, 119
London Zoo, 197, 198, 199, 200,
    203
Louse, 179
Loxodonta, 232, 235, *238*, 239, 242
    adaurora, 232, 235
    africana, 3, 230, 222, 244, 245
        africana, 3, 232
        cyclotis, 3, 178, 188, 206,
        207
    atlantica, 232, 241, 242
Luangwa Valley National Park, 24,
    68, 79, 80, 85, 87, 158, 164

Mahout, 195, 203
Makhna, 6
Male seasonality, 78–9
Mammary gland, 12
Mammoth, 186, *219*, 234–8, *236*
    skull, 235
    tusks, 235, 237
Mammut, 214
Mammuthus, *222, 223*, 230, *232*,
    234, *236*, 238, *238*, 239,
    242
    africanavus, 235, *236*, 240
    armeniacus, 236, *236, 240*

Mammuthus—contd
    columbi, 236, 236
    imperator, 219, 236, 236
    meridionalis, 235, 236, 236,
        240
    primigenius, 5, 219, 236, 237,
        239, 240
    subplanifrons, 235, 236, 240
Mammutoidea, 214, 217–18
Mandible (lower jaw)
    evolution, 223–6
    shape, 14
Marang Forest, 88
Marking, 43–5
Marrow fat, 31, 31–2
Mastication, 7, 226–9, 227, 228
Mastodon, 214, 217, 219
Maternal care, 82–4, 83
Matriarch, 52–7, 72, 113
Measurement of
    blood vessels, 18
    clitoris, 21
    ears, 11
    intestines, 17
    seminiferous tubules, 80
    shoulder height, 26, 27, 35, 128
    Wolffian duct, 19
Measurement techniques, 27
Mechanical advantage, 223–4
Medial sclerosis, 119, 186
Melia volkensii, 149
Metarchidiskodon, 230
Methane, 129–30
Microfilaria, 176
Migrations, 69–70, 157
Mkomasi Game Reserve, 57, 58, 79,
        85, 86, 87
Moerotherioidea, 214, 216
Moerotherium, 214, 216, 217, 219,
        222
Molars
    anatomy, 7–9, 8
    duration in mouth, 9
    eruption, 7, 9
    evolution, 212, 231, 231, 238,
        239, 240, 241, 242
    growths on, 173
    role in age determination, 28
Moniteur, 189
Morillia, 214

Mortality rate, 135–8
Musth, 77–8, 195, 196, 198, 203
Mweya Peninsula, 148, 152

Nares, 18–19, 215, 221
Neck, 15, 16
Nematodes, 176, 178
Nephritis, 182
Nettlerash, 180
Nuchal eminence, 14
Nuffield Unit of Tropical Animal
        Ecology, 23
Numbers of elephants, 244–7
Nuttallia loxodontis, 176

Oestrus, 74
Oestrous cycle, 74
Oozie, 195
Ophthalmia, 184
Optimal foraging, 158
Ovary, 21
Overpopulation, 142–5, 146–7
Ovulation, 74, 76

Palaeomastodon, 219, 220
Parasites, 42–3, 178–80
Pasteurellosis, 177
Pathological techniques, 42–3
Penis, 19–21, 75. 77
Pentalophodon, 214
Phiomia, 220, 221, 222
Physiology, 41, 41–2, 42, 116–30
Piroplasma, 175–6
Piroplasmosis see Tick fever
Placental scars, 38, 86
Plant defences, 101–3
Platybelodon, 215, 219, 221, 222,
        222, 223, 226
Platyhelminthes, 178
Pneumonia, 177
Poaching, 141, 164, 166, 167, 170–
        71, 208
Population
    cycles, 158–60
    dynamics, 132–45
    maximum increases, 134
    models, 134
    structure, 135–42, 136, 137,
        140
Primary forest, 69, 105, 106, 158

Primelephas, 215, 230, 231, 235, 239, *240*, *241*
Proboscidea, 211–13
Progesterone, 2, 21
Protein in
blood, 32, 122–3
food, 123, *124*
Protoungulates, 1
Protozoa in gut, 89, *90*
Puberty, 84–6
Pygmy elephants, 129, 233–4, 242

Rabies, 177
Radio tracking, 44–5, 68, 69, 70, 132
Rainfall and reproduction, 78–80
Rain forests, 97, 103, 105, 106
Recapture, 196–7
Respiration chamber, *41*, 41–2, *42*
Respiratory
rate, 118
system, 18
Resting, 111
Reproduction
breeding seasons, 39–40, 77–81, *79*
mating behaviour, 74–8
study techniques, 38–41
Rhynchorostrinae, 215, 225
Rhynchotherium, 215, *222*, 224
Ribs, 16
Ruaha National Park, 24, 117, 150
Ruhunu National Park, 60, 98, 151
Rwenzori National Park, 23, 24, 31, 68, 69, 79, 85, 87, 92, 103, *108*, 123, 124, 125, 126, 130, 131, 148, 152, 171, 173, 179, 208

Sabi Sand Game Reserve, 68
Saddle, 191, 193
Saddle pad, 193, *193*
Sahara Desert, 186
Salt licks, 69, **7**
Scenting, **5**
Scott, Matthew, 198, 199, 200
Scratching, 180, *181*, **9**
Seasonal breeding, 39–40, 77–81, *79*
Seasonal movements, 69–70

Secondary compounds, 104
Secondary forest, 69, *105*, 105–6, 158
Self-regulation of numbers, 134
Seminiferous tubules, 80
Sengwa Wildlife Research Area, 24, 64, 68, 70, 151, 152, 165
Sense organs, 22
Septicaemia, 175, 177
Serengeti
National Park, 24, 100, 131, 150, 152
Research Institute, 24
Serridentinus, 215, 225
Serum analysis, 32
Sex ratios, 138–9, 142
Sexual dimorphism, 127–8
Shading behaviour, **1**
Shoulder height, 26–7, *27*, 35–6, 128
Sight, 22
Sirenians, 1–2, 216
Skeleton, *15*, 16
Skin, 11–12, 180–81
Skull
anatomy, 14–16
evolutionary changes, 213, *222*, *223*, 224, 226
woolly mammoth, 235
Sleep, 110–12
Smell, 22, 66
Snares, 10, 170–71
Social behaviour, 52–73, 156
Sodium balance, 69
Soolay, 196, *196*
Species characteristics, 3–4
Spermatozoa, 19, 40
Spermatogenesis, 19, 77
Stable limit cycles, 159
Stegodon, 218, 231
Stegodontidae, 214
Stegolophodon, 218, 231
Stegotetrabelodon, 230, *231*
Stomach, 17
contents, 32–4, 103, 123, 237
Stress, 1, 173, 174
Stroke, 174, 175
Strongyloid nematodes, 178
Succinylcholine chloride scoline, 164
Suckling, 83–4

Sulawesi, 234
Surra, 175
Sweat glands, 11, 113, 120
Symphysis, 213

Tabanid flies, 175
Tai Forest, 97
Tapeworms, 178
Techniques, 23–51
Teeth, diseases of, 171–3
Temperature, 118–21
    regulation, 119–21, *120*
Temporal gland, 12, 40–41, 66, 76, 77
Territory, 64, 70–71
Testis, 2, 19, 40
Testosterone, 77, 78
Tetanus, 177
Tetralophodon, 214, *222*, 223
Threat display, 11, 65, **4**
Thut, 175
Ticks, 176, 179
Tick fever, 175–6
Toenails, 12–13
Toes, 2, 12
Tongue, 22
Tooth *see* Molars *and* Tusk
Toothache, 171–2
Torynebelodon, 225
Touch, 22
Trails, 50–51, 106, 113
Training, 191
Translocation, 167
Tree destruction, 145, *146*, 148–57
Treetops, 72, 73, **7**
Trilophodon see Gomphotherium
Trumpeting, 66, 67
Trunk
    anatomy, 9–10
    capacity, 10
    evolution, 221–3
    function, 10, 22, 65, **3, 5**
    injury, 6, 10, 171
Trypanosoma, 175
Tsavo
    National Park, 24, 57, 58, 59, 68, 73, 79, 85, 87, 116, 131, 132, *133*, 149, 158, 162, 164, **5, 6**
    Research Project, 24

Tsetse fly, 175
Tuberculosis, 177, 185
Tummy rumble, 66
Tusk
    abscesses, 171–2, 198
    anatomy, 4–7
    grades, 205
    growth, 4–5, 126
    length, 237
    malformations, 171, 172, *172*
    mammoths, 235, 237
    mandibular, 213
    maxillary, 213
    splitting, 172–3
    trade, 205–10
    weights, 6, 126
Tusklessness, 5–6, 151
Twinning, 74

Ulcers, 182, 183, 184
Unguiculata, 1
Urine
    composition, 116, 129
    growth studies and, 38, 122
    volume, 116
Urino-genital canal, *20*, 21
Uterus, 38

Venae cavae, 18
Vocalization, 66–7

Walking, 14, *108*, 113–14, *114*
Wankie National Park, 69, 85, 87, 103, 127, 165
Water holes, 69
Weaning, 84
Weight of
    body, 26, 127–8
    brain, 16
    food, 99
    heart, 18
    hind leg, 25, 26
    temporal gland, 12
    testes, 19
    tusks, 6, 128
Weight measurement, 25, 35
White elephant, 203–4

Zoos, 197–201
Zyglolophodon, 214